Praise for *Susie*

This is, without doubt, the most detailed, historically accurate, and definitive account on the life of my great-great-grandmother Susie. Ray Rhodes has been meticulous in his research and yet has presented Susie's life in a very readable and engaging way. I came away from each chapter wanting to live life like Susie did. First, and most importantly, to have that strong and abiding faith she had in God. Second, to have the complete devotion to my husband that Susie and Charles had to each other. Finally, to have the unwavering perseverance that she had to the end, despite prolonged illness and the many trials of her life. This book will encourage you to live life looking to Christ to supply and to be everything you need as you seek to serve Him for His glory.

SUSANNAH SPURGEON COCHRANE, great-great-granddaughter of Charles and Susie Spurgeon

I have long wanted to read a biography of Susannah Spurgeon, and Ray Rhodes has given me (and the church) a gift in this biography of a remarkable woman. If you long to know that your trials will be used by God, your weakness is the way to holiness, and your faithfulness in the ordinary and hidden work of ministry is valuable to God, then let Susie be your teacher and your friend. You will find a fellow sister in this book, and you will be encouraged. God will do His intended work in the lives of His people, and Susie is one faithful example of that work.

COURTNEY REISSIG, author of *Glory in the Ordinary* and *The Accidental Feminist*

I read the dedication and thought, "This book will be a delight." On studying the timeline, I thought, "This book will be very helpful." After the introduction, I thought, "This book will be charming." Finishing Susie's early life justified my presumption, "This book is well-researched." Contemplating the vital intersection of Susie's life with Spurgeon surprised me with the observation, "This book opens up new light on the Prince of Preachers himself." When I came to the last remarkable month in Menton and Spurgeon's death, I felt, "This book shows the value of marriage in which two people have so sympathized that they have become virtually of one mind and heart." Looking at the ongoing theme of the Book Fund and the ministries it spawned, I thought, "What an example of practical vision and persevering execution this lady was!" Her independent usefulness in writing prompted the surmise, "This could serve as an example for many a Christian woman in sharing the riches of biblical knowledge, deep fellowship with Christ, and edifying admonition. And men too, for that matter." The church planting venture and her part in the restoration of the Tabernacle inspired the conviction, "That is just right. We should never till the day we die cease working for the glory of God and the extension of the kingdom of Christ." The universal lament following the death of this steel shadow sealed the conclusion in my heart, "In a life matured by grace, she would not have been this person without Charles; and he would not have achieved such stature and received such love and respect without her; and, in fact, all of us need our mates, our friends, our churches, our trials, our triumphs, and the constant awareness of the goodness and wisdom of God to become what we should here and to prepare us for what we will be hereafter."

TOM NETTLES, retired and serving as Senior Professor of Historical Theology at The Southern Baptist Theological Seminary; author of *Living by Revealed Truth: The Life and Pastoral Theology of Charles Haddon Spurgeon*

It has been way too long for the release of a full-length biography of Susie Spurgeon. Ray Rhodes has made it worth the wait! This book is a gem that has the same effect on the reader that Susie had on all the lives she touched: it draws our minds and hearts to marvel at the Lord's goodness. As Charles Spurgeon referred to his wife, this "bravest of women, strong in the faith" was so focused on God's glory that theology pulsed through her veins and out of her heart, mouth, hands, and pen. Susie Spurgeon, queen of the housewife theologians, treated the many obstacles and sufferings in her path as opportunities for the Lord's strength to work through her weaknesses. And he worked mightily through Susie to bless her family and friends, and to minister to pastors, to orphans, and to us as well. I'm thankful for how Ray has enriched my understanding of Christ through the life of Susie Spurgeon.

AIMEE BYRD, author of *Why Can't We Be Friends?* and *No Little Women*

Charles Spurgeon was the most famous name in Christendom in the latter half of the nineteenth century. He is still widely regarded as the "Prince of Preachers" in all of Christian history and is the hero of countless evangelical preachers today, including myself. What is much less known is how much Spurgeon loved and relied upon his godly wife, Susannah. Through both original research and new insights into long-dormant material, Ray Rhodes has restored "Susie" to her rightful place alongside her famous husband. Anyone interested in Spurgeon will enjoy this book, especially for its insights into the home life, family worship practices, and spiritual relationship of the Spurgeons. Anyone looking to read the life of a heroic Christian woman will find it in this biography of the remarkable Susannah Spurgeon.

DONALD S. WHITNEY, Professor of Biblical Spirituality and Associate Dean at The Southern Baptist Theological Seminary, Louisville, KY; author of *Spiritual Disciplines for the Christian Life*, *Family Worship*, and *Praying the Bible*

Admirers of C. H. Spurgeon will be delighted to pick up this new biography of his wife, Susannah. Ray Rhodes's carefully researched account of Susie's life freshly illuminates the story of the woman who upheld the nineteenth century's greatest preacher by her love and prayer. Susie's story exemplifies trust in God in the midst of chronic illness and paints a sweet picture of married love. Readers will also give thanks to God for her Pastors' Book Fund, which supplied thousands of volumes to equip needy pastors. We can learn much from the stories of saints who have gone before, and this book is no exception.

MEGAN HILL, author of *Praying Together* and *Contentment*; editor for The Gospel Coalition; regular contributor to CT Women and *Today in the Word*; and pastor's wife

It is hard to believe that there has been no substantial study of Susannah Spurgeon's life until this work by Ray Rhodes. Her husband and his ministry are so well-known, but for some reason, Susannah and her life have been but a chapter in his story. Thankfully Ray has now corrected this and given us a full account of her inspiring pilgrimage. I hope this book receives a wide readership among both women and men.

MICHAEL A. G. HAYKIN, FRHistS, Chair and Professor of Church History, The Southern Baptist Theological Seminary, and author of numerous volumes, including *Eight Women of Faith*

As modern readers, it's often difficult to relate to the saints of old. Ray Rhodes paints us a picture of a woman who devoted herself to personal piety—an inspiration for women in any age.

SARAH ZYLSTRA, senior writer at The Gospel Coalition

A well-worn adage states, behind every great man is a great woman; and it's often true. Most of us know the great C. H. Spurgeon, but precious few know the godly woman to whom he was married—the woman who raised his children, who kept his house, who was his soul mate, and who helped keep him sane amid the boiling cauldron of local church ministry in Victorian England. In these clearly written, lively pages, my friend and fellow pastor Ray Rhodes brings Susie Spurgeon to life in bold relief and in full color, taking us inside the life of the woman who loved the Prince of Preachers. This is a unique, much-needed biography. It's the best kind of history—written to serve the church of Jesus Christ—and it will serve as the standard biography of the delightful Mrs. Spurgeon for decades to come. There is literally something compelling here for every Christian. Read and rejoice that God gave the great Spurgeon such a lion-hearted helpmate.

JEFF ROBINSON, lead pastor, Christ Fellowship Church of Louisville, KY, and senior editor, The Gospel Coalition

What a joyful, unexpected delight this book is! Immediately engaging, lightning paced, colorfully written, and surprisingly encouraging. Susannah Spurgeon was no second fiddle. Despite her staggering medical challenges, she modeled well that we are all to be faithful until our King returns. This is plain ol' good reading.

TODD FRIEL, host of *Wretched TV and Radio*; author of numerous books

Susie lifts us up from our life of comfort and convenience to a time when the difficulties of daily living, coupled with her health limitations, did not hinder her from using her gifts for the promotion of God's kingdom. What an inspiration she is at the side of her famous husband, Charles Spurgeon, encouraging him in times of depression and ministerial challenges, as well as heeding God's beck and call to send books and supplies to needy ministers around the world! Susie's ministry of encouragement to faithful, humble pastors encourages us to use whatever gifts God has given us, in the situation where He has placed us, for His glory. Ray Rhodes's treatment of the history of Susannah Spurgeon, in the setting of Victorian England, is interesting, informative, and motivating!

MARY BEEKE, author of *The Law of Kindness*, and wife of Joel Beeke (author, and president of Puritan Reformed Theological Seminary)

I love Ray Rhodes's new book, *Susie: The Life and Legacy of Susannah Spurgeon*, for so many reasons. But it's just what I'd expect from a friend who loves the gospel as much as Ray does; loves Lori, his wife, with so much delight and zeal; and is committed to putting as many good books into the hands and hearts of God's people as possible. Susie dispels the caricature of there being a "little woman" behind every great man. Susannah Spurgeon had an amazing story and voice, life, and legacy of her own—a life she gladly lived in the shadow of her world-renowned husband, Charles Spurgeon—but a life from which we all can learn and greatly benefit. Thanks to Ray, I no longer view Susannah Spurgeon as just a supporting character in the ministry of her husband. Thanks to Ray, when I hear the name Spurgeon, I'll now ask, "Are you referring to Susie or Charles?" I cannot overstate the importance, timeliness, and helpfulness of this book.

SCOTTY WARD SMITH, pastor emeritus, Christ Community Church, Franklin, TN; Teacher in Residence, West End Community Church, Nashville, TN; author of numerous books including *Everyday Prayers*

SUSIE

THE LIFE AND LEGACY
OF SUSANNAH SPURGEON
wife of Charles H. Spurgeon

RAY RHODES JR.

MOODY PUBLISHERS

CHICAGO

Unless otherwise noted, all Scripture quotations are taken from the King James Version.

Scripture quotations in the dedication and those marked ESV are taken from the ESV® Bible (The Holy Bible, English Standard Version®), copyright © 2001 by Crossway, a publishing ministry of Good News Publishers. Used by permission. All rights reserved.

All emphasis in Scripture has been added.

Edited by Amanda Cleary Eastep
Author photo: Rachel Rink
Interior Design: PuckettSmartt
Cover Design: Erik M. Peterson
Front cover portrait copyright © KGPA Ltd / Alamy Stock Photo (E7D8CT). All rights reserved.
Back cover portraits are in the public domain.

All websites and phone numbers listed herein are accurate at the time of publication but may change in the future or cease to exist. The listing of website references and resources does not imply publisher endorsement of the site's entire contents. Groups and organizations are listed for informational purposes, and listing does not imply publisher endorsement of their activities.

Library of Congress Cataloging-in-Publication Data

Names: Rhodes, Ray, Jr., author.
Title: Susie : the life and legacy of Susannah Spurgeon, wife of Charles H. Spurgeon / Ray Rhodes Jr.
Description: Chicago : Moody Publishers, 2018. | Includes bibliographical references.
Identifiers: LCCN 2018025669 (print) | LCCN 2018032094 (ebook) | ISBN 9780802496768 (ebook) | ISBN 9780802418340
Subjects: LCSH: Spurgeon, Susannah, -1903. | Spurgeon, C. H. (Charles Haddon), 1834-1892. | Baptists--England--Biography.
Classification: LCC BX6495.S725 (ebook) | LCC BX6495.S725 R46 2018 (print) | DDC 286/.1092 [B] --dc23
LC record available at https://lccn.loc.gov/2018025669

ISBN: 978-0-8024-2284-2

We hope you enjoy this book from Moody Publishers. Our goal is to provide high-quality, thought-provoking books and products that connect truth to your real needs and challenges. For more information on other books and products written and produced from a biblical perspective, go to www.moodypublishers.com or write to:

Moody Publishers
820 N. LaSalle Boulevard
Chicago, IL 60610

3 5 7 9 10 8 6 4 2

Printed in the United States of America

To

My Wife, Lori

You will always be "O most beautiful among women."

You have captivated my heart, my sister, my bride; you have captivated my heart with one glance of your eyes (Song 4:9). I am captivated!

Our Daughters and Sons-in-Law

Rachel (and Adrian), Hannah, Sarah (and Caleb), Mary, Lydia, Abigail

Like arrows in the hand of a warrior are the children of one's youth (Ps. 127:4). I am defended!

Our Grandchildren

Susannah, Josiah, Caleb, Eden Rose

Grandchildren are the crown of the aged (Prov. 17:6). I am crowned.

and

My London Research Assistant

Maureen Gardner

Your devotion to Susie's story is inspirational. I am inspired.

CONTENTS

Foreword

S ometimes, the most revealing lessons of history come from silence. One of the strangest silences of church history is the lack of attention to the wives of ministers and pastors, even the most famous of Christian leaders.

Such a silence should make us think. Why this absence of historical interest?

Of course, the first thought that must come to mind is the reality that for over a millennium, under the Roman Catholic Church's teaching and practice, priests were celibate. Today's evangelical Christians know this, to be sure, but most probably do not reflect on why the Roman Catholic Church—then and now—expects priestly celibacy while evangelical congregations expect their pastors to be married, with relatively few exceptions.

To say the least, this represents a massive shift in both theology and church practice. And to understand this massive shift we must go back to the Protestant Reformation of the sixteenth century, and especially to

Martin Luther and his cherished wife, Katie. Together, they established the model of the married pastor and his joy in both wife and children. In effect, they invented the Protestant family.

When Martin Luther was ordained in 1507, he was already an Augustinian friar. Now he also held priestly status. Having famously made an oath to St. Anne during a frightening thunderstorm, Luther turned from law to theology. No one was more disappointed than his father, Hans Luther, who had expected his son to become a lawyer, to marry, and to bring him grandchildren.

The unfolding of the Reformation came as Luther, especially after his posting of the "Ninety-Five Theses" on October 31, 1517, was convinced by Scripture that so many of the teachings and practices of the Roman Catholic Church were clearly unbiblical. Eventually, Luther came to see mandated priestly celibacy as one of those unbiblical teachings. He began to work as something of a matchmaker for his ministerial students, matching them with former nuns now ready for marriage. Before long, Luther was married himself, and with his wife Katie (herself a former nun), lived out the Reformation both in the church and in their home.

In my study I have a wonderful and historic set of oil portraits of Martin and Katie Luther. They are among the most prized possessions in my personal library. Why? Because Martin and Katie are inseparable in life and legacy. Martin Luther became the first major Christian pastor who simply cannot be known without reference to his wife. Luther made sure of it. We cannot explain Luther without reference to the strength and love he drew from Katie and his children and the warmth of a Christian home.

Luther understood why Paul told Timothy that the man who holds the teaching office in the church should be "the husband of one wife" (1 Tim. 3:2 ESV). As Ray Rhodes makes clear, the same was true of Charles Spurgeon. In *Susie: The Life and Legacy of Susannah Spurgeon*, Rhodes tells her story. Of course, in telling her story, he also tells the story of the most famous preacher of Victorian England, Charles Spurgeon. As we come to know his beloved Susie, we come to know Spurgeon in a way otherwise impossible without the knowledge of her presence, love, and influence in his life.

The best books fulfill a need, and this book does just that. Books worthy of reading tell a story well, and that is true of the book you now hold in your hands.

There is one additional reason I cherish those portraits of Martin and Katie Luther. My ministry would not be what it is and I would not be the man that I am without my own sweet wife, Mary. I have felt her constant support and influence in my life. I know the same is true of Ray Rhodes, who would testify in the same way about his own beloved wife, Lori.

I think it is safe to say that his own happiness in marriage goes a long way toward explaining why he wrote this book, why he knew that telling Susannah Spurgeon's story would be important, and why you will want eagerly to read *Susie*.

R. Albert Mohler Jr.
President of The Southern Baptist Theological Seminary

TIMELINE

Birthdates uncertain: Susannah (Susie) Spurgeon's grandparents were Sampson and Mary Knott and William and Mary Thompson. It is believed that Sampson and Mary married in 1801 and Sampson died in 1860. He was an Esquire, retired miller, and well-off.

1805 or 1806, Jan. 20: Susannah Knott Thompson, mother of Susannah Spurgeon, is born in Ramsgate, Kent. Baptized in the parish church at St. Lawrence in Thanet.

1808, March 9: Robert Bennett (R. B.) Thompson, father of Susannah Spurgeon, is born in London. Baptized at The Tabernacle in June by Matthew Wilks, an English Separatist pastor.

1823, June 2: Henry Kilvington and Mary Knott (Susie's aunt, her mother Susannah's sister) are married. Susie and her parents would briefly live with the Kilvington family.

1829: Susannah Kilvington, Susie's cousin and, later, close friend, is born.

1831, April 16: R. B. Thompson and Susannah Knott are married at St. Giles Church, Camberwell, located in the London borough of Southwark.

1832, Jan. 15: Susie Thompson is born at Old Kent Road, London.

1834, June 19: Charles Haddon Spurgeon is born at Kelvedon, Essex.

1837–1901: Reign of Queen Victoria.

1840: Pastor J. J. Audebez's (French Reformed Church, Paris) wife, Jeanne, dies. Sometime after Audebez marries his sister-in-law in 1842, Susie visits Paris and the Audebez home. She occasionally lived with the Audebez family during her travels between 1845 and March 1854.

1841–1850: Pastor James Smith serves the New Park Street Chapel. The Thompson family attends this church during his tenure.

1842: R. B. (a warehouseman) is unable to meet the demands of his creditors. Sometime afterwards, as early as 1843 and as late as 1851, R. B. went to work for Messers. Cook and Son located in Central London. In the 1840s the Thompsons lived in central London. In 1843, R. B.'s financial problems are resolved.

1848: Susannah Kilvington marries William Olney. The Olneys are significant influences in Susie's life.

1850, Jan. 6: Charles Spurgeon is converted at Primitive Methodist Chapel, Artillery Street, in Colchester.

1850, May 3: Charles is baptized in the River Lark at Isleham Ferry.

1850, Oct. 3: Charles is received as a member of St. Andrew's Street Baptist Church, Cambridge.

1851: The Great Exhibition with its central structure "The Crystal Palace" opens in London's Hyde Park. Charles Spurgeon travels from Cambridge in June to attend.

1851, October: Charles becomes pastor of Waterbeach Chapel just north of Cambridge.

1852: Susie is converted at the Poultry Chapel in central London on a Sunday evening late in the year. Date is uncertain.

1853, Jan. 29: Susie visits Notre Dame Cathedral on the eve of the wedding of Napoleon III and Eugenie.

1852/53–1855: Either late 1852 or early 1853. R. B. and family move in (temporarily) with Henry and Mary Kilvington (Susie's aunt) and remain there until the late spring of 1855. They live at 7 St. Ann's Terrace on Brixton Road, after which they return to central London and live at 210 Falcon Square.

1853: Mary Kilvington, sister of Susannah Knott Thompson, dies.

1853, late summer or fall: Charles preaches at a Sunday school event in Cambridge. This leads to an invitation to preach in London at the New Park Street Chapel (NPSC).

1853, December 18: Charles preaches at the NPSC for the first time as a guest preacher. Susie Thompson does not attend the morning service but at the encouragement of Thomas Olney (William's father) she attends the evening service and hears Charles preach for the first time.

1853–54: Cholera outbreak in London, 11,000 people die. In 1854, Charles ministers to the sick, dying, and grieving.

1853–56: Crimean War

1854: The Crystal Palace is reassembled in Sydenham, South London.

1854, April 20: Charles gives Susie an illustrated copy of *The Pilgrim's Progress*. William Olney tells Charles about Susie's spiritual struggles, which precipitates this gift.

1854, April 28: Charles accepts the pastorate at the New Park Street Chapel.

1854, June 10: Charles and Susie attend the grand reopening of the Crystal Palace. Here Charles, via a book, reveals his love to Susie.

1854, Aug. 2: Charles proposes to Susie in her grandfather's garden.

1854, December: Susie applies for membership at the New Park Street Chapel and writes out her testimony of faith in Christ.

1855, Jan. 23: Susie stands before the church and gives verbal testimony to her faith in Christ.

1855, Feb. 1: Susie is baptized by her fiancé, Charles, at NPSC.

1855, Feb. 4: Susie officially becomes a member of New Park Street Chapel where she is an active member until September 1867. She is ill by late 1867 and rarely attends services at what is now the Metropolitan Tabernacle.

1855: Susie is forgotten by Charles as he prepares to preach at The Horns. She rushes home to her mother in anger. This event likely happened sometime between February and May of 1855. Charles was living at 75 Dover Street. Susie was then living at 7 St. Anne's Terrace, Brixton, just a mile or so from The Horns.

1855: *Smooth Stones Taken from Ancient Brooks* was published by Charles Spurgeon late in the year. In the summer of 1855, Charles enlisted Susie to pull salient quotes from the writings of Thomas Brooks for this work. This was Susie's first literary effort, although she is not credited in the book.

1855, April: Susie visits Charles's parents at Colchester for the first time.

1855, Dec. 22: Charles gives Susie the first published volume of his sermons.

1856, Jan. 8: Susannah (Susie) Thompson marries Charles Haddon Spurgeon. They honeymoon in Paris.

1856, January: Charles and Susie move into their first home together at 217 New Kent Road.

1856, Spring: Susie accompanies Charles to visit his grandparents at Stambourne.

1856: The Pastors' College begins, in seed form, with one student and is more formally developed in 1857.

1856, Sept. 20: Susie gives birth to twins: Charles and Thomas.

1856, Oct. 19: The Surrey Garden's Music Hall Disaster.

1856, Nov. 2: Charles returns to the pulpit at New Park Street Chapel.

1856, Nov. 23: Charles returns to the Surrey Garden's Music Hall to preach.

1857, Fall: Charles and Susie move to 99 Nightingale Lane.

1857, Oct. 7: Charles preaches to almost 24,000 people at the Crystal Palace.

1857–1867: Susie enjoys relatively good health and often travels with Charles. She hikes the Alps, tours art galleries, and enjoys Venice. She is active in church. Susie was with Charles in Geneva in 1860 when he preached in Calvin's pulpit.

1861, March 18: The Metropolitan Tabernacle opens, seating five to six thousand.

1862, April 14: Susie's mother, Susannah Thompson, dies. Charles preaches at her funeral.

1866, August: Charles initiates an orphanage for boys through a gift of 20,000 pounds from Anne Hillyard. From this the Stockwell Orphanage would rise.

1867: The Stockwell Orphanage officially opens.

1868: Susie is seriously ill and no longer able to travel.

1868–69: Around this time, R. B. Thompson moves from Falcon Square to Bell Street.

1869: The Nightingale Lane home is torn down and a new one built at same location.

1868/69: Susie undergoes surgery in Brighton by Sir James Young Simpson. She is an invalid for much of the remainder of her life.

1869: Thomas Olney dies.

1870, Oct. 18: R. B. Thompson marries Mary Ann Kirkwood at Christ Church in Central London. Robert is a wine merchant. Robert and Mary Ann live in Hornsey near London.

1872/73–1892: Charles is often at Mentone, France, during the winter months due to his deteriorating health.

1873, Oct. 5: R. B. dies of a heart attack in Penzance at South Terrace; he is buried there.

1874, Oct. 21: Sons Charles and Thomas Spurgeon, eighteen years old, are baptized at the Metropolitan Tabernacle.

1875: Thomas Johnson, a former slave from Virginia, begins his studies at the Pastors' College.

1875, summer: The beginning of Mrs. Spurgeon's Book Fund, which she manages until her death.

1875: The Girls' Orphanage opens at Stockwell.

1880: In the late summer, Charles and Susie move to Beulah Hill (Westwood) in Upper Norwood South London and near the Crystal Palace at Sydenham Hill.

1881, Jan. 8: Susie and Charles celebrate their silver wedding anniversary.

1884/85: Susie publishes *Ten Years of My Life in the Service of the Book Fund*.

1887: The Down-Grade Controversy begins. Charles resigns from the Baptist Union on October 28.

1888, Jan. 18: The Baptist Union votes to censure Charles.

1888: Charles publishes *The Cheque Book of the Bank of Faith* and in it writes of his suffering over the controversy and also over Susie's affliction. Susie believed that the Down-Grade Controversy resulted in Charles's early death at age 57.

1889: Susie joins Beulah Baptist Chapel, Thornton Heath, London (near Westwood). (Membership disputed by the Metropolitan Tabernacle.)

1889, March: Death of Charles and Susie's granddaughter Marguerite May (Daisy) Spurgeon at three months old.

1890: Death of Charles and Susie's grandson Charles Philip Spurgeon at less than a year old.

1891, June 7: Charles preaches his last sermon at the Metropolitan Tabernacle.

1891, October: During the first part of the month, Charles and Susie travel together to Eastbourne, England.

1891, Oct. 26: Charles *and* Susie leave London for Mentone in hopes that his health will improve in the warmer climate. It is the first time Susie has been able to make the trip.

1891: From October through mid-January 1892, Charles mostly completes his book *The Gospel of the Kingdom*.

1892: On January 8, Charles and Susie celebrate their thirty-sixth wedding anniversary, and on January 15, they celebrate Susie's sixtieth birthday.

1892, Jan. 17: Charles leads his last worship service at his hotel in Mentone. On January 20, Charles goes to bed and remains there until he dies eleven days later.

1892, Jan. 31: Charles dies in his room at the Hotel Beau Rivage at 11:05 p.m. Susie is with him as is his brother, sister-in-law, and Susie's friend Elizabeth Thorne. A memorial service is held in Mentone and then Charles's body is removed to London. Susie does not return to London for a month, but instead she recovers at the estate of Thomas Hanbury.

1892, Feb. 11: Charles is buried at Norwood Cemetery.

1892, March: Susie returns to London from Italy and resumes her Book Fund.

1894, March: Thomas Spurgeon is formally elected as the pastor of the Metropolitan Tabernacle. There is considerable dissent. He accepts the pastorate on April 2.

1895: Susie publishes *Ten Years After!: A Sequel to "Ten Years of My Life in the Service of the Book Fund."*

1895, spring: Susie discovers that there is no Baptist chapel at Bexhill-on-Sea and determines to plant a church there after a season of prayer.

1896: The first building of Beulah Baptist Church at Bexhill-on-Sea is opened, a school-chapel. Church is formally constituted on January 31, 1897.

1896: Susie publishes *A Carillon of Bells*.

1897–1900: Susie coedits and is a major contributor to the four-volume *C.H. Spurgeon's Autobiography*.

1897, April 12: Susie cuts the first sod for the chapel at Bexhill. On July 7, she lays the memorial stone.

1898: Susie publishes *A Cluster of Camphire*.

1898, April 20: The Metropolitan Tabernacle is gutted by fire.

1898, Aug. 17: The Beulah Baptist Chapel is opened at Bexhill-on-Sea free of debt.

1899, Feb. 8: Susie leads a fundraiser in the basement of the Metropolitan Tabernacle. She does so against her doctor's counsel and raises $30,000 for the rebuilding of the Tabernacle.

1900, September: The Metropolitan Tabernacle is reopened.

1901: Susie publishes *A Basket of Summer Fruit*.

1903, Oct. 22: Susie dies at Westwood at 8:30 a.m.

1903, Oct. 27: A memorial service is held at the library of Westwood with the funeral service following at Chatsworth Road Baptist Chapel and burial at the West Norwood Cemetery.

1903: Charles Ray publishes *The Life of Susannah Spurgeon*.

1904: A memorial tablet for Susie is erected at Beulah Baptist, Bexhill. The Book Fund continues under the leadership of Elizabeth Thorne at Westwood.

1917, Oct. 17: Thomas Spurgeon dies.

1926, Dec. 13: Charles Spurgeon Jr. dies.

2018, September: *Susie: The Life and Legacy of Susannah Spurgeon* is published.

Susie, Herself: An Introduction

1832–1903

S usie Spurgeon finished writing the note—she had penned hundreds like it over the years—and placed it carefully inside the cover of the book *The Gospel of the Kingdom*. Her late husband, Charles Haddon Spurgeon, the English Baptist pastor renowned as the "Prince of Preachers," had written the book. She wrapped the parcel and handed it to her longtime friend and assistant Elizabeth Thorne to mail. Like the many parcels sent before, the note and book would eventually find their way to a pastor as part of Mrs. Spurgeon's Book Fund.

This particular pastor, now living in a foreign land, had once sat in a classroom at the Pastors' College and listened intently as college founder Charles Spurgeon lectured. The book, a commentary on the gospel of Matthew, was Spurgeon's final work, which Susie described as "the last sweet, loving labour for the Master's glory of the heart and hand now cold in death."[1] Sometime later, the same pastor would reply in a note to Susie: "The last work of that wonderful brain and those busy hands, I value more than words can express; and I have pasted your letter within the cover."[2]

Another pastor once wrote, "God bless you very, very much, and your work for His ministers, and cheer your heart whenever the desolation of loneliness comes over you, as you see the vacant chair, and the many things in the house that speak of your loved one. Take courage!"[3]

❧

Following the death of her husband on January 31, 1892, and still mourning her deep loss, Susie had wondered what the Lord would do with her, a frail and lonely widow. Would she continue her seventeen-year book ministry to poor pastors? She decided, yes: "God constrained me to the service, and strengthened me for it, in order to keep heart and mind from dwelling too constantly upon my loneliness and grief."[4] Charles had encouraged her to embark upon the book ministry, which Susie described as "an angel of light, to point out to me the consoling power of active service for the Lord and His poor servants."[5]

As the books her husband authored passed through her hands, they stirred memories in Susie's mind. She remembered the early days of their marriage when she and Charles had journeyed across the continent. A smile came to her face as she reflected on rowing in a gondola with her beloved along the Grand Canal through Venice. Romance had filled their hearts in the city that she described as "dreamy." Even ordinary days held joy. Charles tenderly addressed her as "my darling" and "my precious love." Sometimes they laughed so hard that they cried. But now, Susie wiped tears from her eyes. She missed her husband.

They had delighted in each other, despite their many trials. Susie recalled feeling the first signs of her declining health, as sharp pains pierced her body. She had eventually undergone surgery that left her mostly confined to home, and she had wondered if she would ever be useful again to either her husband or her Savior. Years of sickness followed.

From then on, Susie's health prevented her from accompanying her husband on his travels. When Charles left home for another trip to south-ern France, he would look longingly into her eyes, saddened she couldn't go with him. She knew it had been hard for Charles, who was also sickly, to leave her behind as he traveled a thousand miles from home.

In the midst of *her* pain, Susie often comforted Charles as *he* suffered through his own afflictions of depression, gout, and kidney disease. At times she found him weeping though he didn't know why, his depres-sions could be so dark. Susie comforted Charles by reading the poetry of George Herbert to him.

Soon Susie's chance to actively serve others arrived the day Charles handed her the first volume of his newest book, *Lectures to My Students*. She was so delighted with his masterful work that she wished every pastor in England could have a copy, free of charge.

Charles looked at his wife and said, "Well, Susie, will you make it happen?"

Surprised by her husband's challenge, Susie retreated to an upstairs room, paused to catch her breath, and then retrieved a small stash of money that she had stored away in a drawer. "Perhaps the Lord will use this small offering to provide a few books to pastors," she thought. She never dreamt, however, that this experience would lead her to invest the remainder of her days in service to pastors and their families.

☙❧

Knowing the parcel was now in good hands with Miss Thorne, Susie reflected on her almost twenty years of service to impoverished ministers via books, money, and even clothes for their wives and children. God had used Charles to inspire her work, and Susie was thankful. Her chief desire was to honor Christ, but she also believed that her ministry to pastors was "the best memorial of [Charles's] wonderful life of service for God."[6]

With such memories fresh in her mind, Susannah leaned forward in the chair at her husband's desk and considered their thirty-six-year

marriage. Only twelve months prior, on January 31, Charles had died
in his room at the Hotel Beau Rivage in Mentone, France, at the age of
fifty-seven. At his bedside, Susie had bowed her head and "thanked the
Lord for the precious treasure so long lent to her, and sought, at the throne
of grace, strength and guidance for the future."[7] In the year following
Charles's death, she had felt the deep pangs of life as a widow separated
from the "Prince of her life."[8]

Susie carefully lifted one of her beloved's pens, dipped it in ink, and
gently touched the nib to paper:

> I am writing in my husband's study, where he thought, and
> prayed, and wrote. Every inch of the place is sacred ground.
> Everything remains precisely as he left it. His books (now
> my most precious possessions), stand in shining rows upon
> the shelves, in exactly the order in which he placed them,
> and one might almost fancy the room was ready and wait-
> ing for its master. But oh! That empty chair! That grave por-
> trait over the door! Those palm-branches overshadowing the
> clock! The strange, solemn silence, which pervades the place
> now that he is no longer on earth! I kneel sometimes by his
> chair, and laying my head on the cushioned arms, which so
> long supported his dear form, I pour out my grief before the
> Lord, and tell Him again that though I am left alone, yet
> I know that "He hath done all things well." Then wander-
> ing from room to room, looking with tear-dimmed eyes at
> the home treasures my dear one loved and admired, almost
> expecting to hear the sound of his footsteps behind me, and
> the sweet tones of his tender voice in loving greeting.—I
> have, alas to realize afresh how true were King David's
> words when he said in his sorrow, "I shall go to him, but he
> shall not return to me."[9]

Surrounding her as she worked were twelve thousand of her husband's books, of which over half were either written by or about the Puritans that he loved so much.[10] Spurgeon's books, Susie's "most precious possessions," still sprawled through three rooms: the study, the adjoining library, and another smaller room nearby.

Susie pushed back from the desk and remembered her husband's many encouragements to her. She could not—she would not—quit her ministry, regardless of her loneliness and poor health. She missed Charles terribly, but just as God had enabled her to serve Him through physical affliction, He would also help her serve Him as a widow.

Susie administered a book fund and an aid ministry that supplied books, money, clothes, and other supplies to needy pastors. She was a prolific author of five books and a major contributor to other publications (including the massive four-volume *C. H. Spurgeon's Autobiography*). Biographer Richard Ellsworth Day, in his popular book about Charles Spurgeon, imagined that if Susie had not chosen to sink her individuality into Charles and his ministry, "she could have mounted the levels of Elizabeth Barrett Browning" in her own writing.[11] In addition, Susie supported the Metropolitan Tabernacle, opened her home as a place of hospitality, served as the "Mother" of the Pastors' College, and was even instrumental in planting a church.

Though her hopes, dreams, and service were joined to Charles during his life and ministry, Susie also had a life filled with joys, sorrows, hopes, and dreams for twenty-two years prior to meeting the great preacher and for almost twelve years after his death. It was God's provision of her parents, family, Christian leaders, friends, and experiences that helped mold Susie into a godly and persevering woman who became so beloved to her husband and so useful to the kingdom of God. And it was the grace of God that sustained her in the years following Charles's death.

As Susie reflected on her life and ministry, she praised God:

How inexpressibly thankful do I feel now for the sustaining grace which upheld me, and enabled me to testify to them [pastors who received books from her] from my own experience, that every promise of God holds true, and that even in the depths of sorrow and darkness, His light shines round about those who put their trust in Him![12]

Ten years later, on a crisp October day in 1903, Susie, who died at seventy-one, lay in a lily-draped casket, carefully positioned in the middle of the library just outside Charles's study where she had so often sat at his desk writing encouraging words to pastors and reflecting on God's hand in her life.

Recalling that her name, Susannah, means "lily," her son Charles penned a memorial to his beloved mother intimating that her "Christian character partook of the nature and beauty of this sweet plant."[13] His beautiful mother, with her brown eyes and her long chestnut hair, had lived an equally beautiful life. She loved her husband. She loved Jesus. And she had served God faithfully.

Though it is impossible to consider Susie in isolation from Charles Spurgeon, she was a remarkable woman in her own right. Her only prior biographer, Charles Ray, concluded of her that Susie would live on "not only as the wife of Charles Haddon Spurgeon . . . but as herself."[14]

CHAPTER I

Formation and Family

Susie's Birth and Victorian London

The weather was a frosty thirty-four degrees, but the sun was shining brightly outside the Thompson home on January 15, 1832 when Susie was born. However, the warmth of welcoming a newborn to the family more than countered the winter temperatures for Robert Bennett (R. B.) and his wife of only nine months, Susannah Knott Thompson.[1]

The Thompson home on Old Kent Road, London, was not far from where a number of religious dissenters in the sixteenth century were accused of treason and hanged. The Thames River flowed just to the north of Susie's first address, but at various times over the course of her lifetime, she resided on both sides of the famous waterway.

William IV was the reigning king of England, and Victoria, his young niece, was heir to the crown when Susie was born. After an extended illness, William died in 1837, and Victoria, eighteen years old, ascended the throne where she served until her death in 1901. Susie was five when Victoria was crowned, and she died two years after Victoria's death—all of Susie's life was characterized by Victorian culture. Victoria's reign was

mostly ceremonial, but she had an important influence in England, especially as an agent of morality and family life. Victoria, her husband,
Albert, and their nine children were the subject of admiration, curiosity,
and criticism in the nineteenth century. Her long reign directly touched
two centuries, and numerous prime ministers served under her, including
Melbourne, Disraeli, and Gladstone. Though it is unlikely that she ever
met the queen, Susie shared a lifetime with her.

Not only was Susie a Victorian chronologically, she was also one
culturally. In the course of her seventy-one years, she was familiar with
the literature of the day, including the works of Charles Dickens, and
the beloved English author's prose even made its way into Susie's later
writings.[2] Like many upper middle class young ladies, Susie was well read
and expertly versed in literature, music, art, and language.

Susie witnessed many changes in Victorian London—changes that
included some advances for women, such as the women's suffrage movement, gained traction in the later years of the 1800s. However, for much
of the Victorian era, women were mostly valued in the domestic realm.
Upon marriage, the husband legally controlled most spheres of his wife's
life. That said, during Susie's lifetime, progress toward increasing women's
rights was realized.

Susie thrived both socially and educationally, and once she was married, she was contented as the wife of Charles Haddon Spurgeon. She
was blessed with a husband who valued her, not only as his wife but also
as his friend, equal, and partner in gospel enterprises, despite their living
and ministering in a male-dominated society.

Susie's generation experienced massive technological developments
that brought gaslights to city streets, rapid transit via railways, and later
introduced electric lights and the telephone by the end of the nineteenth
century. London was a city of change.

When Susie was born, travel was limited to walking or traveling by
horse, carriage, or boat; but the 1840s cut many miles of train tracks across
Europe, and by 1850, trains raced across the landscapes of both England

and France. Susie enjoyed long walks, and when given the option of riding in a carriage through scenic passageways or walking, Susie chose to go on foot. She crossed most of the Alpine passes, and whenever possible, she left carriage or mule to walk, for she loved to stand and view the towering mountains above and the deep gorges below.

Driven by the Industrial Revolution, England moved from primarily a rural population to having a majority of citizens residing in urban settings. From the early days of the nineteenth century until the mid-1850s, nearly insurmountable challenges confounded the city's leaders and plagued its citizens. London's streets, lined with new residents looking for opportunities, brought burdens to the Royal City, burdens that she was ill prepared to bear.

Sanitary conditions deteriorated. Water from the Thames was contaminated. From an infected well and a filthy river, death was pumped into the homes of the city.[3] The weeping in London was heard in almost every neighborhood due to the resulting cholera outbreak. It is likely that Susie Thompson and her family felt some measure of fear as a result of the widespread death in the city during several such cholera epidemics that afflicted London.

While riches increased for some, with manufacturing advances and the expansion of trade, poverty afflicted many in the overpopulated and often unsanitary neighborhoods of London from early to midcentury. Prostitution and other forms of vice stood in sharp contrast to the age of Victorian morality, which comprised strict sexual ethics, law and order, and a romanticized view of women as the "angel of the house." Religious values permeated Victorian culture and an enterprising work ethic fueled industry.

Susie remained in the city through—as Dickens wrote—the "best of times and the worst of times."[4] Yet she escaped disease, death, and hard labor in the factories, and she experienced many benefits that were inaccessible to lesser-privileged London girls. Even with its problems, Victorianism entered its Golden Age with an expanding economy and, with the exception of the Crimean War, the continent enjoyed a season of relative peace.

Victorian London was Susie's primary context all of her life. On those occasions when she ventured outside London during her youth, it was to pursue cultural experiences and educational opportunities in France. For those journeys, Susie, accompanied by a chaperone, traveled down to Dover via carriage, crossed the English Channel by boat, and proceeded on to the brilliance of Paris with its art galleries, cathedrals, and monuments to military victories. There she learned to speak French and, as she gazed at the towers of Notre Dame or walked along the Seine River and near the Louvre, her English sensitivities were further refined. Perhaps it was as much the "City of Lights" as Victorian London that shaped the poetic quality of Susie's speech and later her writing. Certainly, her cultural proclivities and educational development were nurtured by the two cities.

SUSIE SHINES IN THE "CITY OF LIGHTS"

Like most London girls, Susie was educated in music (she was a pianist), art, manners, etiquette, and homemaking. But as a young woman, she also spent significant time pursuing an education in Paris.

The following advertisement from a London newspaper provides a clue as to why Susie went to Paris and how she eventually connected with Rev. Jean-Joël Audebez, a leader of the French church reform movement, and his family.

> Ladies and Young Ladies desirous of spending a few months in Paris, are informed that they would find a happy and comfortable home in the family of the Rev. J. J. Audebez, French Minister. They would enjoy all the advantages of social and religious intercourse. His three daughters would give them, every day, instruction in the French language.[5]

If the advertisement is an accurate indicator of when Susie began her Paris studies, then she was probably about eighteen years old. However, it is likely that she had visited Paris earlier and, because prior opportunities for study in Paris were available, she may have been as young as sixteen on her first visit.

Regardless, the advertisement placed by Audebez turned out to be a perfect opportunity for Susie to expand her education and to engage in social and theological exchanges. Paris became her schoolroom and her second home as she often traveled there until she was twenty-two years old.

France's capital city fascinated Susie, and she was attracted to its beautiful cathedrals and art galleries. The colors, windows, and spires of the ancient buildings looked heavenly to her. She possessed a keen knowledge of French history, and in her later writing, she nostalgically recalled the glory days of Paris prior to what she described as the "Communistic fires" that had "scorched and blackened her streets" and the "turbulent mobs" that had "despoiled her temples and palaces."[6] Her numerous trips to Paris included excursions to tour its famous attractions, as well as to learn the French language. It was during those Paris adventures that she spent months living in the Christian household of Pastor Audebez.[7]

Susie first came to Audebez's home after the death of his first wife in 1840 and during his second marriage to his wife's sister in 1842. Almost certainly, his daughter Clary Pauline and stepdaughter Maria became friends with Susie, as they were near her in age. They also served as Susie's tutors in French. Audebez was a writer, preacher, and missions leader, as well as pastor of several independent congregations in Paris.[8]

Minister John Yeardly, in his *Memoir and Diary,* writes warmly of Pastor Audebez:

We felt much inclined to hear him for ourselves, and attended in the Rue St. Maur on First-day evening; and we have this testimony to bear,—that we heard the *gospel* preached to the *poor.* He first read the 25th Psalm, and then part of the Epistle to the Romans, which formed the basis of his exhortation. It reminded me of [what I have read of] the preaching of the early Christians. My very heart went with his impressive exhortation to believe in the Lord Jesus as the only means of salvation, and of the necessity of bringing forth fruits unto holiness.[9]

Audebez was also one of the originators of the Evangelical Society of France. In the 1840s, he visited London on several occasions to report on the moving of God's Spirit in France and to raise funds to assist in the evangelistic efforts there. It's possible that during his London trips, Audebez made the acquaintance of R. B. Thompson, who became comfortable entrusting Susie to the pastor's school. Living in the godly home of the Audebez family provided a solid Christian influence for Susie as she enlarged her education, deepened her understanding of the gospel, and attended church with his family.

Susie's numerous ventures to Paris provided opportunities that served her well throughout her life. Some years later, she was in frequent contact with missionaries and pastors from around the world, and her multicultural experiences in France no doubt enhanced her international communication with gospel workers. Paris also proved to be even more memorable to Susie, as she and Charles would spend their honeymoon there.

Susie's early cultural and educational experiences stand in contrast to those of the man she would marry. Charles Spurgeon was a man of books and learning, yet his early years were steeped in rural culture with its green pastures, dirt roads, and small villages. Though he had visited London, he was more at home on his grandfather's land in the farming community of Stambourne, his parents' home in small-town Colchester, and the Puritan world of Cambridge with its outlying villages where he lived as a teenager. Even after he moved to London and was married, he sought homes outside the city that would afford him fresh air, clearer skies, and higher ground. The country life characterized Spurgeon's early experiences in ways that were evident in his speech, writing, and preaching until his death at age fifty-seven.

Susie, though a city girl, nevertheless had a deep appreciation for nature as well. In later years, when she was wracked with physical pain and often confined to Westwood, their home at Beulah Hill, she wrote of wishing that she were an artist so she "could with pencil or brush perpetuate some of the lovely pictures," which she had discovered when wandering with Charles across the grounds of that estate. Such happy memories stirred her to refer to that place as Dulce Domum, sweet home.[10]

Susie's childhood and youth were materially prosperous and socially astute. Charles, on the other hand, was a man of more modest means who, especially because of his impressive mind cultivated by voracious reading habits, could converse with people in either village or metropolis, with farmer or architect. He arrived in London, initially in the garb of a country preacher, to pastor the New Park Street Chapel (NPSC). He had come from a small village church, with even smaller wages, but what resources the members of the Waterbeach Chapel were blessed with, they gladly had shared with their bivocational pastor. Spurgeon recollected to his friend H. I. Wayland:

> I paid twelve shillings a week for my room at Cambridge, and had left seven shillings for all other expenses; but the people, whenever they came to town, would bring potatoes, turnips, cabbages, apples, and sometimes a bit of meat; and so I managed to live.[11]

In contrast, Susie's family enjoyed more prosperous circumstances, which were sometimes improved through her father's business enterprises and, likely, through the generosity of her extended family.

SUSIE'S PARENTS AND FAMILY

[To avoid confusion, it may help to note that this section refers to three different people named Susannah: Susannah (Susie) Thompson (later Spurgeon); her mother, Susannah Knott Thompson; and her cousin Susannah Kilvington Olney.]

Susie Thompson left behind only a few slender passages about her childhood and teenage years. Fragments from her family background can be pieced together through census reports and legal records. Susie's address on Old Kent Road was near her grandparents, Sampson and Mary Knott. The Knotts' home, with its small garden, would later play a role in Susie's romance with Charles.

In a rare glimpse into her childhood, Susie once recalled:

> When I was a little child, and had been troublesome to my mother, reproof or punishment would always be followed by the trembling question, "Mother, don't you love me?" And the mother's reply invariably was, "Yes, I love you: but I do not love your *naughty* ways." Poor mother! Doubtless I tried her very much, and this was the best that grieved parental love could say; but the Heavenly Father has sweeter, choicer words than these for His erring children. His love is Divine, so He says, "I have seen his ways *and will heal him.*" O sweet pitifulness of our God! O tenderness inexplicable! O love surpassing all earth's loveliest affection! Do not our hard hearts yield under the power of such compassion as this? God knows all our wickedness. He has seen all our waywardness; yet His purpose towards us is one of healing and pardon, and not of anger and putting away.[12]

As an only child, it is likely Susie, along with her mother, lived a relatively solitary home life due to her father's job, which required him to travel.

R. B. was employed in the warehousing industry as a foreman and as a traveling sales representative at various times during his career, eventually as an employee for Messers. Cook and Son, a large warehousing and distribution company of silk, linen, woolen, and cotton goods, located at St. Paul's Courtyard in the city of London.[13] For much of Susie's early life, her father, as a traveling sales rep, dealt in fabric, clothing, and accessories.

He rode the expanding rail lines across the country, visiting retailers with a sampling of his company's products.[14]

Susie began the 1840s as an eight-year-old girl and was seventeen as the decade ended. For her and her family, and also for many people in London, those years were times of highs and lows. They included the wedding of Victoria and Albert, but they were also marked by a significant economic downturn resulting in rising unemployment and the highest crime rate of the century.[15] The financial reversal that gripped the nation was felt all the way to the Thompsons' door.

Early in the decade, R. B. was a partner with two other wholesale warehousemen. That partnership dissolved on August 24, 1840. By May of 1842, R. B. was unable to meet the demands of his creditors. *The Morning Advertiser* from October 1842 under the heading "Law Notices This Day. Bankruptcy Court" listed "Robert Bennett Thompson, of Wood-street, warehouseman, audit and dividend at twelve."[16] Undoubtedly, this disrupted the Thompson household. Bankruptcy, debt, and unemployment, though widespread and feared, were viewed unfavorably in nineteenth-century England. Though Thompson avoided the poorhouse, one of the worst-case scenarios connected with such a financial downturn, his temporary inability to meet his obligations must have been a difficult burden for him to bear.

Susie was only ten years old at that time; old enough to feel the emotional blow to her family but young enough to be protected by parents and extended family members from the full impact of her father's financial troubles. Susie never mentioned her father's economic problems in her later writings, nor do any extant letters reveal her feelings during those trying times. It is unusual, given Susie's prolific writing later in life, that she rarely refers to her parents or childhood. Perhaps her reticence came from her sense of Victorian propriety or from sadness or awkwardness she felt in reflecting on such trying times.

The 1850s brought better days for London as rapid train transit created a "national culture," allowing London's daily papers to be read at the breakfast tables throughout the hamlets and cities of England. With the increased speed of steamships crossing the Atlantic, a more international culture developed in England.[17] Perhaps the most visible monument to "British Supremacy" was the Great Exhibition that opened in London's Hyde Park in May of 1851 and ran through October of that same year.[18]

R. B., his wife, Susannah, and daughter, Susie, would almost certainly have attended the Exhibition, along with six million others. Charles Spurgeon lived north of London in June of 1851 and traveled by train from Cambridge to visit the Great Exhibition.[19] For six months, the latest inventions and technological advances from around the world were on display. After the exhibit closed, its central structure, the Crystal Palace, was dismantled, reconstructed, and in 1854 reopened in south London.[20] Built of metal and glass, it was a unique architectural marvel, and the fulfillment of Prince Albert's dream. The massive structure, holding over 100,000 exhibits and three times longer than St. Paul's Cathedral, was "a triumph of engineering and design."[21] In 1854, the Crystal Palace played a key role in the budding relationship between Susie and Charles.

Susie's family lived primarily in the central London area of Falcon Square for much of the decade of the 1850s. With improving financial conditions, R. B. was able to hire a domestic servant for their home. Except when she was away in Paris, Susie resided with her parents until she was married in 1856. However, for two and a half years, the Thompson family again lived on the south bank of the Thames at 7 St. Ann's Terrace on Brixton Road, in the home of Susie's aunt, Mary, and her husband, Henry Kilvington.[22]

The Thompsons joined the Kilvington family, most likely, to provide assistance to them due to the deteriorating health and eventual death of Mary. The Kilvingtons still had children at home, and Susie and her mother, no doubt, would have been a help to them.

Henry and Mary's second eldest daughter, also named Susannah, was Susie's cousin and dear friend. By the time the Thompsons resided with the Kilvingtons, cousin Susannah was married. Her marriage to William

Olney, son of Thomas and Unity Olney, stalwart members of the New Park Street Chapel, would later provide the key connection between Susie and the Olney family and—ultimately—Charles Spurgeon.

Susie was especially close to Susannah and William. At one point during a spiritual struggle, she looked to William for counsel. She writes of that occasion referring to him as "Father Olney's second son" and her cousin by marriage. She described him as "an active worker in the Sunday-school at New Park Street, and a true Mr. Greatheart, and a comforter of young pilgrims."[23]

Susie's close relationship with her cousin Susannah often brought her into the societal circles of the Thomas Olney family, and she was regularly welcomed into their home, as a "greatly-privileged favourite with Mr. and Mrs. Olney."[24] The Olneys' love for the New Park Street Chapel (NPSC), and for the Thompson family, led to Susie and her parents' occasional church attendance at NPSC. Though Susie was not yet a Christian, she was surrounded by Christian influences.

Pastor James Smith served NPSC for nine years (1841–1850). He was the latest in a line of distinguished Baptist pastors stretching back to the 1600s that included Benjamin Keach and John Gill.[25] Smith gained the respect of the Thompsons, including Susie, who described him as "a quaint and rugged preacher, but one well-versed in the blessed art of bringing souls to Christ." Yet, at that point in her life, Susie was unconverted and uncertain. She would observe Smith baptize new believers "wondering with a tearful longing whether [she] should ever be able thus to confess [her] faith in the Lord Jesus."[26]

Thomas and Unity, along with their children, were important to the spiritual development of young Susie. Despite the scarcity of information about Susie prior to her marriage to Charles, a picture emerges of a girl and young lady influenced by godly people.

In his 1903 biography, *The Life of Susannah Spurgeon*, Charles Ray asserts, "The young girl's visits to New Park Street Chapel were no doubt more frequent than they would have been, from the fact that old Mr. and

Mrs. Olney were very fond of her and often invited her to visit them."[27]

However, until she was twenty-one years old, Susie had not yet professed her faith in Christ. In her writings, she often indicated conviction over her sins. Perhaps her sense of guilt clouded her eyes to the grace of Christ, hindering her confession. Many years later, *after* her conversion, Susie still grieved over her "misgivings" and "weaknesses." In her later years, she still considered herself "so forgetful, so unworthy, so inexcusable," yet by that time she understood God's kindness and sought Him for help to overcome her sins.[28]

The depth of Susie's parents' religious commitment remains uncertain; the fact that R. B. was baptized as an infant at an independent chapel and that his wife, Susannah Knott, was likewise baptized in the Church of England offers no resolution. The Thompsons' attendance at NPSC, primarily during the tenure of Pastor Smith, suggests that if they had ever been connected to Anglicanism, they were no longer.

Scripture reading was likely a regular activity in the Thompson family, as it was in many English homes of the day. Though the depth of England's love for Scripture at that time is a matter for debate, the Bible was nevertheless, as Victorian Era scholar Timothy Larsen argues, "a dominant presence in Victorian thought and culture."[29] Victorian literature and its art were saturated with references to Scripture,[30] and Victorian families often participated in both "morning and evening, private and household devotions." Larsen asserts that the Bible "was the lens through which people saw their own experiences."[31] However, the dominance of the Bible within the Victorian world was primarily a cultural veneer.

Regardless, the ubiquity of the Bible for the Victorians is inarguable, which helps to frame an understanding of the childhood and first twenty years of Susie Thompson's life.

When Susie died in 1903, her son Thomas stated at the memorial service that "R. B. Thompson, Esq. and his wife were occasional attendants at New Park Street Chapel,"[32] which indicates they were not members of the church, nor were they overly active participants. This may imply that after Smith left New Park Street, the Thompsons lost interest, or it may be a hint to Mrs. Thompson's developing illness that hindered her participation.

Robert, Susannah, and Susie moved from the Kilvington home to Falcon Square in late spring of 1855.[33] Falcon Square was a busy area of shops and inns where people lived and business was transacted. R. B.'s work headquarters was nearby, and Susie often walked past her father's business and window-shopped the latest wares at the shops. The great dome of St. Paul's Cathedral, a towering monument reflecting back to the days of Sir Christopher Wren's architectural prowess, was likely visible from Susie's home. As she enjoyed walks through the city, she passed by the old cattle and horse trough near her home, and she often strolled down nearby Aldersgate Street where the great Methodist preacher John Wesley was converted in 1738.

THE DEATH OF SUSIE'S PARENTS

Susie married in 1856, and her parents remained at Falcon Square. R. B. continued his work as a warehouseman. Sadly, Susie's mother Susannah entered into an extended period of sickness and suffering by 1862. Mrs. Thompson's affliction was severe, and she died April 14. The death certificate records her cause of death as, "Abdominal tumor of uncertain date. Hemorrhage from the stomach." Her obituary in *The Observer* simply read, "14th, Susannah, the wife of Mr. R. B. Thompson, Falcon-square City, aged 57."[34] Charles Spurgeon, in a letter to his parents in April, mentions Mrs. Thompson's long period of suffering:

> April 21/62
> My dear Father and Mother,
> In the hurry and singular excitement of the past week I failed to do what I should have done, viz to inform you of our loss.
> Poor Mrs. Thompson ceased to breathe last Monday

evening and I buried her this morning. She had suffered so long that her departure is subject of unfeigned joy. The bitterness of death is past. It was far better that she should depart than lie there to become a mass of living corruption and agony. Susie and our poor Mr. Thompson are both resigned as one could wish, indeed they feel as I do that it is well.

She enjoyed much peace, and seemed full of simple childlike faith. She enters glory as we must do solely through the merit of our only Savior.

The poor sinful soul is washed in precious blood and the body waits for the trump of the archangel.

Receive our warmest love. The time when we hope to see you draws near. Let us know your arrangements and consider us always.

Your loving Children,

Charles for both.[35]

Susie felt both relief that her mother's suffering had ended and grief over the loss. In addition to the letter providing Susannah's date of death and the fact that Charles led her funeral service, it also reveals that Mrs. Thompson's illness caused her longtime suffering. That, along with the early death of her sister and, later, Susie's long illness, suggests the possibility of a hereditary disease. Most importantly, Charles's correspondence indicates that Mrs. Thompson had a "simple childlike faith."

The death of Mrs. Thompson appeared to change the dynamic of Susie's relationship with her father. In the late 1860s, R. B. moved from Falcon Square to Bell Street where he was employed as a wine merchant. On October 18, 1870, he married Mary Ann Kirkwood, a widow, at Christ Church, Newgate Street. R. B. and Mary Ann resided at Middleton Street, Hornsey, just outside of London. Surprisingly, neither Charles nor Susie, nor any members of Thompson's extended family, are mentioned as participating in the wedding or being involved with R. B. after he remarried. Instead, R. B.'s accountant, Joseph Ramsdale, served as the legal witness to the marriage ceremony, and later as the executor of Thompson's will. The final known reference about any family interaction with R. B. is from a letter that Charles wrote to Susie in 1869 mentioning that her father had stopped by their home at Nightingale Lane for a visit while Susie was recovering from surgery in Brighton.[36]

With the loss of her mother and the uncertainties in her father's circumstances, Susie contented herself with her own home and pursuits. After she married Charles, she embraced his parents as her own, and she referred to them as mother and father. She even signed her correspondence to Charles's parents with the affectionate descriptor, "daughter."

The 1871 census records R. B. and Mary Ann as still living in Hornsey and Robert as an unemployed wine merchant.[37] For reasons unknown, in 1873, R. B. traveled to South Terrace, Penzance, almost three hundred miles from his home, where he died, at sixty-five, on October 5, from a probable heart attack ("spasm of the stomach and heart").[38] The *West Briton and Cornwall Advertiser* records that he was the "father-in-law of the Rev. C. H. Spurgeon." It is curious that Thompson was buried in Penzance and not London, the city where he had spent all of his life. If the issue was finances, Susie and Charles could have easily provided the necessary resources.

At R. B.'s death, his resources had diminished since his earlier, more successful days as a businessman, and he died in debt to the Mercantile Credit Association.[39] R. B.'s finances seemed to fluctuate throughout his life, though he did enjoy occasions of relative prosperity. In England, wealth was not the sole determiner of one's class in society. Business, property ownership, and job title were often just as important, in regards to determining social status, as one's financial portfolio. Therefore, descriptors of Robert as Esquire and gentleman may be more indicative of his circumstances related to property, work, and position.

R. B.'s story ends with some sense of sadness. Miles away from home and from his only daughter, he died and was buried, although it is likely

that his wife was with him. When he died, Susie was ill and mostly confined to her home. Yet, her godly character leads one to believe that she
loved her father and prayed for him.

Despite the lack of information about Susie's first twenty years, her
declaration that she went to church in her mother's womb and that from
childhood she professed a love for Jesus[40] indicates she was raised in a
home where Christ and His church were honored. And, though she didn't
make a confession of faith until she was twenty-one, gospel seeds had
been planted in her heart by her mother, friends, extended family, and
pastor that eventually sprang up into true faith in Christ that continued
to grow.

CHAPTER 2

A Progressing Pilgrim
1852–1855

$\Large S$ixty-one miles north of London, at Zion Chapel in Cambridge, a nineteen-year-old country preacher addressed a Sunday school anniversary gathering. Charles Haddon Spurgeon, pastor of the Waterbeach Baptist Chapel, just north of Cambridge's spires, preached forcefully, and his sermon made an impression on another young man who was in attendance that day. After hearing the fiery preacher, George Gould imagined what a splash such a talent would make in the city, and he knew just the church. As soon as Gould returned to London, he met with Thomas Olney and urged him to issue an invitation to Spurgeon to preach at the New Park Street Chapel. The rest, as they say, is history.

A few months prior to Gould's experience, a similar life-changing sermon was proclaimed in London. On a Sunday evening in late 1852, Susie Thompson exited her home in the city, made her way over to Cheapside Street, turned left, and entered the Poultry Chapel for worship services. Little did she know that the six-minute stroll among the shadows of St. Paul's Cathedral and to the old chapel in the business district of London that evening would lead her on another journey before the night was over, a journey from spiritual darkness into eternal life.

Though Susie normally attended the New Park Street Chapel, it would not have been unusual for her to join in special services at another church from time to time. The short path to the Poultry Chapel was a familiar one to Susie and her parents since they had lived in the area for some time. The origins of the chapel date from 1640, and it is believed that the Puritan preacher Thomas Goodwin founded it. The nonconformist (dissenting from the Church of England) congregation moved to Poultry, Cheapside in 1819.[1] The area was named Poultry because of the poulterers (poultry dealers) who transacted business there in times past.

Susie's father was born nearby in the Old Artillery Grounds Parish and had been baptized as an infant at George Whitefield's Tabernacle near Moorgate Street. The remains of saints such as Susannah Wesley and John Bunyan lay just north in the Bunhill Fields burial grounds across the street from John Wesley's chapel.

R. B.'s baptism at the Tabernacle, Susie's attendance at the Poultry Chapel, and her and her parents' participation at the New Park Street Chapel are all indicators that the Thompsons were more theologically aligned with nonconformity than they were with the established Church of England. In the Thompsons' case, their nonconformity to the Church of England meant, in part, that they believed in a free church, independent from the state, and that they were evangelical in nature.

That winter's evening, Pastor S. B. Bergne preached from Romans: "But what saith it? The word is nigh thee, even in thy mouth, and in thy heart: that is, the word of faith, which we preach; that if thou shalt confess with thy mouth the Lord Jesus and shalt believe in thine heart that God hath raised him from the dead, thou shalt be saved" (Rom. 10:8–9).

Despite the waning light of the winter's evening, inside the relatively small and "dingy"[2] chapel, Susie experienced "the dawning of the true light" in her soul. As the words of the sermon fell on the ears of the congregation, Susie heard something else too . . . she heard the Lord say, "Give Me thine heart."

"Constrained by His love," she later wrote, "that night witnessed my solemn resolution of entire surrender to Himself."[3] Susie was almost twenty-one years old.

Like so many in the well-mannered and religious English culture around her, Susie had spent her first twenty-one years within an assumed Christianity, reading her Bible, praying, and attending church. The rest of her Christian life would be very different, although initially clouded with doubts about her newfound faith.

Susie looked back on her experience at the Poultry Chapel as the time of her true conversion to Christ and yet, for the next year, she entered into seasons of "darkness, despondency, and doubt." It was difficult for her to face such spiritual challenges so soon after her conversion, but worse still, she kept both her new faith and her doubts bottled up in her heart. She said that she "became cold and indifferent to the things of God" and she described her spiritual condition as "sickly and sleepy."[4]

⁂

Though she was unimpressed the first time she heard Charles Spurgeon preach, Susie later interpreted that first encounter through the lens of God's sovereign governance. She had been trained to appreciate societal propriety in speech, manner, and dress. Charles violated her preconceived notions of what was appropriate for a polite young man in Victorian times, and a preacher at that. Susie found Charles's hair, suit, mannerisms, and his provocative preaching style offensive. Later, reflecting on her earlier sentiments, she wrote:

> Ah! How little I then thought that my eyes looked on him who was to be my life's beloved; how little I dreamed of the honour God was preparing for me in the near future! It is a mercy that our lives are not left for us to plan, but that our Father chooses

for us; else might we sometimes turn away from our best blessings, and put from us the choicest and loveliest gifts of His providence.[5]

It was Sunday morning, December 18, 1853, when Charles first filled the pulpit at the historic chapel. Susie, who was visiting with the family of NPSC deacon Thomas Olney, didn't attend that morning service, but witnessed the family's excitement after they returned home, both bewildered and amazed . . . for "they had never before heard such preaching . . . [for] they had been fed with royal dainties."[6]

Olney and his family were overjoyed about young Charles, and they believed that his first sermon that day was an indicator of great things to come for him and, they hoped, for their church.

Charles, however, had a different reaction to the service. He was discouraged because attendance was scant in a building that seated over a thousand people, and he longed to be back at the Waterbeach Chapel among the people who loved and supported him.[7] The crowd that gathered back at the village church that morning while Charles preached in London far exceeded the small congregation at the prominent New Park Street Chapel that December day. The Olneys, determined to encourage the nineteen-year-old preacher by securing a larger crowd for the Sunday evening service, spent the afternoon enlisting friends to attend the evening sermon.

Susie was one of the people Thomas Olney persuaded to attend.[8] Her mind swelled with fond memories of the historic chapel as she awaited the appearance of Spurgeon at the pulpit. She recalled select memories from her earlier experiences at the church. She remembered everything from a deacon's attire and the "curious pulpit without any stairs" to the way the previous pastor, James Smith, conducted services.[9] Susie had enlightened opinions regarding the appropriate decorum of the service and the pastor.

The Olneys were glad that "little Susie," as they called her, would join them to hear Spurgeon preach. She esteemed the Olney family, but she was unenthusiastic about hearing Charles. Her "ideas of the dignity and propriety of ministry were rather shocked . . . by the reports which the morning worshippers had brought back concerning the young man's unconventional outward appearance!" When she first saw Charles in the pulpit, she was distracted more by his looks than she was drawn to his sermon. She was amused by his "huge black satin stock" and his "long, badly-trimmed hair, and the blue pocket handkerchief with white spots."[10]

Susie's concern about the preacher's exterior spoke to her spiritual immaturity and the cultural perspective formed by her upbringing in London. Such was the case with many parishioners in England's great city who were members of prominent churches. However, Susie wanted to please Mr. and Mrs. Olney and, as she would record many years later, she "was present at the second sermon, which my precious husband preached in London."[11]

Despite her acquiescence to attend, Susie, no ordinary girl of mere modest means or sentiments, "was not at all fascinated by the young orator's eloquence" and thought Spurgeon's "countrified manner and speech excited more regret than reverence."[12]

Years later, after Spurgeon's death, Susie reflected on the ill-informed opinions of her younger days. She admitted that she had been "foolish" and "was not spiritually-minded enough to understand his earnest presentation of the gospel, and his powerful pleading with sinners."[13] But his was a sermon that Susie, so full of uncertainty, desperately needed to hear.

SUSIE AND NEW PARK STREET CHAPEL'S SPIRITUAL CHALLENGES

Susie's offended sensibilities hindered her from being receptive to Charles's message, yet at the same time, she was troubled that she lacked assurance of true faith. Years later she surmised: "None could have more needed the quickening and awakening which I received from the earnest pleadings and warnings of that voice, soon to be the sweetest in all the world to me."[14] Susie needed biblical preaching, and, though reluctant at first, she found help for her travails through Charles.

New Park Street Chapel faced its own problems and was greatly diminished from its former days of vibrancy. Attendance had significantly declined, and a sense of hopelessness tempted the faithful who nevertheless remained active in the church. Among those faithful few was the Olney family, who prayed that God would bring revival to the church. Susie's own parents were now seldom to be found at NPSC and, had it not been for the Olneys, Susie herself would not have been as active a church attender as she was.

Like Susie, the church needed a spiritual renewal. The recorded minutes from a church meeting on December 14, 1853, just four days before Spurgeon preached his first sermon at NPSC, offer insight into difficulties the church faced: "Dear Brethren, We regret that, during the past year, we have made no additions to our numbers in consequence of our being without a Pastor." The minutes, which were sent to the London Baptist Association, closed with these revealing words: "We enclose our statistics. Brethren, pray for us."[15]

After Charles's first sermon, the church had its hopes renewed that better days were ahead. Before even completing an agreed-upon trial period, which began in late January 1854, the church overwhelmingly extended a call for young Charles Spurgeon to serve as their pastor. On April 28, 1854, he sent a letter to the church in which he simply stated, "I ACCEPT IT."[16] He entreated the church to remember him in prayer and requested their "co-operation in every good work; in visiting the sick, in bringing in enquirers, and in mutual edification."[17]

Though he was only nineteen, he demonstrated maturity by his request for help, and by God's grace, he was ready for the task at hand.[18] Little did Charles know that his greatest help would come from a lovely London lady with long, curly brown hair who occupied a pew on that first Sunday evening. Through Charles's ministry, the church was revitalized, and it experienced both numerical and spiritual growth. Susie Thompson too experienced her own spiritual revitalization and growth.

THE PILGRIM'S PROGRESS
AS A MEANS OF SPIRITUAL HELP

Before Charles's influence in Susie's spiritual life, she had sought guidance from her cousin Susannah's husband, William Olney, who had listened carefully as Susie described her concerns about her spiritual state. William was likely the one who informed Charles of Susie's struggles.

Soon after her conversation with William, Susie was surprised to receive an illustrated copy of John Bunyan's *The Pilgrim's Progress*, inscribed: "Miss Thompson, with desires for her progress in the blessed pilgrimage. From C. H. Spurgeon, April 20, 1854."[19]

The Pilgrim's Progress was, in Charles's view, the right book for Susie. She, though twenty-two years old, was a new convert, and a discouraged one at that. Just as Bunyan's writings had been instrumental in Charles's own understanding of the Christian faith, he was confident that Bunyan's allegory would positively counter Susie's uncertainty. She considered Charles's gift to her as indicative of his desire to "help a struggling soul heavenward." She was greatly impressed by his concern, and "the book became very precious as well as helpful."[20] Bunyan's allegory took deep root in her heart, and eventually influenced her own books, letters, and other literary offerings, which often employed Bunyan's descriptors of the Christian life.

Charles insightfully turned to *The Pilgrim's Progress* as a means of spiritual encouragement for Susie. In 1903, the year of Susie's death, their son Thomas Spurgeon wrote that his father was "in love with John Bunyan" and was "akin to him in faith and thought and language."[21] Thomas surmised, "Here [in *Pilgrim's Progress*] is milk for babes and meat for men. . . . Moreover, the meat is such that the 'babes' will enjoy a taste of it, and the 'men' will be all the better for a sip or two of the milk."[22]

Spurgeon scholar Peter Morden explains that Bunyan's writing influenced Spurgeon by providing "a framework for understanding the Christian life" and by offering a way for him to "make sense of particular experiences that occurred along a Christian's journey."[23] Certainly, Charles hoped for such results with Susie.

Since both Charles and Susie were regular visitors at the Olney home, they had occasion to see one another often. As Susie became better acquainted with Charles, she confided in him by sharing her spiritual concerns. It stretches the imagination a bit and is somewhat humorous to think of the refined city girl, sharing her heart's concerns with the more rustic Charles. How ironic that the man who had once offended her sensibilities became the one that she looked to for counsel:

> By degrees, though with much trembling, I told him of my
> state before God, and he gently led me, by his preaching, and
> by his conversations, through the power of the Holy Spirit, to
> the cross of Christ for the peace and pardon my weary soul was
> longing for. [24]

Interacting with Charles and reading Bunyan's *Pilgrim's Progress* helped Susie to better apply Scripture. Thomas Spurgeon, in the foreword to *Pictures from Pilgrim's Progress*, provides a context from which it is easy to understand how Bunyan's classic work would have been helpful to Susie:

> Urging the earnest study of the Scriptures, C. H. Spurgeon once
> said: "Oh, that you and I might get into the very heart of the
> Word of God, and get that Word into ourselves! As I have seen
> the silkworm eat into the leaf, and consume it, so ought we to
> do with the Word of the Lord—not crawl over its surface, but
> eat right into it till we have taken it into our inmost parts. It is
> idle merely to let the eye glance over the words, or to recollect
> the poetical expressions, or the historic facts; but it is blessed to

eat into the very soul of the Bible until, at last, you come to talk
in Scriptural language, and your very style is fashioned upon
Scripture models, and, what is better still, your spirit is flavored
with the words of the Lord. I would quote John Bunyan as an
instance of what I mean. Read anything of his, and you will
see that it is almost like reading the Bible itself. He had read it
till his very soul was saturated with Scripture; and, though his
writings are charmingly full of poetry, yet he cannot give us his
Pilgrim's Progress—that sweetest of all prose poems—without
continually making us feel and say, 'Why, this man is a living
Bible!' Prick him anywhere; his blood is Bibline, the very essence
of the Bible flows from him. He cannot speak without quoting a
text, for his very soul is full of the Word of God."[25]

For Spurgeon, reading Bunyan was "almost like reading the Bible
itself" and "the very essence of the Bible flows from him." Spurgeon
confessed:

Next to the Bible, the book that I value most is John Bunyan's
"Pilgrim's Progress." I believe I have read it through at least a
hundred times. It is a volume of which I never seem to tire; and
the secret of its freshness is that it is so largely compiled from
the Scriptures. It is really Biblical teaching put into the form of
a simple yet very striking allegory.[26]

Obviously, Bunyan's classic made an impact on Susie as her own blood
later could be considered "Bibline," and by 1884 she had read the Bible
through fourteen times, which meant, "reading about three chapters daily
to accomplish this in a year."[27]

Years later, Charles asked Susie if she recommended such a plan as the
one that she used. She responded that a regular reading through of the
Bible was helpful to acquaint the reader with all of Scripture, including

parts that "might otherwise be passed over." However, for her "spiritual enlightenment and refreshment," she preferred meditating on smaller portions of Scripture, such as a "half a verse." It was usually during her times of focused meditation on a few verses that she "experienced more application of the text by the Holy Spirit."[28]

The deepening of Susie's faith is a testimony to the impact of her Bible reading and meditation and the subsequent tutelage of Charles. She considered the words of Scripture "tender words" and the words of "Jesus Christ himself, my gracious Lord and Master, who thus speaks, and I shall do well to ponder every weighty sentence as I listen to his loving voice."[29]

The chain of the events that led Susie to Charles and even to *The Pilgrim's Progress* is a study in the providence of God.

Imagine if Susie's cousin Susannah had not married William Olney, and if Thomas Olney had not married Unity Potter, and if James Smith had continued his ministry at New Park Street Chapel, Charles and Susie may never have met. Yet, the event that first set it all in motion happened on a Saturday afternoon in Cambridge.

George Stevenson, in his *Sketch of the Life and Ministry of the Rev. C. H. Spurgeon,* wrote poetically of George Gould's meeting with Thomas Olney:

> The young speaker at Cambridge is recommended to the New Park-street [*sic*] deacon; hope succeeds; faith is strengthened; the young speaker is applied to, and soon after, while yet in his 'teens,' becomes the appointed pastor of the once largest Baptist church in London. This young man is the Rev. Charles Haddon Spurgeon.[30]

Charles said that his speech at Cambridge and the corresponding request of Gould to Olney was "the hand of God, the means of my transference from Cambridgeshire to the metropolis."[31] It was also his means of transport to the heart of Susie Thompson.

CHAPTER 3

Hearts United at the Crystal Palace

Anticipation in London had been building for months as the news-papers carried regular updates on a massive building project south of the city. June 10, 1854, was to be a day of fanfare with the reopening of the Crystal Palace. The Palace, crafted with iron and glass, was the genius of the famed designer Sir Joseph Paxton (1803–1865) and was an architectural marvel. It had originally been built at London's Hyde Park as a temporary hall for the Great Exhibition of 1851. Constructed in less than a year, it was dismantled six months after the Exhibition and moved to a permanent location in the south London suburb, Sydenham Hill.[1] Beyond the magnificent building itself, the stunning grounds surrounding the palace contained gardens, fountains, and numerous models of extinct animals. In the midst of the excitement of the Palace's grand celebration, a similarly impressive love story was unfolding.

Little did Susie know that Charles's pastoral concern for her in April of 1854 and their subsequent steadily growing friendship would blossom into romance by June. Though Susie testified to being "happier than I had been since the days at the Poultry Chapel" where she had been converted, her joy was centered in her newly found spiritual clarity and the privilege of enjoying friendship with her pastor. It doesn't seem that any romantic thoughts about Charles had yet entered her mind prior to June. Initially, Charles was simply helping a "struggling soul heavenward," through his gift of *The Pilgrim's Progress*, but he must have soon after entertained the possibility of something more regarding his friendship with Susie. Less than two months after presenting his gift of Bunyan's book to her, Charles found a way to creatively communicate to Susie his interest in pursuing more than a friendship.

Susie Thompson and Charles Spurgeon were seated together with friends from the New Park Street Chapel. While the crowd eagerly anticipated the Crystal Palace's opening ceremony, Charles handed Susie a copy of Martin Tupper's *Proverbial Philosophy* and pointed her to a section titled "Of Marriage."

> Seek a good wife of thy God, for she is the best gift of his
>   providence;
> Yet ask not in bold confidence that which he hath not promised.
> Thou knowest not his good will:—be thy prayer then submissive
>   thereunto;
> And leave the petition to his mercy, assured that he will deal
>   well with thee.
> If thou art to have a wife of thy youth, she is now living on the
>   earth;
> Therefore think of her, and pray for her weal; yea, though thou
>   has not seen her.[2]

Susie looked at Charles as he whispered in her ear, "Do you pray for him who is to be your husband?"[3] The intended message surprised her, but it was unmistakable. Susie didn't respond to the question, but her quickening heartbeat sent a telltale flush to her cheeks. She didn't meet

Charles's gaze, afraid he would see "the light which at once dawned in them." She continued to sit quietly beside him, "while the brilliant procession passed round the Palace." But "the glittering pageant" couldn't compete with "the crowd of newly-awakened emotions which were palpitating within her heart."[4]

That Susie seemed to have previously lacked even a hint of his earlier romantic interest may seem surprising to modern readers, but it speaks to her utter lack of presumptiveness regarding her friendship with Charles. The young couple slipped away from the group with whom they were seated, and they walked together throughout the building, around the Palace gardens, and down the outside steps to the lake a hundred yards below. At the lake they viewed the "colossal forms of extinct monsters." These dinosaur models were fascinating to the couple, but, more importantly, God was creating a lifelong bond of love between Charles and Susie.[5]

After Charles died in 1892, Susie described the stroll along the Palace grounds on that June evening: "During that walk, on that memorable day in June, I believe God Himself united us to each other forever. From that time our friendship grew apace, and quickly ripened into deepest love."[6] Susie said of the Crystal Palace that it "was a favorite resort with us;" "It possessed great attractions of its own, and perhaps the associations of the opening day gave it added grace in our eyes."[7]

CHARLES AND SUSANNAH'S ENGAGEMENT

Less than two months following Charles's gifting of *Pilgrim's Progress* to Susie, he pointed to Tupper's poem to communicate his romantic intentions; and two months later, he proposed marriage on August 2, 1854, in her grandfather Sampson Knott's garden.[8] The garden, according to Susie, "was a little old-fashioned garden . . . which had high brick walls on three sides, and was laid out with straight, formal gravel paths, and a small lawn in the midst of which flourished a large and very fruitful pear tree—the pride of old granddad's heart." The garden was not a very romantic setting, and Susie didn't imagine that most people would choose such a location for a "declaration of love."[9]

But for Susie, "dreary" as the garden may have been, it took on a magical atmosphere because it became the setting of her engagement and was forever etched upon her memory. "To this day," she later recalled, "I think of that old garden as a sacred place, a paradise of happiness, since there my beloved sought me for his very own, and told me how much he loved me."[10]

Charles's love for Susie was obvious, but he reserved uttering the three powerful words, "I love you," until the moment of his proposal of marriage. Susie "trembled" at the experience and "was silent for very joy and gladness." Of the "sweet ceremony of betrothal" she declared, "Every loving and true heart can fill up the details either from experience or anticipation. To me it was a time as *solemn* as it was sweet."[11]

Susie, overwhelmed by the experience, felt as if she must immediately seek God in prayer. She quickly exited the quaint garden and retreated to a private upstairs room in her grandfather's house. There, she "knelt before God, and praised and thanked him with happy tears for his great mercy in giving me the love of so good a man."[12] In her diary, dated August 2, 1854, she wrote: "It is impossible to write down all that occurred to me this morning. I can only adore in silence the mercy of my God, and praise Him for all His benefits."[13]

Susie later confessed to not fully knowing, at that time, the extent of Charles's greatness. Had she fully grasped what being Mrs. Charles Haddon Spurgeon would entail, she may have been overwhelmed. In her many reflections on her engagement and marriage to Charles, Susie expressed that God brought them together. She declared, "The perfect love which drew us together never slackened or faltered; and, though I can now see how undeserving I was to be the life companion of so eminent a servant of God, I know *he* did not think this, but looked upon his wife as God's best earthly gift to him."[14]

Charles and Susie acquired season tickets to the Crystal Palace, and, during their engagement, met there as often as once a week to walk and talk together.[15] The Palace with its colorful gardens provided an interesting and beautiful context for their love to grow. Sentimentally, it held a special place in Susie's heart because that was where Charles had so imaginatively revealed his feelings for her in June of 1854. In addition, the Palace itself, with its mesmerizing exhibits from exotic lands and its lovely grounds, was an enjoyable and educational place to visit. Every time they entered the Palace grounds and walked by the lake, the memories of that sweet June day flooded her mind. Susie believed that the weekly retreats helped to brace Charles for the constant demands of his ministry, as well as the depressing effects of London's often dreary weather conditions combined with the smells of industry.

For Charles's weekly meetings with Susie in Sydenham, he took a train at the London Bridge station, and in short order he arrived at the Crystal Palace. Susie, on the other hand, was then living at 7 St. Ann's Terrace, Brixton Road, and she would often walk seven miles to the Palace, that being no small achievement. Though it was a long walk for Susie, she averred that it was "a pleasant task to me, with such a meeting in view and such delightful companionship as a reward."[16]

Charles was clever in the manner that he suggested his weekly rendezvous with Susie. She remembered, "After the close of the Thursday evening service [at the New Park Street Chapel], there would be a whispered word to me in the aisle, 'Three o'clock tomorrow,' which meant that if I would be at the Palace by that hour 'somebody' would meet me at the Crystal Fountain."[17] Charles and Susie's romance was playful and delightful. She described their time at the Palace as "bright blissful hours." During their early experiences, both enjoyed good health, and though Charles was very busy with his ministry, neither he nor Susie were yet hindered by the challenges that would later diminish their physical vitality.

Beyond their regular meetings at the Crystal Palace, their weekly "dates" were centered on Charles's work. Charles made the short drive from 75 Dover Road to Susie's home most Mondays. He brought with him a transcribed copy of his Sunday sermon so that he could revise it for publication and distribution. While Charles worked, Susie sat quietly near him, and she considered their time together as "good discipline for the Pastor's intended wife."[18]

If Susie had ever entertained any independent aspirations for herself, by this time she had embraced Charles's aims, plans, and work, and she found her joy in helping him. Even though women in Victorian times enjoyed little independence and were mostly expected to live beneath the shadow of their husband, Susie's relational perspective was not built on cultural norms; she simply delighted in submitting her life to such a kind man as Charles.

Charles deeply loved Susie, and she was treated queenly under his care; their love story is replete with examples of his tender, thoughtful, and romantic treatment of her. However, he was also uncompromisingly devoted to his work. Susie said that his devotion to his ministry "dominated and even absorbed every other passion and purpose of his heart."[19]

Though Susie was content with her unique circumstances, she nevertheless at times felt lonely. On occasion, Charles was so engrossed in his ministry that he didn't even recognize Susie when she approached him on Sundays at church. There were times that he introduced himself to her as if she were a complete stranger. Susie was good-natured about Charles's distractedness, and she was not prone to attribute ill motives to him. However, there was at least one occasion when Susie was angered over his oversight of her. In the community of Kennington, just a mile or two from where the Thompsons then resided, there was a meeting hall called the Horns, occasionally used as a preaching venue.

Charles was scheduled to preach there one afternoon. He enjoyed lunch with the Thompsons, and then he and Susie took a cab together to the meeting hall. Though he had been in London for less than a year, his fame had skyrocketed, and as a result, the crowds flocked to hear him wherever he was preaching. As Charles helped Susie out of the cab, she attempted to stay near his side so as to not get lost in the mass of people. However, Charles was so intently focused on what was about to transpire, the preaching of the gospel, that he forgot about Susie and inadvertently left her as the crowd pressed inside the building.

Susie ran from the building and back home to her mother, fuming and tears streaming down her face. As she shared her "grief," Mrs. Thompson listened intently to her daughter's account and then tried to soothe her "ruffled spirit." Susie recalled, "She wisely reasoned that my chosen husband was no ordinary man, that his whole life was absolutely dedicated to God and His service, and that I must never, *never* hinder him by trying to put myself first in his heart."

Realizing that she had been "very foolish and willful," Susie was beginning to calm down when Charles burst into the house crying out, "Susie, Susie!" With great emotion, he told Mrs. Thompson that he had searched for Susie everywhere to no avail.

Susie recalled:

> My dear mother went to him, took him aside, and told him all the truth; and I think, when he realized the state of things, she had to soothe him also, for he was so innocent at heart of having offended me in any way, that he must have felt that I had done him an injustice in doubting him. At last, mother came to fetch me to him, and I went downstairs. Quietly he let me tell him how indignant I had felt, and then he repeated mother's little lesson, assuring me of his deep affection for me, but pointing out that, before all things, he was *God's servant,* and I must be prepared to yield my claims to His.[20]

Charles, like his hero George Whitefield, put his public ministry at such a premium that sometimes his personal involvement in the immediate needs of his family came second. A 360-degree view of Charles and Susie's marriage reveals, however, that he didn't neglect his ministerial responsibilities, and yet he also made sure Susie was cared for. For her part, Susie made a strong commitment: "It was ever the settled purpose of my married life that I should never hinder him in his work for the Lord, never try to keep him from fulfilling his engagements, never plead my own ill-health as a reason why he should remain at home with me."[21] Though unique challenges associated with being married to a man who faced "incessant demands of his ministry, his literary work, and the multiplied labours of his exceptionally busy life" were overwhelming at times, the Lord helped Susie to fulfill her secret promise.

After the peacemaking efforts of Mrs. Thompson had proven successful, the three of them enjoyed "a delightfully cozy tea" together that evening. "How sweet was the calm in our hearts after the storm," Susie thought later, "and how much we loved and honoured mother for her wise counsels and her tender diplomacy."[22] A mother with less wisdom might have deepened the breach between Charles and Susie, but Susie's mother, gentle as she was, had stout character and recognized the beautiful and unique relationship between Charles and Susie that was unfolding before her eyes. On that emotional evening, the relationship between Charles and Susie was strengthened, and their respect for Mrs. Thompson deepened.

The couple's engagement period is replete with examples of how Charles took Susie's spiritual growth seriously and how he understood his role in her development in godliness. The gift of *Pilgrim's Progress* was an early evidence of his commitment to Susie's sanctification. The usage of Tupper's book pointed to their need for prayer, and Charles looked to yet another book, this one by Puritan pastor and author Thomas Brooks (1608–1680), as an encouragement to Susie during the months preceding their marriage.[23] Susie was eager to learn, and she was especially delighted to receive counsel from one as dear as life to her.

In the summer of 1855, after the Thompsons had moved to Falcon Square, Charles and Susie met more frequently, and Susie happily declared that their "hearts were knit closer and closer in purest love."[24] Though Susie and Charles enjoyed more time together, he continued to bring his work with him to her home. She was rather stunned one day when Charles said, "I want you to go carefully through this volume, marking all those paragraphs and sentences that strike you as being particularly sweet, or quaint, or instructive; will you do this for me?"[25] Charles' intent was that Susie's collection of quotes from the writings of Thomas Brooks would be published as a book.

This literary undertaking was a first for Susie; however, she described her findings from that volume by Thomas Brooks as "bright diamonds and red gold." She later reflected on the results of her work alongside Charles:

> Love . . . is a matchless teacher, and I was a willing pupil; and so, with help and suggestion from so dear a tutor, the work went on from day to day till, in due time, a small volume made its appearance, which he called, *Smooth Stones Taken From Ancient Brooks.* This title was a pleasant and Puritanic play upon the author's name, and I think the compilers were well pleased with the results of their happy work together. I believe the little book is out of print now, and copies are very rarely to be met with; but those who possess them may feel an added interest in their perusal, now that they know the sweet love-story which hides between their pages.[26]

The book didn't bear Susie's name then, nor do modern editions carry her name now. Susie didn't long for any personal credit or fame that might accompany her by having her name attached to the work; her concern was for the contents of the book and for the "sweet love-story" hidden between the pages. Susie's labor in collecting quotes by Brooks served the purpose of uniting her and Charles on a project, and it was another opportunity for her to glean spiritual wisdom. Charles believed that the sermons and writings of Brooks were solid biblical expositions. A strong foundation was being laid, upon which both Susie and Charles stood as they would weather the storms and navigate the challenges of marriage and ministry.

Under Charles's tutelage, Susie applied for church membership at

New Park Street Chapel about four months after their engagement. The membership requirements necessitated that Susie write out a description of her faith. This testimony was then presented to a church leader who noted his acceptance by signing the official church book. Susie was afterward scheduled for a meeting with the pastor (Charles), visited by church leaders at her home to discern if she was living a godly life, presented to the church where she gave an account of the Lord's dealings with her (January 23, 1855), and was accepted into membership after her baptism. Beside Susie's name in the church book is a simple statement by Charles, "Affirmed by C. H. Spurgeon."[27]

Spurgeon's first reaction to Susie's written testimony was one of delight:

> Oh! I could weep for joy (as I certainly am doing now) to think that my beloved can so well testify to a work of grace in her soul. I knew that you were *really* a child of God, but I did not think you had been led in such a path. I see my Master has been ploughing deep and it is the deep-sown seed, struggling with the clods, which makes your bosom heave with distress. . . . I flatter no one, but allow me to say, honestly, that few cases which have come under my notice are so satisfactory as yours. Mark, I write not now as your *admiring friend*, but impartially as your Pastor.[28]

Charles's joyous prose is infused with emotion. Susie was his fiancée, and she was soon to be a fellow member with him at New Park Street. It is at this point that Charles first encouraged Susie to a life of active service for Christ:

> If I know anything of spiritual symptoms, I think I know a cure for you. Your position is not the sphere for earnest labour for Christ. You have done all you could in more ways than one; but you are not brought into actual contact either with the saints or with the sinful, sick, or miserable, whom you could serve. Active

service brings with it warmth, and this tends to remove doubting, for our works thus become evidence of our calling and election.[29]

Charles, in his letter to Susie, discerningly avoided blurring the lines between his pastoral duties and his growing romantic affection for her. In that letter he wrote, "Mark, I write not now as your *admiring friend* but impartially as your Pastor." He gently encouraged her to engage her faith in acts of service. He believed that active service to fellow Christians would result in Susie finding relief from her doubt and display evidence of her salvation. Through *The Pilgrim's Progress,* Susie had learned that when in "Doubting Castle," remember the promises of God. When "Giant Despair" held Christian and Hopeful captive, they only needed to pray and bring to mind God's promises in order to be set free. Bunyan had written:

> Well, on *Saturday* about midnight they began to *pray,* and they continued in Prayer till almost break of day. Now, a little before it was Day, good *Christian* as one half amazed, brake out in this passionate speech; What a Fool, quoth he, am I, thus to lie in a stinking dungeon, where I may as well walk at liberty? I have a key in my bosom, called *Promise,* that will I am persuaded open any lock in *Doubting-Castle.* Then said *Hopeful,* That's good news, good brother, pluck it out of thy bosom and try. Then Christian pulled it out of his bosom, and began to try at the dungeon door. Whose bolt (as he turned the Key) gave back, and the door flew open with ease, and *Christian* and *Hopeful* both came out.[30]

Susie first needed to ponder the promises of God, and then she had to act upon them. She had to insert the key, open the gate, and return to the "King's Highway."[31] Traveling the "King's Highway" included serving others. Charles encouraged Susie, and then he rejoiced in her joyful testimony of faith. Careful not to flatter her, he nevertheless shared his conviction with Susie that he believed her to be a true Christian: "God in his mercy showed me that you were indeed *elect*." His conclusion about Susie's spirituality came by observation of her life, through reading of her conversion experience, and by her willingness to heed wise counsel.

Susie's spiritual maturity was rapidly developing, so much so that Charles described her as "deeply schooled in the lessons of the heart" and being "so thoroughly versed in soul-knowledge."[32] As Charles contemplated Susie's robust love for Christ, he bubbled over with emotion. He declared, "Dear purchase of a Saviour's blood, you are to me a Saviour's gift, and my heart is full to over-flowing with the thought of such continued goodness." Charles never doubted that God was good, but, upon reading Susie's account of her faith, he could not help "but lift up the voice of joy at his manifold mercies."[33] Charles's sentiments should first of all be read as the joy of a pastor over a fellow Christian's testimony of faith in Christ and, secondly, the double joy he expressed because she was his fiancée. Susie was baptized on February 1, 1855, and became a church member on Sunday, February 4. She described her baptism: "I was baptized there [New Park Street Chapel] by my beloved, upon my profession of repentance towards God, and faith in our Lord Jesus Christ."[34]

Charles was overjoyed with Susie; she was the partner that he needed, prayed for, and increasingly depended on. They visited with his parents in Colchester in April 1855, where Susie was warmly welcomed. Susie's father had only reluctantly agreed to allow her to make the journey with Charles, and she later lamented, "After some trouble and disappointment, my father's consent was obtained and we set off."[35] Perhaps R. B. Thompson was simply being a cautious father, concerned about sending his daughter off with a gentleman, not yet her husband. Or perhaps he felt, as the account below hints at, that Charles had not sufficiently honored him. Regardless, Thompson's feelings about Spurgeon fluctuated, evidenced in this letter that Charles wrote to his mother in November of 1854, two months into his engagement to Susie:

75 Dover Road
November 1, 1854

My Dear Mother,

Polly [likely a relative] went yesterday to the Crystal Palace and I hope enjoyed the day. We met with Mrs. Thompson and daughter and having been very urgently invited by Mr. T. [R. B.] we went home to Brixton.

I have left Eliza [Charles's younger sister] there and am going now to spend the day at said house. Young Mr. Kilvington [Henry and Mary's son] is going to Australia tomorrow and all the family are to meet today, Old Mrs. Knott and all. I hope we shall enjoy ourselves without sin. God still deals bountifully with me. Only think of over £800 being subscribed at once for our chapel. Giving £100 has plucked all my feathers off but by the helping of Providence they will soon grow again. . . .

It is not often that I am out and when I am I drive at other people's hours. Mr. Thompson is all of a sudden become extremely kind and does not know how to serve me enough, he declares that he should have liked me well enough but that I never called to see him so you see I am not given to visiting much.

I am
Your most loving Son,
Charles[36]

The letter, written early in Charles and Susie's relationship, indicates that R. B. Thompson had been slow to warm up to his daughter's young fiancé, but by the time of the letter, he seemed more inclined to show hospitality and even "serve" his future son-in-law. Even so, Thompson again displayed reluctance toward Charles in the spring of 1855 when he hesitated to allow Susie to go with Charles to visit his parents. Although she was nearly twenty-two years old, Susie, obviously, did not make decisions independent of her father. Regardless, R. B.'s hesitation may have simply been concern over his single daughter traveling such a distance with a man not yet her husband. Susie found the reluctance of her dad frustrating.

Charles's parents, John and Eliza, displayed no doubt concerning his choice of a bride. They were overjoyed by Susie's visit and received her gladly. Susie was "welcomed, petted, and entertained most affectionately by all the family," and the family took her "to see every place and object of interest in and around Colchester." Susie was most thankful for the extended time with Charles that the few days afforded and "the joy of being all the day long" with her beloved. That time with Charles, she said, "was enough to fill my heart with gladness, and render me oblivious of any other pleasure."[37] Following their visit with John and Eliza and Charles's siblings, they returned to London. Charles, characteristically, immediately reengaged in his work.

Their weeklong holiday had afforded them meaningful time together, but returning to London meant less opportunity to be in one another's presence. However, as was their custom, along with Charles's visits to Susie's home, they exchanged letters each week. Charles wrote to Susie, "Pray for me, my love; and may our united petitions win a blessing through the Saviour's merit." So soon after a blissful several days with his beloved fiancée, he wisely understood even more the temptation that they might feel to elevate their love for one another to idolatrous heights. He urged, "Let us take heed of putting ourselves too prominently in our own hearts, but let us commit our way unto the Lord."[38] So intense was his love for Susie that he feared idolizing her and thus hindering his relationship with God.

Another portion of his letter also demonstrates one of Charles's most frustrating struggles. For much of his life, Charles had suffered from depression, and this piece of correspondence with Susie reveals that he was at that time "very low in spirits." However, he looked to Scripture and found relief from his despondency. He also recognized his need for prayer. As his fame grew, so did his sense of dependency on God.

Susie responded lovingly to Charles's letter:

My Dearest,

I thank you with warm and hearty thanks for the note just received. It is useless for me to attempt to tell you how much happiness I have had during the past week. Words are but cold dishes on which to serve up thoughts and feelings which come warm and glowing from the heart. I should like to express my appreciation of all the tenderness and care you have shown towards me during this happy week; but I fear to pain you by thanks for what I know was a pleasure to you. I expect your thoughts have been busy to-day about "the crown jewels." (He had talked of preaching on this subject.—S.S.) The gems may differ in size, colour, richness, and beauty, but even the smallest are "precious stones," are they not?

That Standard [newspaper] certainly does not bear "Excelsior" as its motto; nor can "Good will to men" be the device of its floating pennon, but it matters not; we know that all is under the control of One of whom Asaph said, "Surely the wrath of man shall praise Thee; the remainder of wrath shalt Thou restrain." May his blessing rest in an especial manner on you to-night, my dearly-beloved; and on the approaching Sabbath, when you stand before the great congregation, may you be "filled with all the fullness of God"! Good night. Fondly and faithfully yours, —Susie.[39]

Susie shines in her letter to Charles. Recognizing that he was "low in spirits," she did more than pray for him, though certainly she did that.

She encouraged him as he faced the unfair criticism that he received from both the religious and secular press.

Susie, still exulting in the time that she and Charles enjoyed together in Colchester, made specific reference in her letter to how he had cared for her. She assured Charles that she was interested in his sermon preparation and she comforted him with her biblical insights, especially evident in her understanding of God's sovereign control over all things. She offered Charles her prayers as he prepared to preach on the Sabbath. It is a lovely letter and must have lifted Charles up from his sadness. Obviously, he longed to talk to Susie. He wrote: "My love, were you here, how you would comfort me; but since you are not, I shall do what is better still, go upstairs alone, and pour out my griefs into my Saviour's ear."[40] Charles did what he was accustomed to do in times of trial: he prayed. He also set an example for Susie that the "Saviour's ear" was open to hear the requests of his servants.

CHARLES AND SUSANNAH'S LOVE LETTERS (1855–1856)

In June 1855, Charles left for Scotland. His intention was to find rest and refreshment, while engaging in a number of preaching appointments. It turned out that he had little time for rest. While away, he longed for home and to be near to his fiancée. In a letter to Susie he requested of her, "Pray for me, my love."[41] Susie later felt tension as she recounted her love story in the *Autobiography* regarding how much she should reveal concerning her relationship with Charles. However, she chose to allow enough light into her account, through Charles's letters, that the reader might see something of the tenderness, sweetness, and sheer joy of their relationship.[42]

Charles not only poured out his heart to her, asking for prayer, he wanted her to hear the words of a "devoted lover."[43] Susie described their mutual affection and told of the "little rills of tenderness that run between all the sentences."[44] Those sentences she characterized as being "like the singing, dancing waters among the boulders of a brook, and I cannot still the music altogether."[45] Charles's affectionate words to Susie did not "dry up" with the years, she said, but "the stream grew deeper and broader, and the rhythm of its song waxed sweeter and stronger."[46]

From Scotland on June 17, 1855, Charles described the success of his preaching labors and the challenges of his work. However, he quickly brought his thoughts back to Susie and his love for her: "Now to return to you again, I have had day-dreams of you while driving along, I thought you were near me. It is not long, dearest, before I shall again enjoy your sweet society, if the providence of God permit."[47] It is a bit surprising to those only familiar with Spurgeon's sermons to hear him communicate in such a manner. "I have had day-dreams of you while driving along" seems a bit much for the preacher who has been described as having no equal since the apostle Paul.[48]

Susie was constantly on Charles's mind, but he recognized that their relationship, and any future meetings that they might have, ultimately rested on the sovereign providence of God. His letters to Susie unveil how much he viewed her as a true partner to him: "I knew I loved you very much before, but now I feel how necessary you are to me."[49] He depended on her, yet he was also quick to consider Susie and how much she *also* missed him: "My darling, accept love of the deepest and purest kind from one who is not prone to exaggerate, but who feels that here there is no room for hyperbole."[50]

Although he was sleepy when he crafted that letter, he did not want Susie to imagine that "I weary myself by writing."[51] The reason he did not view writing to his beloved as a burden was because "it is my delight to please you."[52] He concluded his love letter by underlining the importance of prayer—that though he was weary and his body desperately needed sleep, he could not, he would not, fail to seek God in prayer and to pray for Susie whose name was "sweet to him."

My eyes ache for sleep, but they shall keep open till I have invoked the blessings from above—mercies temporal and eternal—

to rest on the head of one whose name is sweet to me, and who
equally loves the name of her own, her much-loved,
C. H. S.[53]

His letters to Susie from Scotland contain reports of his preaching
and sightseeing and his reflections on the entire experience. However, it is
impossible to miss in them his growing love for his fiancée. The humility,
honesty, and spiritual neediness that he felt, he shared with his future
wife; Susie was the friend and partner that Charles needed. He counted
on her prayers and anticipated that she would gladly hear his sorrows,
cheer him with words of encouragement, and steel him for the challenges
that he faced. Charles was a sensitive man, and the worst thing for him
to imagine was to have a heart that was cold toward God who had been
so good to him.[54] Movingly he expressed:

> I shall feel deeply indebted to you, if you will pray very earnestly
> for me. I fear I am not so full of love to God as I used to be. I
> lament my sad decline in spiritual things. You and others may
> not have observed it, but I am now conscious of it, and a sense
> thereof has put bitterness in my cup of joy. Oh! What is it to be
> popular, to be successful, to have abundance, even to have love so
> sweet as yours, —if I should be left of God to fall, and to depart
> from His ways? I tremble at the giddy height on which I stand,
> and could wish myself unknown, for indeed I am unworthy
> of all my honours and my fame. I trust I shall now commence
> anew, and wear no longer the linsey-woolsey garment; but I
> beseech you, blend your hearty prayers with mine, that two of
> us may be agreed, and thus will you promote the usefulness, and
> holiness, and happiness of one whom you love.[55]

Indeed, prayer was the glue that bound him close to Susie when miles
separated them.

During the Christmas season of 1855, Charles left London to visit his parents in Colchester—just over two weeks before the day of his wedding. Soon after he wrote to Susie:

Sweet One, How I love you! I long to see you; and yet it is but half-an-hour since I left you. Comfort yourself in my absence by the thought that my heart is with you. My own gracious God bless you in all things, —in heart, in feeling, in life, in death, in Heaven! May your virtues be perfected, your prospects realized, your zeal continued, your love to Him increased, and your knowledge of Him rendered deeper, higher, broader, —in fact, may more than even *my heart* can wish, or *my* hope anticipate, be yours forever![56]

Prior to leaving for Colchester, he gave Susie another book. This time it was not Bunyan, Tupper, or Brooks—the book was from Charles's own hand. Years later, after Charles had died, Susie wrote about that gift:

There is just one relic of this memorable time. On my desk, as I write this chapter, there is a book bearing the title of *The Pulpit Library;* it is the first published volume of my beloved's sermons, and its fly-leaf has the following inscription:

In a few days it will be out of my power to present anything to Miss Thompson. Let this be a remembrance of our happy meetings and sweet conversations.

December 22/55
C. H. Spurgeon[57]

The reason Charles would no longer be able to present a gift to "Miss Thompson" was because on January 8, 1856, she would become Mrs. Spurgeon. Being the wife of C. H. Spurgeon would be challenging. Perhaps the adage "ignorance is bliss" was applicable to Susie, for many trials awaited her, not only due to the loss of her own health twelve years later but also due to the many other trials that came from being married to Charles Spurgeon.

One of the gifts that Susie presented to Charles, just prior to their wedding, was a portrait of the young preacher. She called it a "lover's gift." She recalled her dreamy thoughts of her husband-to-be and how she used to "gaze upon the sweet boyish face, and think no angel could look half so lovely."[58] Eventually the picture was framed and took a place of honor on the walls of their first home together. Later, as Charles grew in fame and was away from home, that portrait brought comfort to Susie, and "its expression of calm confident faith strengthened her heart." Susie expressed that, in the painting, Charles's "up-raised finger [well-known to students of Spurgeon] pointed to the source whence I must draw consolation in my loneliness."[59]

Because both his grandfather and father were pastors, Spurgeon was aware of the various hardships that accompanied the role of pastor and their effects on the family. But on the eve of their marriage, neither Charles nor Susie could have imagined the trials, but also the blessings, that awaited them.

CHAPTER 4

A Marriage Made for Heaven

The air was cold and damp in London on January 8, 1856. However, the weather did not prohibit crowds from lining the streets, blocking the roads, and flooding into the sanctuary of the New Park Street Chapel. Over two thousand people had to be turned away from the overcrowded building, so they then took their places with the rest of the throng who filled the streets, pressing as near to the chapel as possible. The people were gathered in hopes of catching a glimpse of London's famous newlyweds.

Susie had spent much of the morning in prayer. R. B. Thompson took the hand of his only daughter and helped her into the carriage, and then they ventured out on the short journey from Falcon Square, across the Thames, and to the front entrance of the New Park Street Chapel. As they made their way to the Chapel, Susie remembered sitting by her father's side and wondered if those who watched her pass by had any idea "what a wonderful bridegroom she was going to meet."[1]

Police, called to duty for this special occasion, had to clear a pathway through the people so that R. B. and Susie could get inside the church building where the capacity crowd awaited. If Mr. Thompson had once been hesitant about Charles Spurgeon, he now supported the marriage of his daughter to the wildly popular young preacher. Though the clouds hung low on that cold Saturday, it was a day of great joy, for it was the wedding day of Charles Spurgeon and Susannah Thompson.[2]

Susie, in later years, reflected on the wedding ceremony and spoke of her feelings that day as "a deep and tender gladness." She and Charles "clasped each other's hand, and then placed them both in that of the Master." She saw their wedding as the beginning of a "journey," and she was "assured that [God] would be their Guide."[3] Susie considered Charles as "the best man on God's earth."[4] She remembered, with utmost tenderness, the events of that wonderful day that began early in the morning on her knees in prayer:

> I see a young girl kneeling by her bedside in the early morning; she is awed and deeply moved by a sense of the responsibilities to be taken up that day, yet happy beyond expression that the Lord has so favoured her; and there alone with Him she earnestly seeks strength, and blessing, and guidance through the new life opening before her.[5]

This reliance on God for the resources that she and Charles would need in their marriage attested to Susie's godliness, a godliness that would characterize her for the remainder of her life. Charles realized that Susie was no ordinary lady, and he valued her as his wife, friend, and assistant in ministry.

Spurgeon biographer Tom Nettles surmised:

> The revelation of the depth of her Christian experience made Spurgeon evaluate the gift of her hand even more, knowing that God himself loves the gift and he may love it too. . . . Spurgeon's

letters to "Susie" always exhibited an indivisible solution of ardent spirituality, intense love for her, deep desire for greater usefulness, unfettered love of God and the gospel along with a consciousness of the need for more purity and single-minded-ness in his love for Christ.[6]

The wedding service was the sort of gospel-saturated affair that Charles would have approved of. The ceremony, led by Alexander Fletcher of Finsbury Chapel, opened with the congregation singing "Salvation, O the Joyful Sound."[7] Such a salvation-exalting hymn was an appropriate way to usher in the Spurgeons' marriage, and it highlighted the gospel mindset that was so characteristic of Susie and Charles. After reading Psalm 100, Fletcher reminded the congregation that their pastor had often spoken of the smiles of Christ in his preaching: "He [Christ] must surely have smiled upon the bride and bridegroom whose marriage feast was graced by His presence." Turning to the couple, Fletcher exhorted them that God had "more blessings in reserve for their enjoyment, felicity, and usefulness."[8]

Thomas Spurgeon, soon after Susie's death in October of 1903, spoke of his parents' sweet wedding day and marriage: "Thus commenced the union 'till death us do part,' that lasted for six and thirty years, and was throughout of the most tender and loving character. That his wife was a true helpmeet, is proved by my dear father's repeated testimony to her worth, by word of mouth and by the fact that he set it down in black and white, again and again."[9] Quoting Tennyson, Thomas reflected: "She set herself to him like perfect music unto noble words."[10]

For Susie Thompson, 1854–1856 were years of change. Though origi-nally taken aback by Charles's uncouth manner, four months after her first encounter with him, she received a gift from his hand. Two more months passed, and the "boy preacher from the Fens" revealed his romantic feel-ings for her. And, six weeks later, Charles Spurgeon, two and a half years her junior, asked the twenty-two-year-old Susannah Thompson for her hand in marriage. Finally, on January 8, 1856, near the pulpit where he preached each Sunday, he put a ring on her finger to the delight of the crowd packed inside the New Park Street Chapel.

Though the Spurgeons enjoyed much happiness, the couple was confronted with difficulties from the start. Along with challenges in ministry, both Susie and Charles later experienced prolonged health problems. In 1888, Susie described one year of their suffering and wrote that it had brought "a series of varied trials to us, and a great fight of afflictions beset both my dear husband and myself."[11] Such a year was not unusual, but though they faced trials both individually and as a couple, Susie declared that she wanted "with all my heart, and soul, and strength, to praise the Lord, who has been to us 'a very present help in trouble.'"[12]

Early in their marriage, Susie experienced difficulties related to her husband's popularity and the demands of his calling. She truly disliked his numerous overnight preaching trips and was sometimes downcast because she missed him. However, she determined never to be an obstacle to him in his ministry.[13] Charles wrote to her, "I have served the Lord far more and never less for your sweet companionship."[14] Charles suffered throughout his adult life with bouts of depression so severe that his mental health was significantly challenged. Lewis Drummond surmised that Susie was a primary reason that Spurgeon kept his sanity.[15] His assessment underlines again how necessary Susie was to Charles.

With hearts aflame in prayer, grounded in Scripture, and joined together in the bonds of holy matrimony, Charles and Susie began their marriage. They entered upon their labors with joyful hearts and courageous convictions that would last a lifetime. Late in her widowhood, Susie contemplated her wedding service and her thirty-six-year marriage to Charles: "But the golden circlet then placed on my finger, though worn and thin now, speaks of love beyond the grave, and is the cherished pledge of a spiritual union which shall last throughout eternity."[16] Though Susie understood that human marriage has no part in heaven, the "spiritual union" that believers share with one another on earth is but a beginning, and it will never end. She realized that, in Charles, she had a partner with whom she would worship God eternally.

The exceptional nature of the Spurgeons' union is worthy of consideration. It was spiritual purposes that brought Susie and Charles together, spiritual means that they employed on the day of their wedding, and spiritual objectives that kept them together throughout the years. They looked to God, sought His help, and joined their hands together in service to Him. Alexander Fletcher prayed at their wedding ceremony that God would "bless them with increasing usefulness, increasing happiness, increasing enjoyment of Thy fellowship!"[17] Charles often recounted God's kindness in bringing Susie to his side. He referred to her as "the ideal wife" and said she was designed by God "to be the greatest of all earthly blessings to him."[18]

Biographer Russell Conwell analyzed the Spurgeons' marriage and believed that Susie and Charles were especially suited for one another. Charles invited Susie to help him put away his "uncouth eccentricities" and to "correct his mistakes in language or history." She was able to assist him, and Conwell claimed that Spurgeon "could never have attained the eminence which he reached" without the help of his wife. Though Conwell's perspective may have been exaggerated, Susie's value to Spurgeon was inestimable. Conwell maintained that, had Charles "allied himself with a wife who was less pious and sincere," his reputation and ministry would have been damaged. However, Susie "worked with him, prayed with him, believed in him, and most affectionately loved him through those many years of work."[19]

Susie was a loyal friend and helper to Charles. A ministry like her husband's that drew massive crowds was ripe for slander and misunderstanding. Large churches and popular preachers were not rare in London, but Charles's passionate evangelism, Puritan theology, and practical methodology stood in contrast to London's more refined ministers. According to Conwell, Susannah was an encouraging comforter when Spurgeon faced attacks from opponents: "[She] stood like a shield between him and the arrows of wickedness, quenching their fiery darts most easily with the shield of domestic love."[20]

Academician Patricia Kruppa posits, "Spurgeon's marriage helped sustain him through some very rugged experiences during his early years."[21] Perhaps it is not an overstatement to surmise that if Charles Haddon Spurgeon had not met and married Susie Thompson, then his life and ministry would have never reached the heights enjoyed both in his lifetime and ever since. Singleness was not a gift that Charles enjoyed. And, yet, it is not simply that Charles needed *a* wife, he needed a very specific wife; he needed Susie Thompson.

After the wedding ceremony, Charles and Susie were whisked away from the New Park Street Chapel, and they boarded a train to the port at Dover, and from there they caught a boat to Paris for a nine-day honeymoon. They arrived in the romantic city to world-class accommodations at the Hotel Meurice. So grand was this hotel that many wealthy and famous people signed its registry over the years. It was known as "the hotel of kings and queens."

Meurice was removed in 1835 to "one of the most fashionable locales in the city, overlooking the historic Tuileries Garden."[22] The hotel provided "lavish entertainment" with bountiful dinners and extravagant luncheons. During 1855, just a year before Susie and Charles checked into their fabulous suite at Meurice, Queen Victoria had stayed at the hotel. The composer Tchaikovsky had been a guest there, and near the end of the nineteenth century, Hotel Meurice regularly hosted "the elite aristocracy."[23] Relevant to Susie and Charles's stay was the British flavor of the hotel. The hotel teemed with British guests, the hotel staff spoke English, and the luxury hotel was nicknamed "City of London."

The well-known English author W. M. Thackeray described the Meurice:

If you don't speak a word of French, if you like English comfort, clean rooms, breakfast, and *maîtres d'hotel:* in a foreign land, you want your fellow countrymen around you, your brown beer, your friend and your cognac—and your water—do not listen to any of the messengers but with your best British accent cry heartily: "Meurice!" and immediately, someone will come forward to drive you straight to the *rue de Rivoli*.[24]

The newlyweds lodged in luxury. Stunning in its architectural beauty, perfectly situated not far from the Seine River, and near to art galleries and cathedrals of Paris, the hotel served as the perfect romantic oasis for the young lovers. One may wonder how a newly married pastor afforded such accommodations. Susie writes, "We had a cosy suite of rooms (by special favour) in the *entresol* of the Hotel Meurice."[25] Her notation of "by special favor" may indicate that the Spurgeons' hotel stay was a wedding gift from family, friends, or church. Or perhaps, since Charles's fame was increasing, the hotel itself may have offered him the suite at a greatly reduced price desiring to curry his favor.

As Susie and Charles exited through the fabulous doors of the luxurious hotel, the Louvre was in sight a few blocks to their left, and the Tuileries Garden was just across the street in front of them. Susie delighted in showing Charles the sights and sounds of the city; it was especially enjoyable for her since Charles didn't speak French, and he had never been to Paris. Susie, however, had often strolled along the streets of the City of Lights. Her previous trips into Paris allowed her to enjoy the high cultural experiences of the city as well as learn French from Pastor Audebez's daughters. Confidently she asserted: "[I] felt quite at home there, and had the intense gratification of introducing my husband to all the places and sights which were worthy of arousing his interest and admiration."[26] She moved with such ease down the streets and into the galleries, and cathedrals, and to the monuments and palaces that she must have seemed like a resident of the great city to her blissful groom.

Charles's natural curiosity was heightened even more as he hung on every word from the sweet lips of his beautiful new wife. Susie spared no enthusiasm as she led him into her favorite cathedral, Sainte Chapelle, with its brilliant displays and multicolored windows. Charles extoled it as "a little heaven of stained glass."[27] Just a short walk from Chapelle was the majestic Notre Dame cathedral, ancient, strong, and towering into the Paris sky.

Three years earlier, Susie had visited the great cathedral and admired its royal beauty draped in lavish décor in anticipation of the wedding of Napoleon III and Eugenie on January 30, 1853.[28] Providentially, Susie's earlier trips to the city had prepared her for a charming honeymoon experience with Charles. In later years, Charles frequently visited Paris and, due to Susie's earlier influence, was able to serve as an excellent cicerone for his fellow travelers. During those later travels, he emboldened fellow Christians in the city who, though they met in inadequate facilities, nevertheless sought to serve Christ faithfully. [29]

In Charles's autobiography, Susie shared an excerpt from a letter Charles wrote to her that further demonstrates the tender love they enjoyed and offers a flashback to their honeymoon: "My heart flies to you, as I remember my first visit to this city under your dear guidance. I love you now as then, only multiplied many times."[30]

When Susie recalled their honeymoon, she lamented the loss afterward experienced in Paris due to the communistic destruction.[31] Charles, writing around 1872, also grieved the sad sight of the ruins "which commemorate the reign of the Commune in Paris." Everywhere he turned, he saw devastation left by the uprising. He specifically references several sights that he enjoyed with Susie during their honeymoon in 1856 that had been devastated by 1872. "The Hotel de Ville stands a ghastly but classical ruin, in fellowship with the Tuileries, the Palais Royal, the great Granaries, and many other vast and once magnificent public buildings." Furthermore, he wrote, "Churches, houses, and docks have shared the same fate as palaces and courts of justice." Charles was sorrowful over "horrors of civil war" that "sadden any heart capable of feeling."[32]

He grieved over suffering residents who lost homes, belongings, and their livelihoods. Gospel-focused solutions, Charles believed, would positively transform political, moral, and social maladies. Though Paris bore the scars of war and upheaval, it was nevertheless the place where Charles and Susie's romance deepened and the city where they enjoyed the earliest days of their marriage. Along with supporting local church ministry in Paris, the city would always hold a place near the hearts of Charles and Susie. For Susie, the early memories with Charles would later soothe her sadness when many miles separated them and when she could no longer travel with him due to her poor health.

After a delightful trip to Paris, Susie eagerly anticipated the beginning of her married life at their first home at 217 New Kent Road, London, convenient to the New Park Street Chapel. Their first residence together was also where Susie gave birth to twin sons, Charles and Thomas, in September of 1856. She described the anticipation that both she and her husband felt on moving into their own home: "How we thanked and praised the Lord for His exceeding goodness to us in bringing us there, and how earnestly and tenderly my husband prayed that God's blessing might rest upon us then and evermore!"[33] So overcome with happiness was Susie that she described her home as "Love-land."[34] On her wedding day, she said that she was living in a "dreamland of excitement and emotion."[35] Susie was beside herself with joy as she moved from "dreamland" to "Love-land."

It is delightful to consider how much fun Charles and Susie enjoyed during the early days of their marriage. Susie "never regretted" the decision made early in her marriage to employ the best room in the house for Charles's study.[36] The "best room" was just below the upstairs room where their "twin-boys first saw the light of day."[37]

Susie and Charles had to "practice rigid economy" as newlyweds, for Charles's salary reflected that of a first-year pastor in a church that had, previous to his arrival, been struggling financially (though it was quickly on the road to recovery). In addition, it was his desire, early on, to "help young men to preach the gospel," and to do so required money.

The funds that launched the Pastors' College with but one student, T. W. Medhurst, initially came from Charles and Susie's own budget. Susie gladly supported Charles's passion for training pastors and she demonstrated such by her cheerful giving of money from the family budget to finance the work. For her support, she was affectionately known as the "Mother of the College."[38] Susie's "motherly interest" in the college provides a context from which her later ministry to poor pastors was birthed.[39] A positive outcome from Susie and Charles's monetary sacrifices was that it further helped them to learn how to depend on God to supply all their needs.[40]

In 1885, Susie reflected on the history of the Pastors' College:

God ever bless the Pastors' College! Very tender memories linger round its name and work! When the dear President [Charles] first had it laid upon his heart to train men for the ministry, or rather, to help those who were called of God to preach to prepare themselves for their life work, he began with one young brother. We were but newly-married, and had great difficulty in meeting the expense of maintaining such a full-grown son [the first student, Medhurst]; but the help the Lord sent was so direct and marvelous, that our faith was strengthened to ask and expect great things, and we had the joy of not only seeing our grown-up family still growing apace but of receiving proportionate means for its maintenance. Many moving tales could we tell of anxious hearts, and an apparently failing purse, in those first days of trial; but *always*, yes *always*, our God put our fears to flight, and sent the needed funds to us—sometimes from an utterly unexpected quarter. . . . From the first day [1856] until now [1885] more than seven hundred men have been sent forth to preach the gospel. . . . God bless *our* College, and *our* Pastors, and *our* Students, and—emphatically OUR PRESIDENT.[41]

Susie's devotion to her marriage is alluded to in a sermon that Charles preached on November 20, 1870, titled "The Saint One with His Savior." It is not difficult to imagine that he had Susie in view when he declared, "She delights in her husband" and "finds sweetest content and solace in his company, his fellowship, his fondness." He further exhorted, "The domestic circle is her kingdom; that she may there create happiness and comfort, is her life work; and his smiling gratitude is all the regard she seeks." The husband, Charles exclaimed, was one who "lavishes his love on her [his wife]." He continued by saying that both husband and wife enjoy watching "their children growing up in health and strength."[42]

Charles and Susie were of such oneness of mind that they often thought "the same thoughts" and at times both, at the identical moment, spoke the "same utterance."[43] Charles declared of a loving husband and wife that they are "like two stars" who "have shone with such blended rays as to have seemed more one than two."[44] Furthermore, he stated, "One name, one heart, one house, one interest, one love, they have had also one spirit."[45]

Susie and Charles's perspective on marriage and family may seem antiquated, and some people might be tempted to derogatorily describe them as "Victorian." However, though they were both products of their culture, their primary views about marriage and family came not from the world around them but from their biblical convictions. There is no indication that Susie ever felt oppressed or limited in any way because she was a wife and mother whose primary domain lay in the management of her home. She was dearly loved and cherished by Charles, and he did not dissuade her from her desires, aims, or pursuits. It was just the opposite; Charles challenged Susie to actively pursue faithful service to Christ in various realms. He never discouraged Susie in her endeavors; he cheered her on. Susie was not a frustrated housewife, nor was Charles a domineering husband. Both were happy in their marriage and ministry partnership.

Susie was just over four months pregnant in the late spring of 1856 when she accompanied Charles on a visit to his grandfather's home in

Stambourne. James Spurgeon, the aged preacher and the greatest early influence on Charles, delightfully welcomed Susie to his home, and she was likewise thrilled to visit with Charles's extended family and to see the country scenes that he had often described to her. Almost nothing had changed in Stambourne since Charles's childhood. Susie recalled that the rural folks were "delighted and interested" in the "young Pastor and his wife." She found it "charming to see him in the midst of his own people."[46]

Charles's affection for his grandfather's land never wavered. Even though his feet were planted in London, his heart was still in the soil of Stambourne. Many of his earliest memories were connected to the manse and the church building nearby. Susie rejoiced to discover the roots of her husband's earliest influences. She remembered of Charles that he was "just the child again," walking the grounds and conversing with the rural people.[47]

Susie shared a humorous story about her visit to Stambourne that reveals one of her especial detestations: spiders. Surrounded by her doting in-laws, she was enjoying a refreshing cup of tea when she spotted something floating in the bottom of the cup, a spider. She was terrified. She remembered that "his black body swollen to a huge size, and his long legs describing a wheel-like circle in the remaining fluid." Even worse, she fretted: "I had been drinking the boiled juice of this monster!"[48] Such experiences notwithstanding, life was filled with happiness for Charles and Susie as they traveled around, worked in ministry together, and prepared for another significant event in their lives—one that would double the size of their household.

CHAPTER 5

The New Parents

After a flurry of activities from January through September of 1856, including their wedding, traveling to Paris for their honeymoon, and setting up their first home together, Susie Spurgeon gave birth to twin sons, Charles and Thomas, on September 20. Near to Susie's side that Saturday was her young husband Charles. Was Charles at ease when he first held his baby boys? It is easy to imagine that he was as comfortable as any new father might be. After all, Charles was the oldest of seventeen children born to John and Eliza Spurgeon. Therefore, he was well acquainted with the sighs and cries of babies, and he was witness to the love tendered to them by his parents.

When Charles was but eighteen months old, for reasons still unknown, he was sent to live with his grandparents in Stambourne for almost six years, after which he was removed back to his parents. Of the seventeen children born to John and Eliza, nine died in infancy. It is staggering to imagine the suffering, tears, and heartbreak that were felt in his parents' home as time and again they witnessed the grave digger's spade and stood close at hand while their little ones were buried in the soil of rural England. The loss of nine siblings must have forever etched its mark on Charles's mind and heart.

John was busy as a bivocational pastor, and he likely struggled to make ends meet. Charles's removal to Stambourne as a toddler was not due to a lack of love from his parents, but was born of necessity. However, when he left the godly home of his parents, he simply entered the equally Christlike home of his grandparents. Charles's brother James Archer described the family that he, Charles, and their siblings enjoyed: "I cannot remember the time when I was not under holy influence brought to bear upon me, and upon my brother, and upon my sisters, in one of the godliest households that I think God ever gave to a Christian." Furthermore, he declared that his mother was "the starting point of all greatness and goodness that any of us, by the grace of God, have enjoyed."[1]

Charles was anxious to welcome his own children to a home such as he had enjoyed in his childhood. The boys would be the only children that Susie would birth; however, she and Charles would nevertheless help to care for hundreds of children through the two orphanages started under Charles's ministry.

Charles had been concerned for London's poor orphans since he first moved to the city in 1854. As he witnessed homeless and impoverished children lining the streets and alleys around town, wearing threadbare clothes and looking emaciated, his heart went out to them. The first orphanage was born of a prayer meeting in the summer of 1866. Charles challenged his large congregation to do more for the Lord in London. Providentially, soon after the prayer meeting, a gift of £20,000 was given to Charles from a widow of a Church of England minister to help establish an orphanage. These funds resulted in the purchase of land just a few miles from the Tabernacle, with more funds arriving afterward from others to fund the institution. Children from all races and religious backgrounds were received into this home for boys. About ten years later, a home for girls was built on the same property.[2]

As London prepared a tower to house its now famous clock and bell (Big Ben), the cries of the twins filled the Spurgeon house on New Kent Road. For Charles and Susie, the birth of two boys was the latest big event to transpire in their lives. Charles considered the twins "the best of sons."[3] He was once asked which of his sons was superior. He wisely replied, "Charlie is the best boy when Tom is not with him, and Tom is best when Charlie is away."[4]

Charles (Charlie) was the older of the two, as he had been delivered first. As an adult, he became friends with author A. Cunningham Burley, and they shared a "mutual admiration of C. H. S. [Charles Haddon Spurgeon]."[5] At one point, Burley suggested that Charlie write a biography of his father, but he felt that the "power of hero worship was too strong in him to do justice to the many-sided character of his father."[6] Burley recollects that the Spurgeon boys, in their early years, did not experience as much personal time with their father as they would have enjoyed. He surmises, "Loving friendship was there and most happy relations also, but a curious restraint . . . fettered their fellowship."[7]

Charles, no doubt, had some regret over not being able to spend as much time with his sons as he would have liked. In later years, he felt similar regret over not being able to personally care for Susie as he wanted due to the demands of his ministry and the decline of his health. The "curious restraint" felt by the Spurgeon boys was likely due to the weight that their busy father bore on his shoulders as he served the church, managed numerous ministries, answered hundreds of letters each week, and was in demand to preach throughout the continent.

Charles was like his father in the sense that other demands often pulled him from home. John Spurgeon wrote, "I had something to do with his [Charles's] up-bringing, but I was so frequently from home that more of the responsibility was thrown on my dear wife, and with constant and prayerful thought she nobly fulfilled the task."[8]

Surprisingly, it was not Charles who led his sons to Christ. Burley recalls, "One of the deepest desires of Mr. and Mrs. Spurgeon's heart had been to bring a sense of vital religion home to their children. This was their constant aim and prayer."[9] It was not due to neglect that neither Susie nor Charles led their children to Christ at the *moment* of conversion because, as Burley notes, "There were ceaseless displays of tenderness with signs of deep solicitude [in the Spurgeon home] that were sufficient to move one to repentance toward God and faith in the Lord Jesus."[10]

Like Charles's own mother, Eliza, Susie bore much responsibility for training of her sons, and her influence on Thomas and Charles should not be minimized. Charles Ray surmises,

> Mrs. Spurgeon was a faithful trainer of her twin sons in the Christian doctrine, and she had the joy of seeing them both brought to the Lord at an early age. "I trace my early conversion," Pastor Thomas Spurgeon has written, "directly to her earnest pleading and bright example. She denied herself the pleasure of attending Sunday evening services that she might minister the Word of Life to her household. . . . "My dear brother was brought to Christ through the pointed word of a missioner; but he, too, gladly owns that mother's influence and teaching and their part in the matter."[11]

Therefore, though other people led the Spurgeon boys to Christ, both sons remembered the inestimable role that their mother played in their conversion. However, though Susie dearly loved both boys, it seems that Thomas was especially dear to her heart. W. Y. Fullerton asserted, "No son was ever a fonder lover of his mother than he."[12] When Thomas was told that he owed his character and his position to his father, he quickly reminded the gentleman that his mother deserved credit as well.[13]

Fullerton writes of Thomas's letters to Susie that they "overflow with affection for 'Mudge', [and] became almost extravagant in their expressions of endearment. . . ."[14] Perhaps it was because of Thomas's later travels and ministry in Australia and New Zealand taking him thousands of miles from hearth and home and the arms of his mother, that Susie's thoughts about him are more pronounced.

Charlie and Thomas were educated first by a governess; then at a school at Lansdowne Road, Stockwell; then to Lang's School at Clapham Park; and, afterwards, they received instruction by a Mr. Rylands Brown when he was a student at Spurgeon's Pastors' College. Later they were educated at Camden House School in Brighton while the Spurgeon home at Nightingale Lane was being rebuilt.[15] Fullerton recounts a story from Thomas that reveals Susie's commitment to the integrity of her sons and provides insight, in part, to her parenting method.

On Sunday evenings their mother used to take the boys aside and talk to them about the way of life, and with one each side of her at the piano sing the songs of Zion. "I like to tell," her son [Thomas] said years afterwards, "how she bade us sing 'There is a fountain filled with blood' and of how when she came to the chorus she used to say, 'Dear boys of mine, I have no reason to suppose that you are yet trusting Christ: you will, I hope, in answer to our constant prayers, but till you definitely do you must not say or sing 'I do believe, that Jesus died for me.' It is just as wrong to sing a lie as to tell one." Then she used to sing it by herself. Somehow or other it did not seem to me, even in those early days, that a chorus should be sung by one voice only! Perhaps that little thought helped me to long to be able to sing it too, and the Holy Spirit wrought in my heart an earnest craving to be able to sing

I do believe, I will believe,
That Jesus died for me,
That on the Cross He shed His blood,
From sin to set me free.[16]

Thomas remembered:

> Oh, how I longed for that! I remember well the bright morning
> when we came to the breakfast table, I climbed upon her seat
> and put my arms round dear mother's neck—I like to have them
> there still—and I said to her, "Dear mother, I really think that
> I do love Jesus." Thank God, she took me at my word, and said
> to me, "I am so glad to hear it, I believe you do." Then I wanted
> Sunday night to come that I might be able to sing my loudest in
> the chorus.[17]

Even as an adult, Thomas remained affectionate with Susie, and after his mother died, he wrote that he wished he could—as he did as a
child—have his arms around her neck still.

Though Charles was faithful to lead in family worship whenever he
was at home, Susie was also diligent in her ongoing training of the twins.
She taught the Bible to them, instructed them in the hymns, and insisted
on integrity of their Christian profession.

Within their marriage, though Susie was a faithful instrument of
piety, it was Charles who assured that Scripture and prayer permeated
their family's life. Emphasizing to students at his Pastors' College[18] the
importance of family, he urged,

> We ought to be such husbands that every husband in the parish
> may safely be such as we are. Is it so? We ought to be the best of
> fathers. Alas! Some ministers, to my knowledge, are far from this,
> for as to their families, they have kept the vineyards of others, but
> their own vineyards they have not kept. Their children are ne-
> glected, and do not grow up as a godly seed. Is it so with yours?[19]

For Charles, it was important for the father to keep the vineyard of his
own home by not neglecting his family.

Reading Charles's lofty challenge to pastors might cause one to feel inadequate for the task at hand. Perhaps many men do not feel that they are "the best of fathers" nor the kind of husbands "that every husband in the parish" longs to imitate. And it is not uncommon for a mother to feel as if she has failed in her parenting and spiritual influence of her children. Charles, anticipating such a sentiment, simply pointed his readers to Christ. In a sermon titled "A Glorious Church" from Ephesians 5:25–27, he proclaimed,

> The Christian should take nothing short of Christ for his model. Under no circumstances ought we to be content unless we reflect the grace, which was in Christ Jesus. Even as a husband, which is a relationship that the Christian sustains in common with the rest of men, he is to look upon Christ Jesus as being set before him as the picture, and he is to paint according to that copy. Christ Himself being the bridegroom of the Church, the true Christian is to seek to be such a husband as Christ was to his spouse.[20]

Though Charles was primarily addressing men, his emphasis also holds true for mothers. He called all to "look upon Christ Jesus." Charles believed that "Parents—and mothers in particular—have a sweet influence on the family and the little ones."[21]

His friend and student, William Williams, often visited with Charles and Susie at their home. He remembered,

> One of the most helpful hours of my visits to Westwood was the hour of family prayer. At six o'clock the entire household gathered into the study for worship. Usually Mr. Spurgeon would himself lead the devotions. The portion read was invariably accompanied with exposition. . . . Then, how full of tender pleading, of serene confidence in God, of world-embracing sympathy

were his prayers! With what gracious familiarity he would talk with his Divine Master! Yet what reverence ever marked his address to his Lord. His public prayers were an inspiration and a benediction, but his prayers with the family were to me more wonderful still. . . . Mr. Spurgeon, bowed before God in family prayer, appeared a grander man even than when holding thousands spellbound by his oratory. Often have I risen from my knees strengthened, as Daniel was when the mysterious hand had laid its gentle pressure upon his head. I owe much; my people owe much, to the family prayers at Westwood.[22]

Charles said, "A home should be a Bethel. If I had no home, the world would be a great prison to me."[23]

Family Bible reading and prayer were a priority for Susie and Charles from the beginning of their marriage, and this was at the heart of their parenting. Susie remembered that whether they "lodged in some rough inn on the mountains or in the luxurious rooms of a palatial hotel in a city," they did not neglect reading the Bible and praying together.[24] The elements of family worship modeled by Charles included Bible reading/explanation, prayer, and hymn singing. As the Puritan Matthew Henry declared, "They who pray in the family, do well. They, who read and pray, do better. But they who sing, and read, and pray, do best of all."[25]

Susie provided glimpses into their experiences of family worship:

At the tea-table, the conversation was bright, witty, and always interesting; and after the meal was over, an adjournment was made to the study for family worship, and it was at these seasons that my beloved's prayers were remarkable for their tender childlikeness, their spiritual pathos, and their intense devotion. He seemed to come as near to God as a little child to a loving father, and we were often moved to tears as he talked thus face to face with his Lord.[26]

Susie continued to offer to her two sons biblical wisdom even in their adulthood. She and Thomas corresponded frequently, and a number of their letters to one another survive. In 1872, Susie writes, "I thank God for sparing you so long to me and hope that I may live to see you a brave, earnest, devoted Christian man. My highest wish for you is that you may be holy."[27] Thomas progressed rapidly in school, and Susie was thankful for his advancement, but she prayed that as his "privileges and responsibilities" increased that his "grace and wisdom" and his "reliance on God" would also increase.[28]

Still, she was concerned about Thomas as he went out into the world.

You will be thrown now, my son, into the company of elder boys of the school. Oh, I pray you, remember what the burden of my heart was the night you took leave of me at Brighton, "Lord keep my boys from the evil that is in the world." You will hear and see and learn things from elder boys that perhaps you never dreamed of before. Oh, my darling, my precious son, turn resolutely away from everything that looks like vice or wickedness, and keep yourself pure unto the Lord. Temptation will be very strong sometimes, but cry unto God; cry mightily and He *will* deliver you. Something in my heart compels me to say this to you to-day; if you do not feel the force of it now, you will soon; so treasure up my words, darling, and above all, trust Jesus and *dis*trust self.[29]

In his letters to Susie, Thomas, who was skilled in drawing like his father, often sent his mother his latest artistic creations. Susie encouraged him and prayed that all his talents would be "devoted to His service."[30] In her letters to Thomas, Susie sought to point him to Christ and to the importance of serving Him. Regarding his art, Susie didn't want him to take art lessons. A "professional gentleman" who saw one of Thomas's works influenced her in that opinion. She felt that his best teacher was nature and the more that he honed his skill on his own, the better it would be.[31]

Thomas and Charlie remained faithful in their walk with God. Not only brothers, they were close friends and both were devoted Christians. When they were older, they distributed copies of their father's sermons at local events, and they led prayer at their school in Brighton.[32] Once they completed school, their parents counseled them to avoid more advanced education and to take jobs. W. Y. Fullerton surmised that the reason Susie and Charles dissuaded the boys from a "university career" was likely because they held out hope that God would eventually call them into pastoral ministry.[33] Charlie began his career as a merchant and Thomas as a wood-engraver, and they were both successful in their early business endeavors.[34] Eventually, both would serve in pastoral ministry.

On Monday, September 21, 1874, their father baptized[35] the eighteen-year-old twins, and on October 4, they were officially welcomed as new members of the Metropolitan Tabernacle.

Thomas and Charlie wasted no time in faithfully serving Christ. In 1874, just under two miles from their home and about a thirty-minute walk, they helped a gardener, Mr. Rides, with the "informal services" that he was holding in his home. Both young men alternated preaching responsibilities. In 1877, the little congregation became Bolingbroke Chapel, and the church continued to add new members and attendees. Today it is called Northcote Road Baptist Church.[36]

It was during the sons' ministry at Bolingbroke that their father, visiting Mentone, wrote a letter to Thomas underscoring the importance of Susie to the family. He encouraged Thomas to "kiss your dear mother, and try and tell her how dear she is to us all three. Our angel and delight is she not?"[37] Such is the way that he and the twins spoke of Susie.

Preaching a sermon in January of 1898, at a memorial for his father, Thomas proclaimed that he would "exalt my father's God by preaching the self-same truths that he preached by passing on the message that was on his lips."[38] Thomas, like his brother Charles, deeply admired his father and counted him as a wise counselor.

On November 23, 1877, Charles wrote to Thomas from London:

My dear Son Tom, —

I have been greatly delighted with your letters and they
have caused great joy all round; especially has your own dear
mother been much cheered and comforted. Write all you
can for her sake—though we all share the pleasure.

God has been very gracious to you in opening so many
hearts and ears to you. May His grace abide with you that
these golden opportunities may all be used to the best possible result. I am overwhelmed with your reception, accept-
ing it as a token of the acceptance, which my works have
among the people. When I have you and Char [*sic*] at my
side to preach the same great truths we shall by God's grace
make England know more of the Gospel's power.

Char [*sic*] is working well at College [the Pastors' Col-
lege] and will, I trust, come forth thoroughly furnished.
When you come home I hope that your practice in Australia will lessen your need of college training so that one year
may suffice. Still every man regrets when in the field that he
did not prepare better before he entered it. We shall see.[39]

Charles viewed letters from Thomas as a means of cheering and comforting Susie. Thomas was in Australia preaching and would later pastor
in New Zealand (the warmer climate being less deleterious to his own
poor health). Charles encouraged his son to rely on God's grace in his
evangelistic work, imagining a day when he, along with his sons, would
labor side by side in the gospel ministry.

After his father's death, Thomas returned to London to serve as pastor
of the Metropolitan Tabernacle (1893–1908). However, Charles never
realized his hope of the three of them laboring together at the same time
and place. Charlie would also go into the ministry and labor as a pastor
in Greenwich and then later serve in ministries that his father created.
Soon after her death, Thomas remembered that Susie was "both wife and

mother, and a model of what each should be. She has had the joy of seeing her sons grow up to fear God, and to preach the Gospel of His grace; and she knew full well that her patient training had much to do with this."[40]

During their childhood, the sons lived beneath the blessings of God in a home where the Scriptures were honored and read; God was sought in prayer; hymns were sung; godly counsel was given; and Christ was exalted. And though their father was often away from his family, he left the boys in good hands under the care and tutelage of his beloved Susie.

Along with teaching them the way of godliness from the Scripture, praying with and for them, Susie modeled patience and perseverance in trial by pointing them to Christ and the gospel. The lessons that the Spurgeon sons learned from childhood would help to steel them as they witnessed the effects of their parents' faith in the midst of great tragedy.

CHAPTER 6

The Shadow of Sorrow: Tragedy and Faith

Before their first wedding anniversary, Susie and Charles faced a challenge that threatened to undo them. Susie's godly character is one important reason why Charles survived what was both a life- and ministry-threatening tragedy. Charles's fame was skyrocketing in London as crowds flocked to hear his gospel messages. His preaching, which so shook the great city for Christ, was also regularly critiqued by the press. *The Observer* referred to him as "the juvenile enthusiastic preacher from Waterbeach."[1] Although Charles's chief aim was to magnify Christ, he had a distinct style, derided by his detractors in the papers as "grave, gay, grotesque, solemn, fanciful, and even coarse; sometimes provoking the broadcat laughter, yet with touches of deep pathos and sublime appeal to the most sacred feelings."[2] He was dismissed by his critics at *The Observer* as a "preposterous mountebank."[3]

The sanctuary of the New Park Street Chapel was increasingly packed beyond capacity with people wanting to hear Charles preach. This growth led church leaders to consider venues that would be more accommodating for the crowds who clamored to hear his preaching.[4] The church agreed to expand the New Park Street Chapel, and facilities were rented for services that provided space sufficient for thousands to attend Spurgeon's sermons. When the New Park Street Chapel's expansion was completed (it had been enlarged to seat over two thousand people), it was still inadequate for the scores who desired to attend. Eventually church leaders purchased land for the construction of a new building, the Metropolitan Tabernacle.

The Tabernacle opened in 1861, seated over five thousand people, and overflowed with six thousand each Sunday. Yet, even with the much larger facility, numerous people were denied entrance because of the overcapacity crowds inside. During the construction of the Tabernacle, one of the places where the church met was the Surrey Gardens Music Hall. There, one of the defining events in Spurgeon's ministry occurred.

The church's first gathering at the Hall was on Sunday evening, October 19, 1856. Prior to the service, Charles and Susie prayed together at home where Susie was recovering from giving birth to their twin boys only a month earlier.[5] She offered God's blessing to Charles as he departed for the Music Hall.[6] While Charles was away, Susie persisted in prayer for her beloved husband and for the worship service.[7]

Approaching the Music Hall, Charles noticed a swelling crowd lining the streets. It was only with some measure of difficulty that he, himself, gained entrance to the building. Twelve thousand people filled the Hall, and ten thousand more spilled over into the gardens and streets outside. Early in the service, mischief-makers entered the building and yelled, "Fire!," "The galleries are giving away!," and, "The place is falling!"[8] Though there was no fire and no structural failure in the building, the emotional damage was done. Panic ensued, resulting in seven people being trampled to death and twenty-eight others hospitalized with serious injuries. A reporter described the evening:

> But in proportion to the joy and hope thus inspired [the large gathering to hear gospel preaching], were the sorrow and dis-

appointment arising from the terrible catastrophe by which the very first service was attended and cut short! At the most solemn moment of the occasion, the wicked rose in their strength, like a whirlwind, sin entered, followed by terror, flight, disorder, and death.[9]

The next morning, London's newspapers were filled with stories of the great tragedy. Some people believed that death and injury could have been avoided had not so many rushed the aisles, stairs, and doorways. One witness recounted how a lady inadvertently smothered her own sister:

> The sister of one of the females who lost their lives waited upon the police authorities and gave a painful narrative as to how the deceased, who was in advance of her, fell . . . and she was driven upon her, and felt the last respiration she gave, but being so closely pressed by those from behind, she was unable to get off her, or to render the least assistance, although she screamed with all her might for help.[10]

The Observer reported that a woman at almost full-term pregnancy was killed; she was removed to another location where a C-section was performed in hopes of rescuing the baby in her womb, but the baby was already dead.[11] *The Manchester Weekly Times* reported, "The despairing shrieks of women and children were heard above the roar of voices which proceeded from the platform and the ground floor of the building. . . ." Women and children were especially "terror-stricken."[12]

The eyewitness accounts of the Surrey Gardens Music Hall disaster are graphic, heart-rending, and tragic. *The Observer* recorded that Charles was removed to an "apartment used as the vestry" in the building, and there "he stretched himself at full length on the floor, apparently in a state of stupor." He was then awakened and "urged to leave the gardens."[13]

Charles was inconsolable, and the tragedy threatened to undo his ministry. Rumor spread that he died that night. He responded, "I was not dead, thank God, but the bystanders might well have imagined that the terrible shock had killed me."[14] Though Charles did not die on that evening, the effects of it plagued him for the rest of his life. Susie referred to the event as "the black shadow of sorrow which the Lord saw fit to cast over our young and happy lives."[15]

Church historian Mark Hopkins writes that the Music Hall tragedy was "an episode whose importance in Spurgeon's spiritual experience was second only to that of his conversion."[16] Though Hopkins's assessment *may* be an overstatement, the horrific night left its imprint on Charles for all of his days. A deacon rushed to the Spurgeons' home and gave Susie the sad news. She recalls, "He kneeled by the couch and prayed that we might have grace and strength to bear the terrible tragedy which had so suddenly come upon us."[17]

As soon as the deacon left, Susie cried to God in prayer. It was a night of deep sorrow that included "weeping and wailing."[18] Even though she was still weak from giving birth, Susie faithfully cared for her children while also comforting her beloved husband in the aftermath.[19] Charles's pain was deep, and he struggled to make sense of what had happened. Charles Ray recounts that Charles "was taken by friends to Croydon where he stayed in the house of Mr. Winsor, one of his deacons, and Mrs. Spurgeon with the babies joined him there."[20] While at Croydon, Charles penned a letter to his mother, raw with pain yet sprinkled with hope.

> Dear Mother,
>
> I could not write till now for my poor brain was hot with grief—but it is all right now—all right—I shall rest for some days then at it again. God is on my side why should I fear. I am not dismayed for God shall help me. Dear Susie cannot write, she is so ill—The Doctor has been today and says she is very, very ill, and then says but not seriously—Do not mention the accident in the Gardens to me at pres-

ent, but pray for me—I am now almost restored to spirits but I shall never forget this burning furnace. I will thrash the devil yet—I will seek to be yet more valiant for God. The Lord nerved me that evening and no unaided man in the universe could have been as brave, as calm, as fearless as I by God's grace—Ah Mother, this is no small honour to be maligned for Jesus—Tremble not I do not—In God's name I say to timid friends and boisterous foes my word is On, still On—for Christ and for his truth—My most fervent love to you and, my dear father—all. Your much-loved son, Charles.[21]

In the aftermath of the Music Hall disaster, some people blamed Charles. He was criticized for renting such a facility that allowed so many thousands to gather. He was lambasted for continuing the service after chaos had ensued the evening of the disaster. In Charles's defense, he did not independently choose the location, provoke anyone to mischief, and his continuing of the service during the upheaval was due to not fully understanding what was happening and attempting to calm the people down via prayer, singing, and preaching in the midst of the confusion.

Susie was bewildered as she wondered what the future held concerning her own well-being and that of the mental health of her husband. According to Charles's letter to his mother, Susie was sickly. Though the nature of her illness is unspecified, it was considerable but not life-threatening. Perhaps her recovery from giving birth a month prior was thwarted as the stress of the Music Hall disaster weighed heavily upon her. Or maybe she felt the early pains of the physical affliction she would later experience. Susie must have wondered about the effects upon her husband from the tragedy, what would happen to his ministry and, therefore, how their young family would be impacted.

During his stay at Winsor's home, Charles regained his physical and mental strength, and he experienced something of a spiritual revival.[22]

He and Susie were walking together one day and meditating on Paul's letter to the Philippians. Suddenly he stopped, turned to Susie, and said: "Dearest, how foolish I have been! Why! What does it matter what becomes of me, if the Lord be but glorified?" Then he quoted Philippians 2:9–11: "Wherefore God also hath highly exalted him, and given him a name which is above every name: that at the name of Jesus every knee should bow, of things in heaven, and things in earth, and things under the earth; and that every tongue should confess that Jesus Christ is Lord, to the glory of God the Father." He said, "Oh, wifey, I see it all now! Praise the Lord with me."[23]

What Charles saw from Scripture was the exalted and reigning Christ that he so loved. Pondering Christ's exaltation following His crucifixion and resurrection sped hope to his heart. He went from almost resigning his ministry to a renewed strength, passion, and vision for pastoral work.[24] However, Charles overestimated the extent of his recovery, especially emotionally. It is impossible to calculate the extent of the damage to Charles both mentally and physically. Susie's love for her husband stirred her up to minister to him, but her own doubts, her own pain, and her own suffering over her husband, she mostly concealed.

While at Winsor's home, Charles and Susie dedicated their twins to the Lord.[25] Susie remembered the little boys being passed around the room, with prayers offered on their behalf, and lots of admiration and kissing. She said that evening, "our infants were brought to Christ the Lord."[26] She was careful to point out that they were not brought sacramentally and with any water applied to them, just brought with requests *of* God *for* His blessing. Susie must have felt a strong sense of relief as hope was restored. She needed Charles now more than ever. They were the parents of twins, and she had not recovered as quickly as she expected from the delivery of the babies.

Charles's apparent recovery must have struck a chord of joy in Susie's heart. He returned to New Park Street Chapel for services two weeks later, on November 2, 1856.[27] He prayed and referred to the feelings of "joy and sorrow" felt by the congregation. He cried out in prayer, "Thanks to Thy Name! Thy servant feared that he should never be able to meet this congregation again; but Thou has brought him up out of the fiery furnace."[28] The first words from his sermon were, "I almost regret this morning that I have ventured to occupy this pulpit, because I feel utterly unable to preach to you for your profit."[29] Prior to the service, he imagined that "the effects of that terrible tragedy" would not hinder him.[30] However, he lamented, "I feel somewhat of those same painful emotions which well nigh prostrated me before." He then asked the congregation to excuse him if he made "no allusion to that solemn event, or scarcely any."[31]

This was a recurring theme; Charles had not wanted his mother to ask him about the tragic night, and he now imagined that he might not be able to even allude to the event in the course of his sermon. He encouraged his congregation with his intent to preach at the Surrey Gardens Music Hall again, as he was confident God would help him.[32] Charles then did what he was most accustomed to doing: he preached Jesus. The title of Charles's sermon was "The Exaltation of Christ."[33] His text was from Philippians 2, the same passage that God had used to comfort him during his walk with Susie. Charles remarked, "The text I have selected is one that has comforted me, and in a great measure, enabled me to come here to-day—the single reflection upon it had such a power of comfort on my depressed spirit."[34]

His first sermon back in the New Park Street pulpit revealed the tension that he felt. He looked to Christ, and yet he doubted if he should have returned to the pulpit at that time. One wonders what Susie must have been thinking. She, no doubt, had rejoiced at his spiritual revival, but did her heart now sink again as her beloved struggled through the sermon? Today, one might be tempted to think that, indeed, Charles did return too soon; perhaps he should have taken more time away for recovery. However, Charles was a preacher, and he may have felt that he *must* preach. As difficult as it is to imagine him returning to the Chapel only two weeks after the tragedy, it is staggering to realize that in only two more weeks, he also returned to the pulpit at the Music Hall—where the great tragedy had taken place. Susie, no doubt, was concerned for her husband, and rightly so.

Services at Surrey Garden resumed on the morning of November 23, 1856, and the church continued to meet there on Sunday mornings until December 11, 1859. On Charles's return to the Music Hall, his sermon title was "Love's Commendation" from Romans 5:8. From that text he proclaimed, "Christ died for us."[35] That simple yet profound theme anchored Charles in truth and filled his heart with hope even though his grief was not fully dissuaded.

Though Charles experienced God's enabling strength to minister again, remembrance of the tragedy haunted him. Time and again both Susie and a number of Charles's friends witnessed his nervous reactions in troubling circumstances. No one felt the depth of his suffering more than his beloved Susie. She lamented, "He carried the scars of that conflict to his dying day, and never afterwards had he the physical vigour and strength which he possessed before passing through the fierce trial."[36] Charles was a changed man, physically and emotionally, from the day of the tragedy forward. And though he was only twenty-two years old, he suddenly seemed much older. No doubt the struggles with depression he faced prior to the Music Hall disaster were exacerbated as well.

At a preaching event some months later, Charles was "leaning his head on his hand" in the passageway of a crowded hall. It was obvious to his most intimate companions that the impact of the tragedy affected his nervous system.[37] Charles's friend William Williams was convinced that his "comparatively early death might be in some measure due to the furnace of mental suffering he endured on and after that fearful night."[38]

Charles's mind was burdened, and Susie did her best to comfort him. That season of trial reveals important truths about their marriage that are also evident in later experiences of suffering. Prayer and Scripture were the means through which both Susie and Charles found comfort and by which Susie ministered to her husband, helping to bring him out of the depths of despair and restore joy to his heart.

Though Charles was recovering, he nevertheless continued to grieve and struggle with depression related to the disaster. The press was vicious in their attacks on Charles, blaming him for the suffering and death, but Susie comforted her beloved husband. She printed Matthew 5:11–12 in large old English type and "enclosed it in a pretty Oxford frame." Susie wrote, "The text was hung up in our own room and was read over by the dear preacher every morning. Fulfilling its purpose—most blessedly, for it strengthened his heart. . . ."[39]

Charles later recognized how near the brink of mental breakdown he had been: "Perhaps no soul went so near the burning furnace of insanity, and yet came away unharmed."[40] Susie, in this early period of her marriage and with two infants to care for, displayed unusual courage, unwavering faith in God, and deep devotion to her husband, believing, "Though we may not at the time, see His purpose in the afflictions which He sends us, it will be plainly revealed when the light of eternity falls upon the road along which we have journeyed."[41]

This early trial in her marriage to Charles anchored Susie for the storms of suffering that were yet to come. There is an emphasis on the theme of God's grace in suffering in the five books that Susie later authored. Helping Charles through his various challenges and dealing with her own physical pain also served to settle her in greater dependence on God. She later wrote, "No darkness, no distance, no dividing distress of any kind can separate thee from His constant care."[42] She followed with words of encouragement: "Do remember, dear friend, that the God you love, the Master you serve, is *never* indifferent to your grief, or unwilling to hear your cry."[43]

Susie was not content to sit idly by as her husband suffered various trials. Often on Sunday evenings, when Charles was weary from a day of ministry, he "would sit in an easy chair by the fire while 'Susie' would read a page or two of *Good Master George Herbert*."[44]

My God, I read this day,
That planted Paradise was not so firm,
As was and is thy floating Ark; whose stay
And anchor thou art only, to confirm
And strengthen it in ev'ry age,
When waves do rise, and tempests rage.[45]

Sometimes the end of the day found Charles depressed, and then the ministry of "the pastor's pastor [Richard Baxter] was a benediction."[46] Susie was convinced that those times of reading to Charles ministered to him by calming his mind and allowing him to rest. She also benefited: "Perhaps the enjoyment of the book is all the greater that he has thus to explain and open to me the precious truths enwrapped in Herbert's quaint verse; anyhow, the time is delightfully spent."[47]

Often Susie's reading to Charles brought great conviction to their hearts, and they wept together. She wrote of their tears, "He from the smitings of a very tender conscience toward God, and I, simply and only because I love him, and want to share his grief."[48] What a tender wife Susie was; tears flowed down her cheeks simply because she loved her husband.

Their ministry to one another cemented their affections with a bond that no amount of suffering could erode. There are few love stories so tender, so sweet, and so instructive as that of Charles and Susie Spurgeon. Biographer Ernest Bacon described their marriage: "God had certainly made them for each other. It was a love match, but also a spiritual partnership, as every true Christian marriage should be."[49]

The long separations from Charles due to his travels were Susie's greatest trial early in their marriage; his absences were "frequent." She was committed to supporting his ministry, "never hindering him in his work," but on one occasion, she felt the pain of separation especially acutely. She paced up and down the hall of their first home, watching and praying for Charles's safe return. When he finally walked up the steps and opened the door, she was filled with joy.[50]

She also recalled a morning when she allowed herself to cry over Charles's impending departure. As the tears streamed down her face, Charles calmed her by reminding her that her willing encouragement of him to travel in ministry was an offering to God. Though one might imagine that Charles's words lacked compassion, Susie received them in just the opposite manner and found comfort in his gentle reminder that her offering and his service were given to God. She remembered the early days of their marriage as lovely. Susie's memory of that time when "love was young" strengthened her in latter days.[51]

The Music Hall disaster, the greatest test in their young marriage, did not create Susie and Charles's bond of love for one another or their spiritual commitments, but it did reveal the depth and value of both. Because Charles and Susie held to the trustworthiness of Scripture, they were supported when the storms of trial pummeled them, and they were able to see a purpose in the suffering. Had Charles not had the ear, the heart, and the prayers of a godly wife, he may have lost hope.

Charles wrote of suffering, "We have suffered, and can testify that there is a point where suffering and pain are the vestibule of bliss. When they bring men as near to Jesus as they carried us, they are not angels in disguise, but seraphs all unveiled."[52] The purpose of suffering, in Charles's view, was to bring men "near to Jesus" and to a "conscious dependence upon God."[53]

Susie was of like mind with her husband. Looking to Psalm 31:15: "My times are in thy hand," she declared:

> Not one or two important epochs of my history only, but everything that concerns me; —joys that I had not expected, —sorrows that must have crushed me if they could have been anticipated,—sufferings which might have terrified me by their grimness had I looked upon them, —surprises which infinite love had prepared for me, —services of which I could not have imagined myself capable; —all these lay in that mighty hand as the purposes of God's eternal will for me.[54]

Firmly trusting in the Bible, the couple found that their suffering increased their confidence in God and their reliance on each other. Charles offered this perspective of their marriage:

> Matrimony came from Paradise, and leads to it. I never was half so happy, before I was a married man, as I am now. When you are married, your bliss begins. Let the husband love his wife as he loves himself, and a little better, for she is his better half. He should feel, "If there's only one good wife in the whole world, I've got her." John Ploughman [pseudonym for Charles] has long thought just that of his own wife, and after thirty-five years, he is more sure of it than ever. There is not a better woman on the surface of the globe than his own, very own beloved.[55]

Charles had a good wife, and his confidence in her only increased with the passing of the years. Susie loved and trusted Charles and ran to him "in search of counsel, comfort, or wise advice" and she always found what she needed.[56] Spurgeon biographer H. I. Wayland asserted, "Never would Mr. Spurgeon have gone through his unparalleled labors, if he had not found rest and reinforcement in his home, and in the society of a brave, noble, loving woman."[57]

Ironically, during the Sunday morning service at the New Park Street Chapel, before the Surrey Garden's Music Hall service held that tragic evening, Charles looked out over his congregation and said:

> Perhaps I may be one of those who shall live in the valley of ease, having much rest, and hearing sweet birds of promise singing in my ears. The air is calm and balmy, the sheep are feeding round about me, and all is still and quiet. Well, then, I shall prove the love of God in sweet communings. Or, perhaps I may be called to stand where the thunderclouds brew, where the lightnings play, and tempestuous winds are howling on the

mountaintop. Well, then, I am born to prove the power and majesty of our God; amidst dangers He will inspire me with courage; amidst toils He will make me strong.[58]

Charles was not one who was called to "dwell in the valley of ease," but instead he was destined for a lifetime of severe trial. Without the grace of God in providing a friend, partner, and a great love in Susie, Charles may have irreparably fallen. Instead, one of God's many provisions to help Charles in his life and ministry was Susie.

CHAPTER 7

Hand in Hand at Home and Abroad

Charles and Susie resided at three London addresses[1] during their marriage but four different homes. In each of their domiciles, Susie was the "Angel of the House."[2] Their first home was the previously mentioned one on New Kent Road where they resided from January 1856 until the autumn of 1857. It was in this home that Charles and Susie welcomed their twin boys. In 1857, they moved to their second home, 99 Nightingale Lane, Clapham. In 1869, this home was torn down and a new one built on the old site; therefore, this was their third home but second address. In 1880, they made their final move to Westwood at Beulah Hill, near Sydenham in south London.

For twenty-three years of Charles and Susie's thirty-six-year marriage, they worked and prayed, read and wept, laughed and worshiped, and built their marriage and family at Helensburgh House on Nightingale Lane. Charles named the house after Helensburgh, Scotland's lovely gardens, and after the place where his friend Rev. John Anderson resided. In late 1856 or early 1857, Charles preached at Helensburgh to large crowds.[3]

Spurgeon biographer G. Holden Pike wrote that Charles and Rev. Anderson had much in common, "and 'Helensburgh House,' Nightingale Lane, Clapham, was a name which told of a friend far away in the beautiful North—'my own John Anderson.'"[4]

When Charles and Susie moved to their new home, the twins were just over a year old. The new address would be the boys' last one as residing members of the Spurgeon house, for it was almost twenty-five years later that Charles and Susie would move again, and that for the last time. Nightingale Lane in those days was a quiet and semirural neighborhood on the outskirts of London surrounded by wildlife and gardens. It was just the sort of homey place that made for an enjoyable and serene setting for the young family.

Helensburgh House, the property surrounding it, and the quiet Nightingale Lane neighborhood provided a retreat for Spurgeon, an idyllic setting for Susie to manage her home and tend to their children, and lovely grounds on which the twin boys could play. It was also a resourceful place; Charles and Susie had a milk cow and gardens on the property. The loveliness and size of the home is indicative of Susie and Charles's improving financial situation. It was at this house that they first hired household employees.

In Victorian London, it was common for a middle-class family to employ at least one servant and, based on position, land ownership, and/or income, they might enjoy the benefit of several. It is not known exactly when Charles and Susie first enjoyed the help of domestic employees, but the 1861 census, the first census taken after their marriage, indicates that they had three at that time. That number increased over the years, and when Charles died in 1892, there were at least six servants, probably several more. This is a strong indicator that Charles and Susie were upper-middle-class citizens for much of their marriage.

Things were tight financially for Charles and Susie in their early years, but it was in part because they were benevolent with their money by investing in various ministries, such as their church, first of all, and then the Pastors' College. A later example serves to illustrate this point: in the mid-1870s, a new building was constructed for the Pastors' College at a cost of £15,000. Spurgeon gave sacrificially to the project from his own funds.[5] It is difficult to compute the monetary value of £15,000 in modern currency; however, $1,500,000 is a modest estimate of the cost of the new building in today's funds.[6]

Even before Charles and Susie were married, he delightfully shared what resources that he had to help others. The seed of his future Pastors' College was planted in 1854 when Charles assisted T. M. (Thomas) Medhurst with living arrangements and personal instruction. Other such men who felt called to preach were likewise helped.

Funding for Charles's new venture was a challenge, as he intimated, "Now I find it no easy task to get money, and I have been thinking I must get friends to give me a good set of books, which I shall not *give* you [Medhurst], but keep for those who may come after; so that, by degrees, I shall get together a good Theological Library for young students in years to come." Furthermore, Charles states: "If I were rich, I would give you all; but as I have to bear all the brunt of the battle, and am alone responsible, I think I must get the books to be always used in the future."[7]

Susie writes of their first home: "We began housekeeping on a very modest scale, and even then had to practice rigid economy in all things, for my dear husband earnestly longed to help young men to preach the gospel, and from our slender resources we had to contribute somewhat largely to the support and education of T. W. Medhurst, who was the first to receive training for the work."[8] Such was the beginning of the Pastors' College and Susie's contribution to it. She recalled sweet memories of working with Charles in planning for and contributing to the future of the college. She said that "together, we planned and pinched in order to carry out the purpose of his [Charles's] loving heart; it gave me quite a motherly interest in the College, and 'our own men.'" She saw the stretching of their finances as "God's way of preparing us to sympathize with and help poor pastors in the years which were to come."[9]

The 1861 census records Charles H. Spurgeon as the head of house, Susannah Spurgeon as his wife, and Charles and Thomas as their sons. After the family listing, the census includes the names of either two or three servants: Mary Arnold (visitor), Eliza Phillips (housemaid), and Ellen Bond (cook). It is likely that the Spurgeons also employed a yardman, but he was either away from the home at the time of the census, or he was a contract laborer instead of household staff. Their presence provides a clue as to how Charles was able to accomplish so much, travel so widely, take care of Susie, and keep his property maintained. Charles was a diligent worker; however, if it had been necessary for him to maintain the yards and house, he would never have been able to lead his ministries, pastor the Tabernacle, and write so prolifically. He needed help and, with God's provision, he was able to employ people to assist him. As well, he enjoyed the benefits of those who helped him in serving his church, thereby freeing him up for his ministry of preaching, writing, and leading.

Nightingale Lane was a lovely place, and Susie and Charles took walks together on the property and down the street.[10] Susie described the house as old and its construction odd. Even with its uniqueness, she appreciated it, and she considered it all that she could have desired. Both she and Charles thought it a "delightsome place," and though the yards and gardens had fallen into disrepair at the time of their move, they enjoyed putting it all back into shape. Susie warmly remembered: "No two birds ever felt more exquisite joy in building their nest in the fork of a tree-branch, than did we in planning and placing, altering and rearranging our pretty country home."[11]

In 1858, Charles was stricken by an illness that removed him from the pulpit for almost a month. Even with that, the early years at Nightingale Lane were the healthiest of any of Charles and Susie's years together. With relatively good health, deep love for one another, and happy children, Susie spent much of her time helping Charles in his work. She said, "I deemed it my joy and privilege to be ever at his side, accompanying him on many of his preaching journeys, nursing him in his occasional illnesses, his delighted companion during his holiday trips, always watching over and tending him with the enthusiasm and sympathy which my great love for him inspired."[12]

From 1857 to 1868, Susannah devoted nearly all of her energies to her husband: "I was permitted to encircle him with all the comforting care and tender affection which it was in a wife's power to bestow."[13] Then, those early years at Nightingale Lane and her travels with Charles across the Continent came to a screeching halt. Susie's health declined and no longer could she minister to Charles, as she desired. To best understand the depth and results of her affliction, it is important to first consider her relative good health during the more comfortable years of her marriage.

Years of Good Health and Travel

For one appreciative of beautiful works of art draping the walls in the great galleries of Europe, the mountain passes along the Alps, the dreamy experience of Venice, and romantic walks in Paris, the dark clouds of suffering that would soon envelop Susie and keep her mostly confined to home would be doubly painful.

During those afflicted years, she often recalled their earlier days of travel, writing that her memories were even sweeter when "my husband could spend a little time by my couch, and the talk turned to these sunny days, and we together recalled our most amusing adventures, and laughed heartily at the blunders and mistakes we either made or mastered."[14]

Susie cherished every minute with her busy husband whose work schedule from the beginning of his ministry in London staggers the imagination. Their early travels found the young couple crisscrossing Europe where they savored the sights and sounds of the green pastures, majestic mountains, and winding rivers. "Twice we visited Venice to-gether," wrote Susie, "and all the dreamy delights of our sojourn there return with their old fascination, by an effort of the will, or a glance at the pages of Mr. Ruskin's *Stones of Venice*." Susie recalled that their time there was "enshrined in my memory as a creation of exceeding loveliness, glowing with the prismatic hues of a gorgeous sunset, and enwrapped in a veil of golden mist."[15]

Susie relished accompanying Charles to the art galleries in the major cities. She valued the work of the classic artists Raphael and Rubens, but she was more infatuated with the Dutch Interior paintings, such as those by Teniers and van Ostade.[16] Their paintings depicted scenes from the everyday lives of hard working people and families of modest means. Susie's appreciation for fine art is quite understandable given her cultured upbringing. Yet, her love for simple things, hard work, and the love of family are evident in her artistic preferences.

During her travels with Charles, Susie displayed tremendous energy and stamina in hiking many of the major passes along the Alps. Likely, when most people think of Susie Spurgeon, the term "mountain hiker" doesn't come to mind. While visiting St. Gothard Pass, she walked by herself in advance of the carriage carrying her husband and his publisher Joseph Passmore. She recalled an occasion when Charles and Passmore were discussing various theological and publishing matters while riding in their carriage. Susie, on foot, disappeared out of sight and turned a corner to spot, for the first time, the Devil's Bridge, which wound between "mighty masses of granite rock" and crossed a "savage gorge where the Reuss foamed and boiled."[17] She described the sight as "the grandest part of the route," yet felt lonely and fearful in the midst of the majestic mountains.[18]

As she hiked the numerous Alpine passes, she preferred walking or riding a mule to the less taxing seating experience of a carriage. Walking allowed her to survey the sights and ponder deeply the beauty of God's creation, as evidenced in the towering mountains and the valley's depths. She exclaimed, "I preferred to toil up the well-made roads whenever it was possible, and stand silently amidst the stupendous heights and depths."[19] The idea of Susie climbing hills, descending into valleys, and crossing rough bridges deep in the mountains is a testament to her courage and resilience. Physically, perhaps her long weekly walks to the Crystal Palace to meet with Charles during their engagement helped to prepare her for these mountain adventures. Obviously, she had recovered sufficiently from giving birth to the twins to accomplish such a feat.

Charles enjoyed taking in the beauty of the great land with his dear wife. Yet, even the most blissful of experiences could turn on him if he was confronted by danger. In those times, memories of the Music Hall disaster would rush to mind and could temporarily paralyze him, both mentally and physically. Susie recounted an occasion when one of their baggage mules lost his footing and partially slid down the slope of a mountain. Though the donkey survived, Charles was emotionally stricken and, nearly collapsing, sunk to the snow-covered ground to sit and recover. Charles, Susie, and their party were eight thousand feet above sea level on a sharp ridge with barely enough time to reach their destination below before dark. After some time and much coaxing, Charles was persuaded to get up and move forward.

Susie was perplexed and dismayed by the experience, until later when she surmised that the experience had conjured up dreadful memories of death and destruction from the Music Hall tragedy and caused Charles's mental unrest. She believed that "the delicate organism of his wonderful brain had then sustained so much pressure in some part of it, that any sudden fright, such as the swift descent of a mule down the mountain, would have the power, for a moment or two, to disturb its balance."[20] A modern psychological analysis of Spurgeon's condition might conclude that he suffered from post traumatic stress disorder. Regardless, the Music Hall episode was often replayed in Charles's mind to ill effect.

Toward the end of his life, he published his devotional book *The Cheque Book of the Bank of Faith*. For the November 10 reading, he includes a telling section:

The way of life is like travelling among the Alps. Along mountain paths one is constantly exposed to the slipping of the foot. Where the way is high the head is apt to swim, and then the feet soon slide; there are spots which are smooth as glass, and others that are rough with loose stones, and in either of these a fall is hard to avoid. He who throughout life is enabled to keep himself upright and to walk without stumbling has the best of reasons for gratitude. What with pitfalls and snares, weak knees, weary feet, and subtle enemies, no child of God would stand fast for an hour were it not for the faithful love which will not suffer his foot to be moved.

Spurgeon then included a selection from an Isaac Watt's hymn:

> Amidst a thousand snares I stand
> Upheld and guarded by thy hand;
> That hand unseen shall hold me still,
> And lead me to thy holy hill.[21]

Although Charles never could quite shake the Music Hall tragedy, he nevertheless trusted that God would not allow his foot to slip into ultimate disaster. Charles's health would fail, his depressions remain. Susie would also suffer; she would suffer the pains that Charles felt, and she would suffer from her medical condition. Yet neither Charles nor Susie was content to live beneath the tears of sadness; they pressed forward with faith and bountiful joy in Christ as they engaged in hard and fruitful work.

Their travels provided Susie with pleasant memories that helped her face the howling storms of suffering that would soon blow across the Thames River and into her home. The story of her greatest physical and emotional difficulties will be later explored, but the things that she valued, the loveliness that she enjoyed, and the happiness that characterized the first years of her marriage all worked together with her sundry trials to weave together, in Susie, a simple but beautiful perspective that is evident in her character and in her later devotional writings.

Returning home from one of their Continental trips, the Spurgeons embraced their sons, and then they walked together as a family to the garden, eager to see the treasures that had sprung up while they were away. Susie remembered that "it looked very quiet, peaceful, and lovely; and we felt the sweetness of God's mercy to us, in bringing us back to safety to such a fair and comely home."[22] The Spurgeons' gardener had "thoughtfully" planned a surprise as a homecoming gift—he had painted the vases and even the fount—centrally placed in the gardens—bright blue and yellow. For a moment, Susie and Charles were speechless.

Susie wrote: "Fresh from the land of art and artists, and from beholding all that skill and good taste combined could provide of beauty of design and charm of colouring in every small detail of decoration and embellishment, our recoil from our disfigured belongings can be easily imagined."[23] Charles delicately handled the matter with his gardener, and soon the pots and the fount were restored to their original whiteness, and the gardener, gently dealt with, had his feelings protected.[24] A happy note was struck at the Spurgeon home as family was reunited and their routine returned.

The story of Susie's early years of marriage and the freedom good health afforded to her is surprising to those who think of her primarily as the suffering, yet godly, wife of Charles Spurgeon. She was both. However, to see Susie relatively free from pain helps one to better understand her plight when, as a thirty-six-year-old woman, she is removed from experiences that she once robustly enjoyed.

Both Susie and Charles appreciated their years of traveling together. Charles was never an athletic type, always preferring his books to physical exercise, although he loved the outdoors, and his library contained many volumes devoted to nature and birds specifically, books such as *The History of the Robins, The Illustrated Natural History,* and *My Feathered Friends.*[25] Susie preferred her feet to carriages, trains, and mules. When later she could no longer embark upon her mountain hikes, she returned to France, Italy, and England via the pages of books and the memories stored for ready retrieval in the inner recesses of her heart. Such memories and books would help her as she walked through a dark and deathly valley.

CHAPTER 8

The Great Sufferer

Susie's love for travel never waned; however, her years of crossing land and sea with Charles met their sunset. It was then, as son Thomas described it, "that my dear mother first became seriously ill."[1] Susie lamented, "In 1868 my travelling days were done. Henceforth for many years, I was a prisoner in a sick chamber . . . "[2] Susie's description rings with despair and indicates that her circumstances were bleak.

Not only did Susie's own pain and suffering weigh upon her back, so did the fact that her beloved Charles's health also diminished even as his responsibilities increased. Along with leading his church and its auxiliary ministries, Charles wielded the pen of a bestselling author.

Additionally, many people pressed upon him to preach, write, endorse books, give money, and even to travel to the United States (which he never did). His workload was enormous though his body weakened and forced him at times to cease from his labors. He was often driven out of London by two necessities beyond the invitations he received to preach in various places: First, he needed fresh air and a beautiful setting to help him reset his mind for writing and regain his strength for pastoring. Also, he needed the bright sun and warmer environment of southern France to work healing on his body *and* mind. Charles struggled with gout and kidney disease; he was overweight, and he was often depressed. As a Spurgeon scholar stated: "One psychiatrist has noted that if he lived today, Spurgeon would be diagnosed with bipolar disorder and treated with medicine."[3]

Though he loved London, sometimes the overcast skies clouded his spirit. One writer sarcastically opined that the sun was an "aerial phenomenon sometimes witnessed in England."[4] Susie's sufferings were doubled; her body was wrought with pain, and Charles was often a thousand miles from home. It was too much for Susie to bear. "My beloved had to leave me when the strain of his many labours and responsibilities compelled him to seek rest far away from home." She remembered, "These separations were very painful to hearts so tenderly united as were ours, but we each bore our share of the sorrow as heroically as we could, and softened it, as far as possible by constant correspondence."[5]

Susie's health deteriorated so significantly that her biographer, Charles Ray, described her as a "great sufferer."[6] Eventually, her condition seemed desperate and surgery was opted for. Though the way ahead was uncertain, Susie looked to God for help. When she and Charles awoke each morning, their eyes focused in on a framed verse that hung on their bedroom wall, Isaiah 48:10: "I have chosen thee in the furnace of affliction." Charles intimated that the passage was not only fixed upon the wall, but it was "written on our heart."[7]

In 1869, church leaders suggested to Spurgeon that the old house at Nightingale Lane should be torn down so that a more suitable one could be constructed on the same site. Susie and the boys relocated about sixty-five miles south to the popular seaside city of Brighton while the house was being constructed. Charles traveled back and forth some but mostly maintained his responsibilities in London. As ladies walked along England's southern shore at Brighton beneath their parasols, Susie wrestled with a medical condition that is believed to have affected her reproductive organs. No known records specify Susie's condition or diagnosis, although her ailment caused severe pain and mostly kept her confined to her temporary residence.

Susie's long confinement meant that she would likely never see the Alps, walk the streets of Paris, sail in a gondola in Venice, or tour the great art galleries across Europe again. So severe was her illness that until late 1891, she seldom ventured out at all. However, when listening to others converse of their travels, Susie summoned her own memories and would exclaim, "Ah, I too have been there."[8]

On the occasion of her surgery, she wondered if she would live:

> I was moved to Brighton, there to pass a crisis in my life, the result of which would be a restoration to better health—or death. . . . The experiences of that trying time need not be described but mention must be made of the great kindness of Sir James Y. Simpson, who travelled twice from Edinburg to Brighton to render all the aid that the highest surgical skill could suggest. When the operation was over, Mr. Spurgeon asked Sir James about his fee, and he replied, "Well I suppose it should be a thousand guineas; and when you are Archbishop of Canterbury, I shall expect you to pay it. Till then, let us consider it settled by love."[9]

Susie's surgery was referred to as a "difficult operation."[10] She expected that it would result in either "better health or death." The operation, arduous as it was, rendered some relief to Susie, but it was not entirely successful. Two facts hint at the type of surgery Susie underwent. First, Charles and Susie had no more children after the birth of their twin boys.[11] It is reasonable to assume, especially since both loved children, that the Spurgeons *would* have had more children if they *could* have. Secondly, the choice of Sir James Young Simpson (1811–1879) as the surgeon offers an important clue: he was primarily known for his work as an obstetrician. Peter Masters notes, "In his teaching he had laid the groundwork for the advanced study of gynecology, so much so that some of his written work continued to be the finest exposition on the subject for the best part of a century."[12]

Simpson was Queen Victoria's favorite doctor, Charles's friend, a devoted Christian, a prolific author, and a sought-after surgeon. A brief glimpse at his remarkable life provides some insight into why Charles chose him for Susie's surgery.

Simpson was raised in a poor family in Bathgate, Scotland. In 1825, at the age of fourteen, he entered Edinburgh University, and soon after he decided to pursue a career in medicine. It was during an academic clinical that he witnessed an operation occurring without anesthesia: "Terrifying screams rent the air, and buried deep into the mind of Simpson a longing to see the end of consciousness and suffering in surgery."[13] This experience haunted him.

At the age of twenty-four he was named the Senior President of the Royal Medical Society of Edinburg.[14] His professional advancement thereafter was rapid. Peter Masters writes, "Aged only twenty-seven, he became a lecturer in obstetrics at the university. In terms of both content and communicational skill, these lectures were universally considered brilliant."[15] As his reputation grew in stature, so did the number of his students, patients, and his income. In 1839, he was elected to the post of professor of midwifery at the university.

Though a member of St. Stephen's Church, Edinburgh, Simpson was not a Christian, but the death of his daughter prompted him to ponder the meaning of life.[16] Pushing those thoughts aside, he gave himself to academics and to further developing his medical practice. His earlier experience, viewing a surgery without anesthesia, continued to burden him about the lack of a successful anesthetic for surgical patients. At the recommendation of a pharmacist, Simpson experimented with chloroform and, along with two of his peers, he breathed its fumes. One of his friends laughed uncontrollably, the other began dancing, Simpson himself felt drunk, and they all collapsed into a deep sleep. When Simpson woke up, he knew that he had made a discovery that would provide relief to many of his surgical patients and to pregnant women during delivery. Soon this anesthetic was introduced to hospitals and successfully applied.[17]

Simpson's first patient to receive chloroform was a woman in labor, with positive results. Simpson received pushback from some of his fellow doctors as well as from Christian theologians about the rightness of using anesthetics to relieve the pain of childbirth. One writer asserts that it wasn't Simpson's usage of anesthesia, per se, that earned him his position but, rather, it was "his work and energy as a propagandist and apologist and as an expositor of the principle that it is right and proper deliberately and scientifically to allay the pain of surgical operations and the discomfort and distress of women in childbirth."[18] Susie Spurgeon was extremely thankful to Simpson for his "great kindness" and his surgical skill.

Simpson, though brilliant, increasingly famous, and successful in his profession, was again troubled by the state of his soul. Through a series of circumstances and a summons to the bedside of an invalid Christian lady who witnessed to him, Simpson was converted. Feeling the weight of his sin and longing for forgiveness, he turned to Christ.[19]

A journalist asked Simpson about his greatest discovery. The journalist expected that Simpson would point to one of his medical accomplishments. However, Simpson replied that his greatest discovery was "that I am a sinner and that Jesus is a great Saviour!" He testified:

But again I looked and saw JESUS, my substitute, scourged in my stead and dying on the cross for me. I looked and cried and was forgiven. And it seems to be my duty to tell you of that Saviour, to see if you will not also look and live: How simple it all becomes when the Holy Spirit opens the eyes![20]

Simpson, though previously religious, dated his *actual* Christian conversion to 1861 and declared that year was his "first happy Christmas" because Christ forgave him of his sins.[21]

How did Simpson and Spurgeon become acquainted? C. D. T. James in *The Baptist Quarterly* writes:

> Mr. Spurgeon and Sir James Young Simpson bore no little re-semblance to each other physically and mentally and it is not surprising that, given the opportunity, an affectionate friendship should spring up between them. They first met in 1864 at the house of a mutual Scottish friend, Mr. William Dickson, and here they continued to meet whenever Spurgeon visited Edinburgh. Quite soon Spurgeon was to become acquainted with the medical and surgical skill of Sir James and to know the warmth and sympathy of their friendship.[22]

Charles turned to Simpson, a godly man and a skilled physician, to serve as Susie's surgeon. By September of 1867, Susie's condition was worsening, and Charles was attempting to get in touch with Simpson. In a note of deep concern, Charles appeals to a mutual friend to help him communicate with the doctor. He wrote, "I am no small trouble to you but what can I do? . . . My dear wife grows worse."[23] Finally, Simpson was able to visit Susie and eventually to perform her surgery.

Charles's correspondence communicates his joy in the outcome of Susie's surgery:

> My very Dear friend, I am writing far into the night to tell friends how my dear wife has sped. That dear angel of mercy, Sir James Simpson, has been very successful, as usual, and the operation is well over; patient, very patient, and in good spirits! If you know ten thousand eloquent men in Scotland I would give them work for the next hundred years, viz. to praise the Lord for sending to us such a man, so skillful and so noble a Doctor.[24]

Simpson gave the graduation address to the Edinburgh students in 1868. He spoke as one who had often seen death's deep valley in the faces of his patients. Perhaps he knew that his own death was near. He proclaimed:

> At that solemn hour, as we cross the river of Death, may He by whom "all things were made" lead and protect and sustain you by the might of His hand—that hand which hung up the sun in the firmament—which spun the planets and stars in their courses—which created this bright and beautiful physical world—and which, in human form, was nailed up to the Cross of Calvary to ransom back the Dark and Desolate moral world, and atone for man's transgressions. May the infinitude of the Saviour's love guard and claim you then, and now, and always.[25]

By March 1870, Simpson's health was deteriorating. He was of calm demeanor as "Just as I Am" and "Immanuel's Land" were sung and Scripture was read at his bedside. Simpson had been an "enthusiastic reader" of Spurgeon's sermons for some time. His friend Dr. Duns read to him from Charles's sermon on Mark 9:8, "Jesus Only." Simpson responded: "That's nice, read it again." Simpson died on May 6, 1870, at his house at 52 Queen Street, Edinburgh.[26]

Whether Susie had suffered damage to her reproductive or other organs when she gave birth to Charles and Thomas in 1856 or had a cyst or tumor, we simply do not know. Pregnancy and childbirth were more dangerous during the Victorian era than they are today. At times, one in two hundred women died during pregnancy,[27] and in maternal hospitals where doctors often transmitted infection from patient to patient, deaths were more frequent.[28] One author surmised that the descriptions of Susie's problems seem similar to endometriosis,[29] in part, the inflammation of the uterus. Severe pain, one of the main symptoms of the condition, is not limited to the abdominal area but is often felt throughout the entire body.

Though the etymology of endometriosis is uncertain, historians of the disease trace it back to antiquity. About 2,500 years ago, what is now classified as endometriosis was sometimes referred to as the "strangulation of the womb."[30] Historically, it was often misdiagnosed as a mental disorder, even hysteria.

Spurgeon's library included a book titled *A Practical Treatise of Inflammation of the Uterus, Its Cervix and Appendages, and Its Connection with Other Uterine Diseases.*[31] Patricia Kruppa writes that this work by Spurgeon's friend James Henry Bennet is "rather glaringly out of place amid the Scriptural commentaries" and that it "suggests the nature of her problem."[32] She further states, "The exact nature of Mrs. Spurgeon's illness remains shrouded in those twin phrases dear to the prose of Victorian chroniclers, 'delicacy forbids,' and 'there are some things too sacred to discuss.'"[33]

J. Y. Simpson was a doctor, author, teacher, and poet. In the June 1870 edition of *The Sword and the Trowel*, Charles included one of his poems.

Rest

Oft mid this world's ceaseless strife,
When flesh and spirit fail me,
I stop and think of another life,
Where ills can ne'er assail me.
Where my wearied arm shall cease its fight,
My heart shall cease its sorrow,
And this dark night change for the light
Of an everlasting morrow.
On earth below there's nought but woe,
E'en mirth is gilded sadness;
But in heaven above there's nought but love,
With all its raptured gladness.
There till I come, waits me a home,

All human dreams excelling,
In which at last, when life is past,
I'll find a regal dwelling.
Then shall be mine, through grace divine,
A rest that knows no ending,
Which my soul's eye would fain descry,
Though still with clay tis blending.
And, Saviour dear, while I tarry here,
Where a Father's love has found me,
O let me feel, through woe and weal,
Thy guardian arm around me.[34]

Simpson's poem was certainly reflective of Susie's own convictions. She accepted that her life on earth would be filled with many sorrows, yet her trials pressed her to look upward to God and to anticipate one day being with Him, absent of suffering. Though Susie's body was wracked with pain, she believed that God "ordered it."[35] She compared suffering Christians to the disciples whose boat was tossed to and fro in a sea gale and who cried out to Jesus in desperation. The Christian's faith sometimes fails, Susie declared; however, God never forsakes His people. If it seems as if He is asleep while His people suffer, it should be remembered that "the pillow beneath His head is His own Omniscience, and, as surely as He ruled those winds and waves on Galilee's lake and reigned in the tempest with a word, so certainly does He manage all the affairs of His children and appoint or permit all that concerns them."[36]

It is difficult to ascertain the tremendous strain placed on the Spurgeons' marriage as a result of Charles's growing sphere of ministry, his own health issues, and a wife so severely afflicted that she could no longer publicly participate in his ministry. However, even under the stress of physical affliction, there is no indication that their love for one another ever faltered. Kruppa writes, "The constancy of the Spurgeons' affections for one another remained undiminished through a series of crises."[37] Charles and Susannah not only learned to face grief patiently, but also their love for one another deepened. Kruppa surmises,

> To the end of their lives, they were lovers; and what could be more touching than these two old invalids, she had grown plump and looking slightly absurd wearing the girlish curls, he prematurely tired and aged, yet writing each other love poems as though they were still twenty and courting under the dome of the Crystal Palace.[38]

Charles grieved over his dear Susie's suffering. Years later, he wrote to his son Thomas, "When you see a lady of your own age who is at all like what your mother *was* be sure to pop the question at once. If you get her and she lives to be what your dear mother *is*, you will lament her weakness and yet reckon her to be better than the strongest of women."[39] Despite this, Charles disclosed to his father, John, "My poor wife is wasting to a shade."[40]

Charles, though often separated from Susie during their hardships, was nevertheless sensitive to her situation. He wrote love letters to her almost every day.[41] She remembered their frequent correspondence as a means that God used to help her through her tribulations. How uplifting it was for Susie to receive such tender epistles from the hand of her beloved describing the sites and preaching places where he proclaimed the gospel and never failing to underline his love for her.

His book *The Cheque Book of the Bank of Faith* was written in the aftermath of the Down-Grade Controversy. (The Down-Grade Controversy was a controversy over the nature of Scripture in which many Christians, including some in Spurgeon's own denomination, downplayed the authority of the Bible. Charles considered anything less than full subscription to the Bible as errant). In this work, Charles reflected on his own dark troubles, the Down-Grade, and adds that his pain was "accompanied both by bereavement, and affliction in the person of one dear as life."[42]

As Charles's own health diminished, he regretted not being able to provide sufficient personal attention to Susie. He wanted her with him as he traveled. However, she could no longer make lengthy journeys with him.

None of her writings, at least, indicate that Susie felt bitter or angry with her lot in life; on the contrary, she said that she was "so unworthy" of the kindnesses of God.[43] Similarly, a year after Charles's death, she wrote: "Dear fellow-Christian, do not faint or fear when the blessed Husbandman cuts, and grafts, and wounds thee!" She encouraged her readers to not be as much concerned about the pain the grafting causes but more that fruit should come through suffering. She was convinced that God does not forget His people but "watches with loving scrutiny every indication of developing fruit-buds" and that "great will be His joy, when, in full strength and beauty, thou shalt glorify Him by thy abundant fruitfulness."[44] She declared, "Yet how good God has been to me! He has upheld me through days of darkness, and seasons of sorrow, of which none knew but Himself and my own soul."[45]

Though Susie was often confined to her home, the Lord sustained her by His Word, through prayer, and by the support of her faithful husband. For the first years of her marriage to Charles, she had faithfully attended church services and served the female candidates at their baptism. After her affliction set in, it was only on rare occasions that Susie returned to the Metropolitan Tabernacle. She considered attending church one of the great happinesses of a Christian's life.[46]

Church records reveal that Susie was active in church (NPSC/Metropolitan Tabernacle) from her membership in February of 1855 through September of 1867. The records have "ill" written in pencil for the year 1868. The records also indicate that she attended services in November of 1868, March of 1869, and then there is no mention of her attending again until December of 1874. (Records from 1875–1894 are unavailable.) She didn't attend between 1895 and her death in 1903.[47] The book contains a note beside Susie's name: "Called Home, Oct. 22. 03." However, as will later be considered, Susie became a member of a church closer to her home in the late 1880s.

Though she missed congregational gatherings, Charles ministered to her on Saturday evenings. She remembered her discipleship "in my own sweet home, and by my husband's side, and by that husband's hand." She said that through Charles, God led her "into green pastures, and beside the still waters."[48]

After Charles chose his texts for Sunday, he called Susie into the study and asked her to read various commentaries on the chosen passages. She said:

> Never was occupation more delightful, instructive, and spiritually helpful; my heart has often burned within me, as the meaning of some passage of God's word has been opened up, and the hidden stores of wisdom and knowledge have been revealed; or when the marrow and fatness of a precious promise or doctrine has been spread like a dainty banquet before my admiring eyes.[49]

Susie's testimony provides further insight into Spurgeon's discipleship of her. Charles also benefited from Susie's spiritual encouragement of him whether through her reading aloud, decorating their home with Bible verses, or by her prayers.

Though he was busy, Charles gladly welcomed Susie to use his study. In addition, his library brimmed with the Puritan divines, and when Susie read from one of their works, she was feasting on the same spiritual food that had nourished Charles so well from his childhood. She considered her time in her husband's study as "gracious hours" that were well spent and "unspeakably precious" to her soul. She explained that while Charles was "reaping the corn of the kingdom for the longing multitude who expected to be fed by his hand" that she could "glean between the sheaves, and gather the 'handfuls of purpose' which are let fall so lovingly."[50] "I listen to the dear voice of my beloved as he explains what I cannot understand, or unfolds meanings which I should fail to see," she said, "often condensing into a few clear, choice sentences whose pages of those discursive old divines in whom he delights, and pressing from the gathered thoughts all the richest nectar of their hidden sweetness."[51]

Charles perceptively opined, "A wife will not be put off with maintenance, jewels, and attire, all these will be nothing to her unless she can call her husband's heart and person her own."[52] Finding in Charles a true encourager and supporter in her labors, Susie worshiped and served God faithfully from their home.

She said Charles offered to her "sweet sympathy" in her troubles. He had a "great heart of love and plenty of room for the bestowal of my burdens and fears."[53] And he saw to it that she was instructed in the Bible. Yet Charles felt that he could not serve his dear wife as much as he wanted to: "Incessant occupations demanded by my sphere of labour give me but scanty opportunities to pay the attentions which are the natural due of a sickly wife; but far from complaining because of this, she surrenders me with real heroism . . ."[54]

One might wonder whether Charles's love for Susie was as practical as it might have been. Perhaps he should have curtailed more of his activities because Susie needed him at home. However, although he was often away from home, he still attended to Susie's care. From early in Charles and Susie's marriage, household servants attended to them, including Elizabeth H. Thorne, who not only worked for the Spurgeons but also became one of Susie's dearest friends. Charles also benefited from the help of assistants: he generally had two secretaries working with him at home, two more at the Tabernacle, others at the college, and still more helping with the other ministries that he was involved in.[55]

Susie received as much attention as she needed, though there was no substitute for Charles. He did, however, correspond with Susie frequently, sent her gifts, prayed for her diligently, and ensured that she had the provisions that her health demanded as well as many of the comforts she desired. One delightful story of his practical care for her is found in his preparation of their new home built at Nightingale Lane. Susie was still away in Brighton recovering, and Charles spared no energy outfitting the house to please his dear "wifey."

> I have been quite a long round today, if a "round" can be "long." First to Finsbury, to buy the wardrobe—a beauty. I hope you will live long enough to hang your garments in it, every thread of them precious to me for your dear sake. Next, to Hewlett's for a chandelier for the dining room. Found one quite to my taste and yours. Then to Negretti & Zambra's to buy a barometer for my very own fancy, for I have promised to treat myself to one. On the road, I obtained the Presburg bisquits, and within their box I send this note, hoping it may reach you the more quickly. They are sweetened with my love and prayers. The bedroom will look well with the wardrobe in it; at least, so I hope. It is well made; and I believe, as nearly as I could tell, precisely all you wished for. . . . I bought also a table for you in case you should have to keep your bed. It rises and falls by a screw, and also winds sideways, so as to go over the bed, and then it has a flap for a book or paper, so that my dear one may read or write in comfort while lying down. I could not resist the pleasure of making this little gift to my poor suffering wifey, only hoping it might not often be in requisition, but might be a help when there was a needs-be for it. Remember, all I buy, I pay for. I have paid for everything as yet with the earnings of my pen, graciously sent me in time of need. It is my ambition to leave nothing for you to be anxious about. I shall find the money for the curtains, etc., and you will amuse yourself by giving orders for them after your own delightful taste.[56]

Charles detested any postulating that the husband was the center of all things. He denounced men who believed that "their wives exist; for them, their children are born; for them, everything is placed where it appears in God's universe; and that they judge all things according to this one rule, 'How shall it benefit me?'"[57] Nevertheless, Charles was a man of his times and his understanding of Christian ministry was cultivated by reading writers from antiquity who equated love for Christ with putting one's ministry first.

Charles took care of Susie, as best he could, and, therefore, she didn't suffer alone.

Susie was indeed the "great sufferer," not only because she endured intense physical pain, but also because she persevered in her trials and still found avenues to faithfully serve God.

CHAPTER 9

Mrs. Spurgeon's Book Fund

Amidst her trials, Susie discovered comfort, delight, and purpose in a ministry that became her "life work." At times Susie felt inadequate due to her health problems. Thomas Spurgeon asserted, "The good Lord Himself had, however, in His heart the best alleviation of her woes and pains; and, in due time, He put it into her hands."[1] The Lord's care for Susie was demonstrated in establishing her as the caretaker of "Mrs. Spurgeon's Book Fund,"[2] a means by which she ministered to poor pastors throughout the British Isles and in other places by providing books (primarily, though not exclusively, written by Spurgeon) for them.

The Book Fund began in 1875 when Susie invested a few shillings to purchase the first one hundred books to give away. She considered her work as "the joy of my life" and as a "sweet service" given by God.[3] It was through the Book Fund that God led her to "green pastures and beside still waters."[4] It was a sustaining grace to Susie during her long years of suffering. How did the fund begin?

Upon the completion of volume one of Spurgeon's *Lectures to My*

Students in the summer 1875, Susie longed to provide a copy to "every Minister in England."[5] Charles challenged her to be the first donor for the enterprise. Susie was taken aback by her husband's request; however, it reminded her that such an endeavor afforded her an opportunity to practice her faith. She said, "I was ready enough to *desire* the distribution of the precious book; but to *assist* in it, or help to pay for it, had not occurred to me."[6] Emboldened by her husband's suggestion, Susie went to work. She inaugurated the book ministry, which, over the next twenty-eight years, distributed 200,000 books free of charge to needy pastors whose libraries were essentially bare. Based on Susie's requirements for receiving books a pastor had to be:

Poor—meaning that his total income could not exceed £150 per year, which equates to about $17,000.00 per year today.

Evangelical—this requirement was rather broadly applied.

A leader—in "actual charge, wholly devoted to the ministry."[7]

The following letter provides an illustration of how Susie responded to one who was not quite qualified to receive a full parcel of books from the fund.

> July 25. 78
> Dear Sir,
> As soon as you are a <u>Settled Pastor</u>, it will give me, should the Lord spare my life, the greatest pleasure to respond to your request: till then, I can do no more for you than send the two books which accompany this letter.
> My Book Fund was established <u>only</u> for the aid and comfort of <u>poor Pastors</u>, and much as I feel for, and sorrow over the needs of other workers for God, I must keep to the prescribed limits, in order to do my work <u>efficiently</u> and completely,
> Very truly Yours,
> Susie Spurgeon[8]

When an application was accepted, Susie sent a parcel consisting of "seven or eight books, several single sermons and often bundles of stationery that had been donated to her by a generous benefactor. The poorest pastors also received copies of *The Sword and the Trowel*."[9]

In some dire cases, a needy pastor's entire library could be inventoried by counting "the *books* upon your fingers." Susie portrayed the pastor as sitting in his study with "bowed head, and weary body" and of "scanty sustenance." He feels a "deep sense of responsibility" and "the weight of souls on his heart" and seeks God for his sermon. He is "weary and faint" and "*very, very, poor*" and "almost overwhelmed by the difficulties of his way."[10] Such was the situation that compelled Susie to act on her wishes to place a copy of *Lectures to My Students* into the hands of pastors across the Isles.

Much of Charles and Susie's relationship was cultivated in his study as she joined him on Saturday evenings to assist him in sermon preparation by reading to him from commentaries. Their times together on Saturdays were inspirational in her book fund work. She intimated that her "happy Saturday evenings" revealed to her "the value and helpfulness of good books in sermon-preparation." Those times helped her to better understand "how great is the privation of those to whom such gracious assistance is denied by their poverty."[11]

As she reflected on her Saturday experiences with Charles, Susie felt deep pity in her heart "for those poor bookless ministers, who sit sighing for thoughts in the face of their unfurnished shelves." She longed to "lay at their door also the provision which is so stimulating and needful, so important to the minister, so refreshing to the people."[12]

Susie described a scene that was repeated many thousands of times of a destitute minister receiving a parcel of books from the Fund. This passage provides a glimpse into Susie's heart of compassion, her skill in writing descriptive prose, her sense of the goodness and providence of God, her value of the pastor's work, her love for the church, and her vision for the Book Fund.

The bell rings, and a large parcel is left "For the Pastor," and is taken at once to his room. In a moment he feels that relief has come; he knows the superscription, and divines the contents; in his joy he almost caresses the package; then, with trembling fingers, he cuts the string, and spreads the treasures out before the Lord. Yes, literally "before the Lord;" for now you see him kneeling by the side of the open parcel, thanking and blessing God for such opportune mercy, for such streams in the desert, such blossoming roses in the wilderness. While prayer and praise mingle on his lips, his hand rests upon a small book of Mr. Geo. Müller; this he takes up and opens, and the first words which meet his eye, standing out in bold relief, shining as it were with heaven's own light, are these—

"OPEN THY MOUTH WIDE, AND I WILL FILL IT."

This is what he needs, this is God's message, this is "the word with power." And the command is obeyed, and the promise is fulfilled, in that first rapturous moment of enlightenment. He has broken down completely now, the tears are running down his cheeks, but they are rills from the fountains of joy, not of sorrow, and will refresh and heal his spirit. The Lord Himself has spoken to him, an angel has strengthened him, and after a season of adoring communion, he rises from his knees strong to labour or to suffer, as his gracious Master wills. That Saturday night will never be forgotten by him, so well-timed was the mercy to relieve his misery, so precious was the light which shone in upon his darkness.

If we could have gone with him, to the house of God on the Sabbath morning following, we should have seen that the blessing so graciously given was resting on him still; nay, more, that it was so abundant in the plentitude of its life-giving power, that it overflowed from his heart into the souls of his people; for saints and sinners alike wept, some over sin, some over recovered joy, and both over the goodness and grace of God in the face of Jesus Christ. God's message to one heart repeated itself to many, and there was rejoicing in heaven and earth that day![13]

Susie's convictions about God are obvious in the passage: it is God who is willing to fill the open mouths of His children who ask of Him; it is God who provides for all their needs; it is God who sends sustaining grace to his broken-down and burdened pastors. Every line of the passage is rife with the premium that she placed on pastors and for pastoral ministry. Her vision for the book fund is evident. Mrs. Spurgeon's Book Fund blessed pastors who, in turn, blessed their congregations.

Though it is unclear what role books played in Susie's life prior to her marriage, regardless, after she met Charles, books and writing were front and center of the Spurgeon home. Susie was married to a man who read six substantive volumes each week, who was constantly editing his sermons and penning new works for publication, who had his mind and heart saturated in Scripture, and who prayerfully studied in preparation for the preaching moment. She experienced the benefits of marriage to such a truth-saturated, well-studied, and gospel-driven pastor. And though writing was sometimes tedious for Charles, he grasped the value of being a writing pastor for the benefit of his church, family, and multiplied millions more.

Susie mirrored Charles's book-important attitude, and she benefited from the Lord's work through his ministry. Therefore, she knew that by investing in pastors, the dividends would pay off with interest. She witnessed the returns firsthand in her home, church, and via Charles's wider ministry; these experiences fueled her vision for the Book Fund.

VISION

Susie's vision for the Book Fund was that pastors would be helped, churches would be strengthened, and the gospel would go forth with greater zeal than it otherwise would have if pastors were left to scrape together mere crumbs from the few morsels of books that they possessed. Her attitude in no way disparaged the pastors who did the best that they could with the resources that they did have, though sometimes she did subtly (and not so subtly) chastise churches that, she felt, could be doing more to financially support their pastors. Nor did Susie minimize the power of the Bible *alone* in the hands of a godly minister. However, her heart bled for poor and often uneducated pastors who not only struggled to provide bread for their wives and children but also found it difficult to manage time and resources to bake spiritual bread for their congregations. These were pious men, able to teach, but lacking aid that would assist them to greater strength in their preaching.

Susie lamented the financial burdens that so many pastors were forced to carry; she knew that it was difficult for them to focus on their ministries when bills were stacked up and their wives and children needed clothing and medical care.

RESPONSIBILITIES

Charles delighted in Susie's book ministry, which involved correspondence, choosing books, overseeing packaging, and keeping a detailed accounting record. Susie often referred to her husband as John Ploughman—Charles's descriptor of a wise rural sage in his popular *John Ploughman's Pictures,* a work somewhat autobiographical of Spurgeon himself but also reflective of his beloved grandfather in Stambourne. Susie's desire was "to see dear John's face beam so radiantly, at the idea of my scattering his books far and wide."[14]

If Charles smiled over her work, Susie said that it was "worth any effort; and love, even more than obedience, constrained me to carry out the suddenly-formed plan."[15] Charles asserted that God "directed my beloved wife to a work which has been to her fruitful in unutterable happiness."[16] He believed that the fund "supplied my dear suffering companion with a happy work which has opened channels of consolation for her, imported great interest to the otherwise monotonous life of an invalid."[17] Charles's

Charles and Susie Spurgeon, "Silver Wedding Portraits." *[From the Spurgeon Library. Used by permission.]*

Susie and her parents lived here, 7 St. Ann's, Brixton, from 1853 until spring 1855. Her actual home, destroyed in WWII, was on the opposite end of the building and reverse in design.

Some of the extinct creatures that Charles and Susie viewed at the grounds of the Crystal Palace on the night Charles revealed his feelings for her.

View of London and St. Paul's Cathedral. This view is from the area of the New Park Street Chapel. Susie lived near St. Paul's at Falcon Square at the time of her wedding.

Susannah Spurgeon's baptism and attendance entry at New Park Street and then at (as it was later called) the Metropolitan Tabernacle. *[From the Metropolitan Tabernacle. Used by permission.]*

Part of a letter from Charles to his mother about the music hall disaster, written soon after the event. *[From the Metropolitan Tabernacle. Used by permission.]*

Nightingale Lane home (front view). Susie and Charles's third home but second address together (the first home here was torn down and rebuilt in the late 1860s).

Nightingale Lane,
Clapham Common, S.W.
Balham   July 26. 78.

Dear Sir,

As soon as you are a settled Pastor, it will give me, should the Lord spare my life, — the greatest pleasure to respond to your request; till then, I can do no more for you than send the two books which accompany this letter.

My Book Fund was established

July 1878 letter from Susie to a pastor. *[From the Metropolitan Tabernacle. Used by permission.]*

only for the aid & comfort of poor Pastors, and, much as I feel for, & sorrow over the needs of other workers for God, I must keep to the prescribed limits, in order to do my work efficiently and completely.

Very truly yours
Susie Spurgeon.

P.S. I would just say that the books I send you prayerfully studied, will yield you a rich harvest of instruction and profitable delight —

July 1878 letter, part two. *[From the Metropolitan Tabernacle. Used by permission.]*

Ruins of Christ Church where Susie's father, R. B. Thompson, remarried in 1873.

Westwood: Susie and Charles moved here in 1880. *[Used by permission from The Angus Library and Archive, Regent's Park College, University of Oxford.]*

Susie's book room, where books were kept and selected to send to pastors. *[Courtesy of The Angus Library.]*

Susie in her boudoir at Westwood. *[Courtesy of The Angus Library.]*

Seven Sisters cliffs in Eastbourne near Bexhill and where Charles and Susie visited together in early October of 1891.

Walkway at Hanbury Gardens, "La Mortola." Susie and Charles (in a wheelchair) walked this passage a month before he died on January 31, 1892. In February, Susie walked it alone.

Mentone, France. Charles visited from the early 1870s until his death in 1892. Susie was with Charles here when he died.

The home (as it is today) where Susie recovered the month after Charles died. At the time, it was owned by Thomas Hanbury and is located near Mentone, France and Ventimiglia, Italy.

Entrance to West Norwood Cemetery in south London, where both Charles and Susie are buried. This entrance is well-known to students of Spurgeon.

Susie's letter to Pastors' College Conference in April of 1893. *[Used by permission from The Angus Library and Archive, Regent's Park College, University of Oxford.]*

Westwood Beulah Hill
Upper Norwood
April 1893.

My dear friend

I give you the "Conference present" for this year, with feelings which fail to find expression in words, because of their depth, both of tenderness and sorrow. Let the book be to you a very precious legacy from your beloved Leader and President; — still living, but "on Christ's other side". I give it to you by his express desire, and you may therefore look upon it as his last loving thought for you, before he went home.

God keep you firm and stedfast in the old faith, for which he lived and died

Yours in Christian love

S. Spurgeon
(Mrs C. H.)

Beulah Baptist school chapel foundation stone at Bexhill-on-Sea placed by Susie's sons, Charles and Thomas.

THESE FOUNDATION STONES WERE LAID
AUGUST 11TH 1896
TO THE GLORY OF GOD
AND IN TENDER MEMORY OF
THAT PRINCE OF PREACHERS
C. H. SPURGEON
BY HIS TWIN SONS
CHARLES AND THOMAS
ON BEHALF OF THEIR BELOVED MOTHER
SHEWING TO THE GENERATION TO COME
THE PRAISES OF THE LORD

Thomas Spurgeon and family, 1902. *[Used with permission from Hilary Spurgeon.]*

Susie cuts the sod for Beulah Baptist, Bexhill-on-Sea larger chapel, April 12, 1897. *[Courtesy of the Archives and Special Collections, James P. Boyce Centennial Library, The Southern Baptist Theological Seminary, Louisville, Kentucky.]*

Stone laid by Susie for the larger chapel at Beulah Baptist Church, Bexhill-on-Sea.

THIS STONE WAS LAID 7TH JULY, 1897,

BY

MRS C.H.SPURGEON,

TO THE GLORY OF GOD,

AND IN PERPETUAL REMEMBRANCE OF

HER BELOVED HUSBAND'S BLAMELESS LIFE,

40 YEARS' PUBLIC MINISTRY,

AND STILL-CONTINUED PROCLAMATION OF THE GOSPEL

BY HIS PRINTED SERMONS.

"I have hallowed this house, which thou hast built, to put My name there for ever, and Mine eyes and Mine heart shall be there perpetually."

I Kings IX.3.

JOHN S. HOCKEY, PASTOR.

RESTA. W. MOORE, ARCHITECT.

CHARLES THOMAS, BUILDER.

Beulah Baptist, Bexhill-on-Sea as it is today, and essentially the same as in Susie's day.

Monument to Susie at Beulah Baptist Church at Bexhill-on-Sea.

Library at Westwood where Susie's coffin was first placed and a memorial service was held.
[Courtesy of The Angus Library.]

Susie's cemetery monument at West Norwood Cemetery. Both Charles's and Susie's remains were laid to rest here.

Susie Spurgeon. *[From the Metropolitan Tabernacle. Used by permission.]*

words are instructive: "By this means He [God] called her away from her personal griefs, gave tone and concentration to her life, led her to continual dealings with Himself, and raised her nearer the center of that region where other than earthly joy and sorrows reign supreme."[18]

CHALLENGES

Susie found that her efforts to aid poor ministers indeed helped her to avoid meditation on her own problems and, therefore, she found a "tone and concentration to her life" that drew her nearer in fellowship with Christ and "brought her boundless joy."[19] The hard but delightful work delivered to Susie much happiness, but, as Charles noted, it was also painful and challenging to her.[20] His perspective is important. Just as he was concerned for Susie's spiritual growth early in their relationship, he maintained his commitment to her physical and spiritual health throughout their marriage. Charles considered the Book Fund as "needed," "useful," and "urgently called for."[21] However, occasionally the work placed an overwhelming burden on Susie. It was during those times, Charles rushed to her aid: "I must place an urgent veto upon the continuation of this labor *at its present rate*."[22] However, he balanced his "veto" by faithfully encouraging his dear wife:

> I think of you as one that gathers herbs and distils them that
> they may be medicines for the spreading sicknesses. If you cannot be the surgeon to deal with the patients, you are the herbalist, to send in a supply of heal-alls for them. The epidemic of
> spiritual influenza can only be met by holy influences which will
> stream from voices and pens, which the Lord has filled with His
> saving health; and you do your part by sending out the sacred
> drugs in book form.[23]

The strain of the book ministry was felt beneath the burden of Susie's afflictions and, facing mountainous responsibilities with the fund, she sometimes felt "overpowered." Occasionally she faced the "constant pain" of "head and hand" in writing reports.[24]

In September of 1880, soon after moving to their new home, Westwood, Susie lamented, "The intervening days of this month are regretfully passed over without record of Book Fund experiences or correspondence, because affliction, both personal and relative, has prevented my usual entry of events." Yet she also said that she was thankful that "the beloved work has not suffered through our [Charles was having problems during that time as well] suffering, nor have its loving gifts failed on account of my weaknesses." In the midst of her pain she "managed to write the necessary letters, and keep all the machinery in motion."[25]

Insightfully, Charles discerned when Susannah needed relief from her book work: "It cannot long be possible to wake up every morning with a dread of that pile of letters; to sit all day, with scarce an interval, writing and book-keeping; and to go to bed at night with a sigh that the last stroke has hardly been made before the eyes have closed."[26]

An example of the heroic effort that the Fund required is seen from February of 1883. Susie declared, "I have received, during the twenty-eight days of this month of February, SIX HUNDRED AND FIFTY-SEVEN LETTERS; the figures are easily written, more easily read; but they give faint notion of the amount of labour involved in the correspondence they represent."[27]

Susie was a meticulous record keeper; she recorded in her journal every pound and shilling that came across her desk, every book that entered her book room, and every volume that she sent out to pastors. She also responded to her mail, and she sent a letter with every box of books that she mailed to pastors. Her dearest friend and coworker, Elizabeth Thorne, assisted her.

The Book Fund, though very useful to pastors, also brought difficult burdens to Susie's book room. She wrote, "For, dear friends, Book Fund work is not *all* composed of pleasant fruit and flowers, there are some thorns concealed here and there which wound the hand which inadvertently touches them." Sometimes the wound came in the form of a demand for books by a prideful pastor. Susie charmingly compared the Fund to her lemon tree; the thorns on the tree illustrated challenges. She lamented, "The flowers of Paradise will doubtless be thornless, but here on earth one cannot gather many roses without pricking one's fingers, nor have a splendid lemon tree without seeing and bewailing its sharp spikes, nor possess any unmingled good but God's love."[28]

Charles believed in rest and in the annual vacation. He asserted, "Our mind grows jaded, and our spirit depressed, our heart beats with diminished vigour, and our eyes lose their brightness, if we continue, month after month, and year after year, without a rest."[29] He ensured that Susie had the help and the rest that she needed, especially so when the mixture of work and suffering became too much for her drooping shoulders to bear and her tender heart to sustain. However, in the midst of Susie's "school of affliction," the Lord provided "holidays" from her suffering that resulted in even greater productivity.[30]

AUXILIARY MINISTRIES

Through the Book Fund, Susie entered into the homes of poor pastors by her parcels of resources. She envisioned their empty shelves, bare cupboards, and scant wardrobes, and she was moved with compassion toward the pastors and their families who lived and worked under such circumstances. As Susie became more acquainted with the severity of the needs of pastors' families, she enabled the Book Fund to spawn other auxiliary ministries, such as the Pastor's Aid Fund.

Through the Pastor's Aid Fund, Susie distributed money and clothes to needy pastors' families. Unexpected supplies sometimes arrived at Susie's doorstep, and she received items such as a "huge package of gentleman's clothing" as tangible evidence of God's goodness. The pastors who received grants of clothing and funds from Susie were those whose wardrobes were threadbare. Upon the delivery of the aforementioned package, Susie received letters from six different pastors who were destitute of clothes. Susie praised God for His provision, and she quickly distributed the clothes.[31]

One pastor wrote to Susie: "My wife and two girls have but one dress each for week-day and Sunday. None of us have more than one pair of boots, and these are in bad repair." Susie was angry that his congregation had not found a way to make sure that he and his family were properly provided for. However, she recognized it was not her anger that the pastor needed but instead money and something to wear. Therefore, she sent him five pounds and a package full of clothes.[32]

Other ministries were spun from the Book Fund, such as the Pastor's Conference book ministry that provided books, chosen by Susie, to students at the annual conference; the Auxiliary Book Fund that sent books to lay preachers; and the home and foreign sermon distribution in which parcels of individual sermons were sent out and often passed out like tracts in London and around the world.

A letter from a missionary in New Guinea provides perspective:

Dear Mrs. Spurgeon . . . Many years have your beloved husband's "Sermons" been to us a feast in seasons of poverty of means of grace. We have been blessed, strengthened, fitted for new work, through them, and not to be regularly supplied with the source of such great blessings is a boon, the result of which only the glorious future can unfold.[33]

THE BOOKS

The books most desired from pastors sprang forth from her husband's prolific pen, works such as *Lectures to My Students, The Treasury of David, Sermons,* and others. With ardent love for Charles, Susie said, "Much of the charm of my work lies in the delightful consciousness that I am daily spreading abroad the precious works of my dear husband." She knew that they were "works which God has so signally blessed to the conversion of sinners and the comforting of the saints, —works, too, so full of holy instruction and spiritual suggestiveness, that no minister's library is complete without them."[34]

Beyond Charles's works, Susie also gifted copies of Thomas Watson's *Body of Divinity*, Dr. Fish's *Handbook of Revivals*, and numerous other well-chosen works that she deemed profitable to pastors. She was selective in her choice of books, and she minced few words concerning people who displayed either a lack of discernment or a lack of compassion in sending her worthless books that would not help a pastor in his sermon preparation and preaching. People sometimes mailed her works that were essentially useless due to their superficiality, faulty theology, or some other problem. Those books were discarded.

One recipient's correspondence with Susie indicates how much he treasured Charles's writings: "The Psalms of David are ever a tower of comfort to tried saints, and your honored husband's work is to my own mind the best book that I have seen."[35] Susie posited that Spurgeon's *Treasury* and his *Sermons* were considered as the "*summum bonum* of their [the pastors who received them] happiness."[36] Her vision was that someday "all the churches awaken to a sense of the urgent need there is that the poor minister's bookshelf should have plenty of books upon it, many a noble volume, ancient and modern take its place beside *The Treasury of David*."[37]

THE CHURCH OF ENGLAND

Surprisingly, Charles's books were sought after by some Church of England clerics. Numerous clergymen in the Established Church applied for books, and they especially wanted *Sermons*, *Treasury of David*, or some other offering from Charles's hands. Susie was happy to receive such requests, and she recognized in them a sincere desire for sound doctrine by the clergymen. She pondered the applications of the "young divines" who solicited "the gift of the works of the once despised Baptist Pastor from the willing hands of his wife." Susie joyfully declared, "It pleases me most to place 'The Treasury,' the 'Lectures,' or the 'Sermons' within the reach of their hands and hearts."[38] She received positive reports about her gifts from the young ministers, and sometimes they preached, in abbreviated format, Charles's sermons from their pulpits.

Ironically, a number of Established Church curates, whose ire had earlier been raised against Spurgeon, especially after his sermon "Baptismal Regeneration,"[39] later welcomed him in their studies and to their pulpits through his books. Susie's tender touch through her letters and gifts no doubt helped to warm many ministers to the possibilities raised from employing Spurgeon's sermons in their church services.

Susie writes of a "young curate" who "asked me for 'The Treasury of David.'" It was his desire to use the work "both devotionally and as a help in the preparation of my sermons."[40] He thanked Susie: "After opening your parcel I could not help kneeling down and thanking Him who is the Giver of every good and perfect gift, and asking Him to bless the books to my soul and future ministry."[41]

By distributing Charles's books, Susie believed that she was providing essential works for pastors. Such a lofty assessment was not developed in isolation, nor was it *merely* because she so dearly loved Charles, but testimonies from pastors near and far away confirmed her estimation.

Susie provides a humorous story of a pastor who wished to purchase "extra" [beyond her gifts] books from her. This particular pastor was poor, and yet he very much enjoyed smoking a pipe. However, his library was quite bare and he determined to sacrifice his tobacco budget so that he could add precious volumes to occupy his lonely bookshelves. He put away his much-enjoyed tobacco and sent Susie the money instead. His letter to her became one of her favorites, and she declared, "I do not know when I have had a letter which so much pleased me: not that I should ever grudge a good man his comfortable smoke, but that I so heartily admire the self-denial and determination, which after a hard battle, conquered the daily, and as some might put it, the dirty habit of a lifetime."[42]

Obviously, Susie was not opposed to smoking; her beloved husband enjoyed cigars "to the glory of God." Charles declared, "When I have found intense pain relieved, a weary brain soothed, and calm refreshing sleep obtained by a cigar, I have felt grateful to God and have blessed his name."[43] Though smoking was not a moral issue against which she railed, she did appreciate the poor pastor weighing the value of tobacco versus that of a good book, and she felt that he made the right choice. She used his example as a means to draw attention to the kindness of God:

> And although the graceful blue wreaths no longer curl lazily up from beside the sturdy fire, nor the long-accustomed lips any more press the slender, seductive pipe stem, the better incense of prayer and praise will not slacken; for the Lord will command that His servant's lips be "touched with a live coal from off the altar"; and such an inspiration will more than make up for it all.[44]

Susie was concerned that churches took too lightly the ministry of their pastors. She exhorted, "People of God, let your love for your Pastors flourish again; hold up the hands that hang down, and strengthen the feeble knees; help them with sympathy, prayer, and temporal blessings."[45] She encouraged all within her circle of influence: "Help some poor Pastors yourselves, dear friends, and you will find that the blessings you bestow upon them for the Master's sake will return to you like richly freighted ships, bringing you a heavenly cargo of spiritual recompense."[46]

Susie served the Book fund for eleven years after the death of Spurgeon, and though she had her own needs to consider, she invested heavily in this ministry. Passmore and Alabaster, longtime friends and publishers of Charles's books, also published Susie's works. They did not accept any profits from the sales of Susie's two books on the Fund; instead they sent the profits to her. She, in turn, gladly invested her author's royalties back into the fund. Mrs. Spurgeon's Book Fund brought many smiles to Susie and gave her an arena in which she accomplished much for God's kingdom.

The hand that holds this pen is very weary; and the brain, which tries to think the thoughts that guide it, is jaded and overstrained. Soon the midnight chimes will be ringing, and "each breeze that rises from the earth be loaded with a song of Heaven." It is meet and wise to say ADIEU now, softly and tenderly, to those who have for so many years been partakers with me of the joy of this sweet service, and then to go alone before the Lord, and bless Him for the immeasurable love and goodness which have ensured so blessed an ending to a year of blessing.[47]

CHAPTER 10

The Move to Westwood: The Book Fund Continues

After living at Nightingale Lane for twenty-three years and stacking up a houseful of memories, new vistas awaited Charles and Susie. Their adventures began with a move farther out from the city, which was encroaching on their neighborhood, to one of the highest and loveliest points in metropolitan London, a place that offered fresh air and wide-open spaces. Westwood, located on Beulah Hill and near the Crystal Palace, afforded Charles the more rural setting that he desired, and the spacious house was ideal for Susie to manage her Book Fund and to receive guests. Of course, one of her first orders of business was to help Charles choose the prime interior real estate for his new study.

Charles and Susie imagined numerous benefits from the move to Westwood. If only the new location would bring improvement to their health, it would be worth the inherent challenges of packing up furniture, personal items, Spurgeon's massive library, and the stacks of Book Fund volumes. Certainly the proximity of the Crystal Palace was an added bonus, for it was there on a June evening twenty-six years prior, that Susie and Charles's romance was born.

There was no shortage of emotions in leaving their old home where they had raised their twin boys, celebrated countless joys, and weathered many storms together.

Susie kept a diary of that time in 1880:

August 1 to 18—Amidst the confusion and inconveniences attendant upon a speedy removal to a new residence, the dear work of the Book Fund must suffer a temporary suspension. Correspondence may be continued, and promises of future bounty may make glad the hearts of longing Pastors; but for some few weeks there can be no regular preparation and dispatch of parcels. Every Thursday of every week for these four years past has hitherto been devoted to this pleasant business, the labour of many willing hands being impressed for the service, and punctually every Friday morning the "Globe Express" van has come to receive and transmit the loving gifts. But alas for all order and rule in such times as these! Rooms are dismantled, shelves displaced, the books themselves are consigned to vast cases, and discomfort reigns paramount.

"What a stirring up of one's quiet nest this removal is!" . . .The heart yearns over a place endeared by an intimate acquaintance of twenty-three years, and full of happy or solemn associations. Every nook and corner, both of house and garden, abounds with sweet or sorrowful memories, and the remembrance of manifold mercies clings like a rich tapestry to the walls of the desolate rooms. On this spot nearly a quarter of a century of blissful wedded life has been passed, and though both husband and wife have been called to suffer severe physical pain and months of weakness within its boundary, our house has been far oftener a "Bethel" to us than a "Bochum." The very walls might cry out against us as ungrateful did we not silence them by our ceaseless thanksgiving; for the Lord has here loaded us with benefits, and consecrated every inch of space with tokens of His great lovingkindness.[1]

Though she was saddened to leave her "Bethel" behind to move to a home that had long been occupied by others, she was convinced that God was leading her and Charles to "go forward." Before they left the Helensburgh House, Charles penned a bit of poetry that he left behind for the new owners.

> Farewell fair room, I leave thee to a friend:
> Peace dwell with him and all his kin.
> May angels evermore the house defend.
> Their Lord hath often been within.[2]

Describing their first view of Westwood, Susie intimated that they "were reminded of Bunyan's description [in *The Pilgrim's Progress*] of the 'Delectable Mountains . . .'"[3] At Westwood, Susie found "sweet surprises of beauty" in "garden, fields, and orchard." They all yielded "their store of pretty sights to those who watch for them."[4]

Their home on Beulah Hill also conjured up Bunyan's imagery as his characters Christian and Faithful enter into the country of Beulah where "the air was very sweet and pleasant."[5] Westwood was all that Charles and Susie could have desired and, though they both suffered with poor health, they were still relatively young. Charles was forty-six and Susie was forty-eight—they anticipated many more years remaining, serving Christ together.

Westwood overlooked nine acres and a small lake. The house itself could almost be described as palatial with its ornate designs and numerous rooms. In fact, Charles initially dismissed the idea of attempting to purchase it out of fear that it might overly tax the family budget and that it might even stir up some measure of criticism from people who imagined that he was living frivolously. However, the circumstances were such that the house and property turned out to be a bargain. With the increasing city footprint that stressed the quiet neighborhood at Nightingale Lane came an increase in property value for the Helensburgh House. Therefore, Charles was able to sell their home and move to Westwood at an almost break-even deal that didn't burden him with any debt.

The first important event to be celebrated at Westwood was to be Charles and Susie's silver wedding anniversary on January 8, 1881. Though plans were set into motion to mark the joyous occasion, they were thwarted because dark clouds of sickness fell over Charles. Nevertheless, Susie could see the "silver lining":

> I look out from the window of the sick-chamber over the broad landscape which is the joy and glory of Beulah's hill, and I see across rolling fogs and billowy mists, far away on the plain, or upon the side of the distant hills, some favored spots where the sun is still "lighting his beacon fire," and where warmth, and light, and beauty, like angels in Jacob's vision, are ascending and descending a ladder of sunbeams set from earth to heaven.[6]

Turning to Charles, Susie offered encouragement: "Take courage, my beloved, the sun has not ceased to shine, nor has our God forgotten to be gracious."[7]

As Charles convalesced and the couple settled in at Westwood, Susie pressed forward with the work of the Book Fund, for many pastors across the British Isles remained in poverty, and she longed to relieve their burdens, at least in some small measure.

Though the Book Fund could not remedy *all* the maladies that were faced in the pastors' homes, it did bring *some* relief. Charles asked, "How can many of our ministers buy books? How can those in the villages get at them at all? What must their ministries become if their minds are starved? Is it not a duty to relieve the famine which is raging in many a manse?"[8]

Susie asserted, "It is the joy of my life thus to serve the servants of my Master."[9] Susie felt that her affliction, rather than hindering her service, provided her greater opportunities: "My retired life shuts out the pleasures of social intercourse but opens a world of glad delight."[10] Shut out from social pleasures, Susie found happiness in serving from behind the walls of her beautiful home.

Mrs. Spurgeon's Book Fund account from 1886 described a year in which she had distributed 9,941 volumes. Charles was at Mentone, France, recovering from another bout of sickness.

> I write the concluding sentences of this year's record under almost precisely similar circumstances to those of many preceding years. The dim and silent study, —the Pastor's empty chair, —the long, grim rows of unused books, —the closed inkstand, in which the very pens have a forlorn and drooping pose, —the lack of scattered papers, and other signs of a busy life-work, — all these proclaim the dear husband's absence, and my solitude. Anxieties, too, concerning my beloved have again assailed me. Ill, and a thousand miles from wife and home! Oh, this were indeed hard to bear for us both, but for the given grace to commit all into the Father's loving hand, and the granted faith to believe that, "He hath done all things well."[11]

Charles's strength returned, and Susie praised God for hearing her prayers: "And verily God answers prayer, for almost before we had time to pour out our complaint before Him, He turned the captivity of His dear servant, and sent forth His Word, and healed him! Surely, 'His mercy endureth for ever!'"[12]

The long separations that Susie and Charles experienced were a heavy burden for both of them to carry. Even the items in Charles's study seemed to personify him and daily remind Susie that Charles was gone and she was alone. The lonely and sickly wife longed to be with her hurting husband, yet providence forbade it, sometimes for long periods. However, in the depths of their loneliness, they found that God's mercy was abundant and enduring.

It was common for Susie to write both from and about Charles's study. Her account in 1887 is another example: "I went into my husband's study, to fetch from his inkstand the pen which he had been lately using."[13] Of his pen she writes, "It bore the traces of recent work; it had written words which would kindle the spiritual fire in men's hearts; it had transcribed weighty sentences which would move sinful souls to seek a waiting Savior."[14] She recognized, of course, that there was no magical value in the pen because it was "but a shapely piece of steel, inert, disabled."[15] Yet, reminded of how Charles used the pen to help people look to the Savior, Susie looked to God to supply her needs: "I laid it [the pen] down, and in my helplessness looked up entreatingly to Him who alone could move brain, and heart, and hand; and the answer to my unspoken prayer will be found in the following pages [her report on the Book Fund]."[16]

In some ways, the study is an apt picture of Susie and Charles's marriage and ministries. How busy their pens were in answering correspondence and in writing books, articles, and reports! In the study, they read Bible commentaries together, prayed together, and grew spiritually together. When Charles was absent, Susie seemed to find a sense of comfort as she sat behind his desk, took one of his pens, dipped it into an inkwell, and then employed the steel for writing beautifully.

Her regular reports, covering the facts yet thoughtfully written, conveyed her deep regard for Scripture and sound doctrine. In 1889, she described her commitment to supply pastors with books that were sound in the faith:

Not to help them find a "new theology," but to enable them better to extol the old "Gospel of the Grace of God," is the one main object of my gifts; and not a single book whose author would dare to tamper with God's holy truth, or profess to know more, and see deeper, and understand more clearly than all the prophets and apostles![17]

Susie penned those lines in the aftermath of the Down-Grade Controversy. Charles first wrote about theological "down-grade" in 1887 in his magazine *The Sword and the Trowel*. The theological decline was centered in doubts concerning the inspiration of the Bible. When Charles challenged his own denomination concerning its acceptance of error and offered a remedy, his solution of adopting a confession of faith was rejected. Charles withdrew from the Baptist Union on October 28, 1887.[18] As a result, he lost many old friends, including some who had been students at his college. It was a heartbreaking experience for both Charles and Susie.

Westwood was a place of work, a place where family worship was practiced, a place where hospitality was extended, a place where Pastors' College students sometimes gathered with Charles and Susie beneath the "Question Oak," a place where marital love prospered, and a place where many thousands of books sped to the empty shelves of poor pastors, bringing with them hope and joy. It was also a place where Charles and Susie welcomed grandchildren.

Charlie and his wife, Sarah, had three children during the Spurgeons' Westwood years: Grace Susie, Dorothea (Dora), and Constance. All often enjoyed the company of "Grandmama." In 1885 (before Constance was born), Susie received a package from Grace Susie and Dora. Inside was a coin and a note: "A New Year's Gift to dear Grandmama's Book Fund from Susie and Dora."

Susie found it a "new and very amusing experience" to have Charlie's little ones help her in her lifework. She saw this as good training for the children and imagined the possibility that one day they might "take up 'Grandma's' work" and expand it after she had died. Growing nostalgic, she wrote:

"*Grandmama*"! Ah me! How the days are going by! It seems but as yesterday that the father of these two little maidens was my own bonnie baby, laughing, ay, and weeping too, in what I then thought a most wonderful and exceptional fashion; yet so many years have flown away, and he has travelled so far on life's journey, that now *his* babies crow and cry even as he once did, and make sweet childish music in his house, *and call me "Grandmama"!*[19]

Upon receiving the gift, Susie wrote a letter back "to the dear son whose love for his mother is one of the joys of her life."[20]

Charles also enjoyed the grandchildren. He referred to them as "the three darlings." In a letter to his daughter-in-law, Sarah, from Westwood on May 31, 1889, he wrote about what seems to be a gift to deliver to his granddaughters: "Dear Daughter, If it is a fine day, and I am well enough, I shall hope to drive over with the dolls, and reach you about 3:30 Saturday. I will also bring your letters. Your loving father, C. H. S."[21]

In September 1889, Charles and Susie welcomed a grandson, Charles Philip Spurgeon, Charlie and Sarah's first son. The couple brought the child to Westwood to be dedicated. With Charles leading the service, he "gave the child to God."[22] Over a year later, in 1891, God took the child to Himself. Susie writes, "One of the brightest, bonniest babies ever seen, he was the delight and expectation of our hearts; but the gift was claimed suddenly, and the child who was to have done, according to our ideas, so much service on earth, went to sing God's praises with the angels."[23] (Charlie and Sarah would have another son in October of 1891 and name him Charles Oliver Spurgeon.)

Little Charles Phillip Spurgeon wasn't the only grandchild of Susie and Charles who died as a baby. Thomas and his wife, Lila, had been married for less than a year when Marguerite May (Daisy) was born on Christmas Day of 1888 in Auckland, New Zealand, where Thomas served as a pastor. The Christmas baby brought much joy to the Spurgeon home but joy was turned to sorrow by March as Daisy died. Thomas's biographer, W. Y. Fullerton, wrote: "The sorrowing parents had no picture of her, save the image engraven on their hearts, for the intention of having a photograph taken was postponed until she should have been a little older."[24] Although Thomas was brokenhearted over Daisy's death and having delayed the photograph, he developed a lifelong ability to relate with parents who lost a child.[25] Thomas and Lila later welcomed two other children, Thomas Harold (1891) and Vera (1893).

For all her grandchildren, Susie most desired to be "as wise and tender a grandmother as the Lord would have me be."[26]

Just prior to Charles and Susie moving to Westwood, Thomas had left for Australia. It was hoped that the warmer climate would strengthen his frail physical health. There, Thomas had numerous ministry opportunities, and he ultimately settled as a pastor in New Zealand. After a five-year separation from his parents, Thomas returned to London, this time to Westwood, for a visit. Susie wrote:

> About ten this evening, my darling son was in my arms. The pain of five years' absence was almost annihilated. Sixteen thousand miles to come home to see father and mother! Many prayers were ascending to heaven from both sides of the world that a safe and prosperous voyage might be vouchsafed to the beloved traveller.[27]

Thomas was delighted to finally get home to "the best parents in the world."

⁂

Just as Westwood received Thomas back to the arms of his mother, it also received people from all walks of life. Susie opened her home generously for hospitality, and Charles warmly welcomed many visitors. The Beulah Hill location was private enough to protect Charles from too many curiosity seekers, but near enough to the great city for welcomed guests to sit for a while beside the fireplace or to join in family worship with Charles and Susie. Students, authors, poor pastors, dignitaries, and religious leaders such as D. L. Moody, were warmly welcomed to Westwood. Moody, the great American evangelist, was one of Charles's dearest friends. After Charles died, Susie sent Moody one of her husband's most treasured Bibles. A friend of Charles's remembered,

> How he delighted to gather about him there a little band of brethren, and after the evening meal propose a few "tales of mercy"! With what interest he would listen to each in turn, and the starting tear would soon tell how his tender trusting heart was touched. What "tales of mercy" he could tell! Can we ever forget them? How they come crowding the memory.[28]

It was Charles's common practice to treat his guests for a walk by the pond to see the swans and to the stable where the horses were boarded. The names of two of Charles's ponies were emblazoned over their stalls: Brownie and Beauty. [29] Westwood held a fernery, garden, and a farm with ten cows. Susie superintended the cow industry; milk was sold, and the profits helped to support a local colporteur.[30] A guest to the Spurgeon home was served "pears, peaches, plums, and honey, all from his [Charles's] own garden. After tea, the family and the servants were called together for family prayers." The guest said of Susie that "she kindly allowed me to see her workshop where she does all the correspondence about the Book Fund, and also the little store-room where the books are kept, and where parcels are done up."[31] He referred to Susie as "a born angel."[32]

Spurgeon's friend Jesse Page remembered one of his days at Westwood:

> It was after a committee meeting held in his house. Business was over. We had risen from tea and walked through the beautiful grounds, and were once again in the house. He opened up the Bible and read, read and expounded as only he could,

opening up the very heart of the Scriptures. Dear Mrs. Spurgeon, slowly recovering from a long and wearisome sickness, was lying on the couch, sharing our joyful communion. Reading finished, the dear one said, "We are part of the family of God: Shall we draw near and talk to Him?" As we turned to kneel, he moved towards the couch, and with one arm around the loved form [Susie], he poured out his soul in a passion of importunate prayer. Never can we forget that hour. It was as if heaven's gates had been widely opened, and some lustrous beam, alight with our Father's smile, had strayed into the room.[33]

Such was the love and welcoming atmosphere that surrounded Charles and Susie's home and was felt by all of their guests.

Westwood was a place of flowers, and those were not *only* for the enjoyment of Charles and Susie, though they enjoyed them very much; they were also for dwellers in the poor neighborhoods near the Metropolitan Tabernacle. The Tabernacle had many ministries, including a "flower mission." Regularly, servants in this unheralded ministry made the seven-mile trip to Westwood to gather flowers for their baskets to bring a bit of joy to the suffering and discouraged poor.[34]

As with many aspects of Charles and Susie's life together, Westwood was a place of variety, from farm animals to gardens, fruit trees, ferns, and flowers. It was a place of ministry, and it was the headquarters of Mrs. Spurgeon's Book Fund throughout the rest of her life and for some years later.

Westwood was also the place where Susie was comforted in the years following the great separation.

CHAPTER II

Mentone: Happiness and a Sad Goodbye

Charles Spurgeon first visited Mentone (located on the French Riviera) in 1871 as just one stop on a larger tour of cities, towns, and villages.[1] From 1872, Spurgeon retreated to Mentone, usually for at least three months at a time, to escape the cold London winters and to write, rest, and to seek restoration of his health.[2] Mentone had become famous as a resort, geographically situated so that it enjoyed a moderate weather pattern, which contributed to the improving health of those who visited.

The famous London physician Dr. James Henry Bennet popularized Mentone as a place of healing. It was his own suffering, which began beneath the brutality of London winters, that first led him to the coast of France. Bennet experienced a health crisis in 1859 of such magnitude that he imagined it would result in his death. He provides a striking account of the crisis in his book *Winter and Spring on the Shores of the Mediterranean*.

Five-and-twenty years devoted to a laborious profession and the harassing cares which pursue a hard-worked London physician, broke down vital powers. In 1859 I became consumptive [with tuberculosis], and strove in vain to arrest the progress of disease. At last, resigning all professional duties, I wrapped my robes around me and departed southwards, in the autumn of the year 1859, to die in a quiet corner, as I and my friends thought, like a wounded denizen of the forest. It was not, however, to be so. The reminiscences of former travel took me to Mentone, on the Genoese Riviera, and under its genial sky, freed from the labours and anxieties of former life, to my very great surprise, I soon began to rally.[3]

Bennet experienced a vigorous recovery from tuberculosis at Mentone, and he considered returning to "professional studies and to professional pursuits."[4] He concluded, however, that it was unwise for him to re-start his work in London full-time; therefore, he determined to "adopt Mentone as a permanent winter professional residence, merely resuming London consulting practices during the summer months."[5]

Charles discovered the potential health benefits of the French Riviera from reading Bennet's book, and he and Bennet became friends. An undated letter from Charles to Bennet offers some insight into their friendship:

> Dear Dr. Bennet,
> ... My wife is pining away. She is so weak & thin & suffers so much that it is a great pain to think of it. To-day she sits over a great fire & cannot get warm at all. She commands me <u>not</u> to write you but yet ever since I returned from Mentone she has longed to see you, & I have made up my mind to let you know this & ask you if ever near here to call on us. If she could move out I would bring her to you, but this is impossible.
> Is it too far for you & Mrs. Bennet to come? Or am I too bold?

I have been ill again & am not getting strength, your prescriptions piloted me through.

I hope Mrs. Bennet is well . . . C. H. Spurgeon[6]

Though the letter is undated, it almost certainly is from the mid-1870s, after Susie's surgery and during the time that Charles is regularly visiting Mentone. It is dated June 3, which is consistent with Bennet being back in London for the summer months. Regardless, it paints a picture of Charles and Susie's relationship with Bennet and is a strong indicator of why Charles chose Mentone as his own place of healing.

Spurgeon's secretary, Joseph Harrald, wrote of Mentone as a "charming region."[7] For Harrald, the true beauty of the place could not properly be described by words or photography. To grasp "a full idea of the loveliness" of Mentone, it must be seen.[8] Even today, it remains a place of amazing beauty filled with lemon and olive trees and flowers galore. With the Maritime Alps towering behind and the blue waters of the Mediterranean Sea splashing upon its shores, Mentone was and is an inviting resort.

As the 1870s progressed, Spurgeon's retreats to the Riviera for lengthy winter stays became frequent. Nigel T. Faithfull asserts that Spurgeon found Mentone "charming" and, as he had read in Bennet, he found it to be conducive as a "place for convalescence."[9]

Mentone's warmer climate gave Charles a brighter outlook. London's cold, damp winters could be debilitating for those, like Charles, who suffered physically and emotionally. Mentone, with its bright sunshine, majestic mountains, varied fruit trees, lovely flowers, and deep blue water, fit the bill as a place of recovery for Spurgeon.

During Charles's first visit in 1871, he enjoyed companionship with his friend George Müller and also with Bennet. Spurgeon relaxed by lying on the beach, walking in gardens and olive groves, and viewing the city from the heights above. While there, he corresponded daily with Susie.

As Susie sat behind Charles's desk viewing his stacks of books, she read each one of his letters from Mentone over and over again. Charles desperately wanted Susie with him, and she also longed for him. However, her health issues were so severe, and she was so delicate, that it was deemed unwise for her to travel. The pain of separation from Susie was a burden too heavy for Charles's shoulders. In a letter home, Charles's loneliness for Susie is striking: "Mentone is charming, but not very warm. It is, as I like it, and is calculated to make a sick man leap with health. How I wish you could be here!"[10] Spurgeon, bold and animated in the pulpit, was sentimental and tender as he considered his suffering wife back at home.

Bennet and Spurgeon were not the only Londoners who traveled to Mentone on a quest for healing; many others from England's great city imitated them and made the pilgrimage to the shores of southern France. Charles and Bennet enjoyed a warm friendship and Charles was encouraged by Bennet to visit his property (just across the Italian border and near Mentone) when he was in the area. Bennet's estate was picturesque with a lush landscape, a restored garden tower, and a stunning view of the sea from the tower. It is surmised that Charles's most beautiful writing, during his times at Mentone, occurred while he worked away in the garden tower, his secretary Joseph Harrald usually by his side.[11]

The aftereffects of the Down-Grade Controversy left Spurgeon emotionally scarred and facing an even greater decline physically. It may well have been that this last great controversy of his life was the instrumental cause of his death at age fifty-seven. One might surmise that, without Mentone, Charles would have died sooner than he did.

Though his trips to the coast strengthened him for his work, Susie suffered back at home. And though he rested at Mentone, the theological battle was never far from Charles's mind, as his letters to Susie reveal. For years, a generous benefactor had supported Charles's ministry financially. However, the controversy found his benevolent friend on the other side of the argument. The benefactor withdrew his support due to a "failure of friendship and sympathy," and he sent a letter letting Charles know.[12] The letter first arrived at Westwood, and Susie opened it:

At once, I took the letter and spread it before the Lord, pleading, as Hezekiah did that He would "hear and see" the words written therein; and He gave me so strong a confidence in His overruling and delivering power that, as I knelt in His presence, and told Him how completely I trusted Him on my husband's behalf, the words of petition ceased from my lips, and I absolutely *laughed out loud,* so little did I fear what man could do, and so blessedly reliant did He make me on His own love and omnipotence![13]

The withdrawal of financial support might have cast a less spiritually minded woman into a sea of despair, but Susie responded in prayer and reliance upon God. She even laughed in the face of trouble. Rapidly, she mailed a letter to Charles in Mentone and told him of the loss of financial support and of her laughter in the face of trouble. He wrote back, "I laugh with you. The Lord will not fail us, nor forsake us. . . . You are as an angel of God unto me. . . . Bravest of women, strong in faith, you have ministered unto me in deed and of a truth. God bless thee out of the seventh heavens!"[14]

Susie viewed the event as a testing in which God "found that his [Charles's] faith did not fail." God supplied the financial need through a woman who, not knowing about the situation, felt compelled to deliver money to Charles.[15] He wrote to Susie, "What a dear soul you are! How I love you! Our inward and spiritual union has come out in this trial and deliverance. We will record all this to the glory of the Lord our God."[16]

Charles's letter to his wife of over thirty years conveys the depth of their relationship as a spiritual union, revealing how their trials called forth from within them the employment of spiritual means. Charles did not ignore the pain that the Down-Grade Controversy had caused him, but he saw the hand of his faithful God in the midst of it all. He said to Susie, "Send a check to [the] bank. Sing the Doxology. Keep all my love, and rest under the blessing of the Lord our God."[17]

Charles knew that in Susie he had a godly wife, and he felt her strengthening hand of encouragement. In the midst of the Down-Grade Controversy, Spurgeon wrote his well-known book *The Cheque Book of the Bank of Faith*. In it he includes a revealing paragraph that displays how deeply he felt Susie's physical affliction, even as he faced the battering of the controversy.

> I commenced these daily portions when I was wading in the surf of controversy. Since then I have been cast into "waters to swim in," which, but for God's upholding hand, would have proved waters to drown in. I have endured tribulation from many flails. Sharp bodily pain succeeded mental depression, and this was accompanied both by bereavement, and affliction in the person of one dear as life. The waters rolled in continually, wave upon wave. I do not mention this to exact sympathy, but simply to let the reader see that I am no dry-land sailor. I have traversed those oceans, which are not Pacific full many a time: I know the roll of the billows, and the rush of the winds. Never were the promises of Jehovah so precious to me as at this hour. Some of them I never understood till now; I had not reached the date at which they matured, for I was not myself mature enough to perceive their meaning. How much more wonderful is the Bible to me now than it was a few months ago.[18]

The Down-Grade Controversy accelerated Spurgeon's suffering, and Susie believed that it was the impetus that finally pushed him into his grave, notwithstanding his various other physical ailments and emotional strains. The tribulation that he encountered was impossible for him to carry in his strength and, therefore, he trusted God to uphold him though waves of suffering crashed on him and threatened to undo him. Charles felt his own pain but perhaps even more difficult for him was the knowledge that Susie was suffering as well.

Twenty years had passed since Susie yielded to surgery by the famed specialist in gynecology, James Y. Simpson. Charles's physical, emotional, and relational struggles, which all reached high marks during the controversy, were exacerbated because his beloved Susie was bereaved over his sorrow and remained in her own valley of deep physical pain. Charles asserted that "every year of my life has had a winter."[19]

Of his emotional challenges, he said, "I am sometimes lifted to the very heavens, and then I go down to the deep: I am at one time bright with joy and confidence and at another time dark as midnight with doubts and fears."[20] Charles left Mentone and journeyed back to London and to the dear one that he had left behind the gates of Westwood.

THE SAD GOODBYE

Wracked with pain and burdened over controversy, Charles departed for southern France again on November 11, 1890 and remained there until February 5, 1891. Once again, Charles needed and benefited from the beautiful scenery and restful shores of his home away from home. He sent an epistle of love from the "charming region" to Susie:

> What an immeasurable blessing you have been to me, and you
> are still! Your patience in suffering, and diligence in service, are
> works of the Holy Spirit in you, for which I adore His name.
> Your love to me is not only a product of nature, but it has been
> so sanctified by grace that it has become a spiritual blessing to
> me. . . . My love to you grows, and yet I do not know how at any
> time it could have been greater.[21]

As usual, Susie remained behind at Westwood. That Charles missed her is obvious in his daily letters home. He called her "my sweetest and best," "my darling," and "best-beloved of my heart." He declared, "I wish I were at home! I must get home." After a drive, he wrote Susie and said, "Oh that you had been at my side." And Charles treasured Susie's letters to him. He replied, "You write so sweetly. Yours is a hand which sets to music all it writes to me."[22]

Though many prayed for Charles's recovery, and he occasionally rallied and resumed his ministry with vigor, his health deteriorated, although eventually, he regained strength sufficient for him to return home. Not long after, he fell ill again. Sunday, June 7, 1891, was the last time he would preach at the Metropolitan Tabernacle.

Following that sermon, Charles, feeling nostalgic for his grandfather's land, began a journey to Stambourne on June 8. He traveled with a photographer to capture pictures for an upcoming book, *Memories of Stambourne.* Perhaps he imagined that seeing the old Meeting House and Manse and catching a glimpse of the pastures and farmland might revive his energy. Instead, he relapsed, and his gout became so severe that he had to quickly return home where he was mostly bedridden for three months.[23] The religious and secular newspapers covered Charles's sickness, and prayers were said at the Tabernacle three times a day. Churches across the world also gathered to pray. Prayers also were offered at St. Paul's Cathedral and Westminster Abbey. Letters were received from people of all stations of life, including the Prince of Wales and W. E. Gladstone.

By fall of 1891, he determined to make yet another trip to Mentone, where he hoped he would more fully recuperate.[24] Every previous trip he longed for Susie to join him but, due to the seriousness of her health, she was forced to remain behind in the stately home, full of books and memories, while Charles made the journey without her. Nevertheless, he found it necessary to leave behind the dreariness of London's climate, referring to it as "Gog, Magog, and Fog."[25]

Charles said that he was "frequently depressed in the sea of smoke-damp in which we swim in London." Yet, with all of her "fogs" he said, "I love her still."[26] To leave behind the thick air of London for the land where "everlasting spring abides" was a hopeful vision of recovery for Charles. What *was* difficult was leaving his dear Susie at home. He had also lamented before previous trips:

What we have left behind in that dear abode! Could *she* but go with us who has been under God, the good angel of our life, then our vacation would lose that one sad vacancy which takes from it its full content; and then all our enjoyment of nature's beauties would be doubled as we marked the pleasure of that kindred spirit, whose appreciations of the divine handiwork are even keener than our own. We have both learned to bow before our Father's will; and whether in one home or with a thousand miles between, we are one in a full and intense yielding to the divine ordination, and in one undivided desire to do, and to be, that which is most for the glory of God. May the dew of heaven fall ever on that house where she abides, who, in great weakness, has not ceased these many years to feed the minds of those who feed the flock of God.[27]

Charles would leave for Mentone on October 26 after first making a shorter journey to Eastbourne, a coastal town just south of London, to test his strength before making the much longer trip to France.

Remarkably, Susie experienced a transformation of health that, perhaps, can best be described as miraculous. Though she wasn't healed of her afflictions, she nevertheless gained strength sufficient to travel with Charles to Eastbourne. Charles imagined that Eastbourne with its stunning white cliffs might be sufficient to restore his strength and to refresh his mind that he might preach again.

On Monday, October 26, 1891, a long-time dream came true for Charles in what is surely one of the most amazing displays of God's providence in Charles's fifty-seven years. On that October day, Charles left London for Mentone *with* Susie, his secretary Joseph Harrald, and his brother J. A. Spurgeon and his wife. They arrived on October 29, 1891. This was the first and only time that Susie had ever visited Mentone with her beloved, and they enjoyed three months of "perfect happiness" before the "sorrowful separation."[28] Upon arriving, Susie "began work, on perforated cards, a series of texts, selected by her dear husband and herself, to be fastened around the cornice of their sitting-room, as a grateful memorial of the Lord's goodness to them in bringing them both in safety to the sunny South, after the terribly trying summer and autumn in England."[29] Susie was accustomed to such decorating, for at Westwood she had a number of framed Bible verses hanging on the wall.

While at Mentone, Charles wielded his pen when he could, but he was happiest in serving as Susie's tour guide, taking her to his favorite places. Thirty-six years prior, his young bride had clasped his hand as she led him to the famous sites of Paris. As Paris was special to Susie, and a place that she longed for Charles to enjoy with her, Mentone was the same for Charles. Year after year he had dreamt of her walking with him through the olive groves, lush gardens, and along the shoreline. Susie remembered her time at Mentone with Charles as "glorious days." Sincerely she promised, "Never shall I cease to bless God for His tender mercy in permitting me to be with my beloved, and to minister to his happiness and comfort during those three blessed months!"[30] She describes Charles as "full of fun and child-like pleasure," finding ways to surprise her and laugh with her. She intimated that at meal times "he was the life and soul of the party, with a cheerful smile, and a kind word," and everyone appreciated the "sweetness of disposition" that Charles conveyed.[31] Susie recalled,

I can never describe the pride and joy with which he introduced me to his favourite haunts, and the eagerness with which he showed me each lovely glimpse of mountain, sea, and landscape. He was hungry for my loving appreciation, and I satisfied him to the full. . . . We took long daily drives, and every place we visited was a triumphal entry for him. His enjoyment was intense, his delight exuberant. He *looked* in perfect health, and rejoiced in the brightest of spirits. . . . Not a care burdened him, not a grief weighed upon his heart, not a desire remained unfulfilled, not a wish unsatisfied; he was permitted to enjoy an earthly Eden before his translation to the Paradise above.[32]

Charles turned to Susie during one of their walks, pointed to a lovely scene, and asked, "There, wifey, isn't that worth coming all the way to see?"[33] After Charles's death, she remembered his words and penned her thoughts: "Yes, truly, and if there had been nothing else to see than his exultant happiness at my long-desired presence with him, this would have well repaid any effort of love on my part."[34] At Mentone they were together and as happy and playful as two schoolchildren on a playground. Susie played the piano for a group of Charles's acquaintances that were lodging in the Hotel Beau Rivage, and she "sang some of her favorite hymns."[35]

From October 1891 through mid-January 1892, Charles was able to mostly complete his final work, *The Gospel of the Kingdom*, an exposition of Matthew's Gospel. Susie wrote in the introductory note that the book was his "last precious legacy" and "the last sweet song from lips that were ever sounding forth the praises of his King." Of the later portions of the book, she mused that it "was written on the very border-land of heaven . . . almost within sight of the Golden Gates."[36] Though Charles did not live to fully revise the manuscripts, Harrald, "with loving care, entirely from his [Spurgeon's] own spoken and written words" finished the work in January of 1893.[37] Susie's "Introductory Note" provides a rich insight:

Few and simple should be the words which introduce this ea- gerly, expected book to the many friends who will welcome it.

The beloved author has gone to his eternal reward, he is "the blessed of the Lord for ever"; but he has left with us this last precious legacy, which draws our hearts heavenward after him.

It stands alone in its sacred and sorrowful significance. It is the tired worker's final labour of love for his Lord. It is the sweet song from lips that were ever sounding forth the praises of his King. It is the dying shout of victory from the standard-bearer, who bore his Captain's colours unflinchingly through the thickets of the fight.[38]

In a letter published in *The Sword and the Trowel* in March 1892, Susie wrote of their last three months together. She disclosed how Charles had often desired for her to accompany him: "For fifteen years my beloved had longed to bring me here; but it had never before been possible. Now, we are both strengthened for the long journey; and the desire of his heart was fully given him."[39]

On New Year's Eve of 1891, and New Year's Day of 1892, Charles gave two addresses to a small gathering of friends, and on January 10 and 17, he conducted two brief services in his room. Susie recalled:

On the second Sabbath evening, January 17, 1892, before offering the closing prayer at the final service in which he took part on earth, he gave out the last hymn he was ever to announce to a company of worshippers here below. If he could have foreseen what was to happen only a fortnight later, he could hardly have chosen a more appropriate farewell than the poem founded on some words of the sainted Samuel Rutherford,

> The sands of time are sinking,
> the dawn of Heaven breaks,
> the summer morn I've sighed for,
> the Fair, sweet morn awakes.
> Dark, dark hath been the midnight,
> but dayspring is at hand,
> and glory, glory dwelleth
> in Immanuel's land.[40]

During January of 1892, Charles and Susie celebrated their thirty-sixth wedding anniversary (January 8) and Susie's sixtieth birthday (January 15). On Wednesday January 20, Spurgeon went to bed, due to his declining health, and there he remained. Toward the end of the first week in bed, he was able to muster the strength to tell his longtime secretary, Joseph

Harrald, "My work is done."[41] By Tuesday, January 26, he was in and out of consciousness. He rallied a bit and posted an offering to the Metropolitan Tabernacle with the message, "Love to all friends."

On Sunday night, January 31, 1892, Charles died; Susie was by his bedside. The *Autobiography* records, "Then all was over, Mr. Harrald offered prayer, and Mrs. Spurgeon thanked the Lord for the precious treasure so long lent to her, and sought, at the throne of grace, strength and guidance for the future."[42]

With a broken heart, Susie looked to God in prayer: "Oh! My husband, my husband, every moment of my now desolate life I wonder how I can live without thee! The heart, that for so many years has been filled and satisfied with thy love, must needs be very empty and stricken now that thou art gone!"[43]

After Charles died, Susie reflected on the sense of deepening loss that she felt but she also testified to the "divine power of healing to my sorrowing soul." Pondering Scripture, she pondered that, "It is 'far better' for him to be 'with Christ,'" and that helped her to "patiently and even cheerfully endure" what she described as her "lonely life."[44] Painfully, Susie recalled again the tragic episode in Spurgeon's ministry, the Down-Grade Controversy. She asserted:

> I can bear my testimony to the fact that his last conscious moments were embittered by grief over those who had departed from the faith. The Baptist Union and "our own men" who had turned aside from the truth, were specially mentioned and our dear sufferer was only comforted by the knowledge that he had done all he could to bring about a better state of things.[45]

Susie's emotions fluctuated between joy and sorrow: "I can sometimes dwell with such joy on the thought of his eternal glory 'with Christ,' that I forget to sorrow over my own great and unspeakable loss."[46] Movingly, she wrote about Charles, "Thou wert the most tender, gracious, and indulgent of husbands, ruling with perfect love and gentleness. . . ."[47] With such expressions of thanksgiving, Susie was also moved to tears. She cried out, "God took my treasure from me."[48]

Though her pain was intense, Susie rejoiced in God's comfort that came via letters and telegrams from friends and admirers of Spurgeon from around the world. In her message of thanks to the readers of *The Sword and the Trowel* she wrote, "You have strengthened and helped me wonderfully. My loss is your loss, so we could weep together. You loved my beloved, and we could rival one another in his praise. You will miss his dear face, his sweet voice, his gracious, genial presence, not so *much* as I do, but as *truly;* and here, too, we mourn together."[49]

Susie described her final months with Charles:

I will tell you of one fact, which has greatly comforted me in my deep grief; it will ever be a precious memory to me, and a theme of praise to God. It may rejoice your hearts also to have such an assurance from my pen. It is that the Lord so tenderly granted to us both three months of *perfect earthly happiness* here in Mentone, before He took him to the "far better" of His own glory and immediate presence! . . . He was hungry for my loving appreciation, and I satisfied him to the full. His enjoyment was intense, his delight exuberant. He seemed in perfect health, and rejoiced in the brightest of spirits. Then, too, with what calm, deep happiness he sat, day after day, in a cosy corner of his sunny room writing his last labour of love, *The Commentary on Matthew's Gospel!* Not a care burdened him, not a grief weighed upon his heart, not a desire remained unfulfilled, not a wish unsatisfied; he was permitted to enjoy an earthly Eden before his translation to the Paradise above. Blessed be the Lord for such sweet memories, such tender assuagement of wounds that can never quite be healed on earth! Up to the last ten days of his sweet life, health appeared to be returning, though slowly; our hopes were strong for his full recovery, and he himself believed that he should live to declare again to his dear people, and to poor sinners, "the unsearchable riches of Christ."

But it was not to be, dear friends. The call came with terrible suddenness to us; but with infinite mercy to him. The prayer, "Father I will that they also whom Thou hast given Me, be with Me where I am; that they may behold My glory," was answered in this case. His Saviour wanted him higher, and could spare him to us no longer. He is gone to his everlasting reward, and the hallelujahs of heaven must hush, and rebuke the sobs and sighs of the earth.

Looking up, with tear-dimmed eyes, to the God and Father of our Lord Jesus Christ, we can say, "Even so, Lord, for thou hast made him most blessed forever. Thou hast made him exceeding glad with Thy countenance." Yours, "sorrowful yet rejoicing," Susie Spurgeon.[50]

With Christ,
Which Is Far Better

When Charles Spurgeon addressed a small group of Christians gathered in his hotel in Mentone, on January 1, 1892, he did not know that before the clock struck midnight on the last day of the month, he would be in heaven. Charles's conviction was, "Great mercy has hung up a veil between us and the future; and there let it hang."[1] Though Charles suffered physical and emotional pain throughout his adult life, during previous trips to Mentone, his health had been sufficiently restored, enabling him to return to his ministry. During his final three months, he had again expected to recover. Joseph Harrald wrote of Charles and Susie's experience at Mentone:

> Those last three months seemed to make their earthly bliss complete; husband and wife often said it was their honeymoon over again. They celebrated together at Mentone their thirty-sixth wedding-day, also Mrs. Spurgeon's birthday, and from the family standpoint . . . it was all that one could have desired.[2]

Charles was thrilled that his dear Susie was with him in Mentone, and he was convinced that he would be able to return with her to London in February 1892 to resume his ministry, stating to his friends, "I shall be home in February."[3] However, a "veil" hid the timing of his death from him. His friend and biographer, Robert Shindler, concluded that, indeed, Spurgeon *was* at home in February "in a far more real sense than any of us had supposed when we heard the words."

Charles went to his *real* home, heaven, just before midnight on January 31, 1892, where his beloved Susie would join him in 1903. News of his death spread quickly, and Susie was inundated with messages from friends and dignitaries, including a message from the Prince and Princess of Wales.[4] Plates were attached to Spurgeon's casket, inscribed, "I have fought a good fight, I have finished my course, I have kept the faith," a verse chosen, not by Spurgeon, but by Harrald.[5] Harrald had suggested the inscription to Susie, and she responded, "How is it that you always think of just what I have been thinking? There is no other text for him."[6]

Charles had indeed fought a good fight, but his fight, including his final battle with suffering, was not waged alone. Near to his side was his beloved Susie, who had been a true helper, fellow sufferer, comforter, wife, and friend to him. In later years, Susie often looked with "tear-filled eyes" at the framed portrait of Spurgeon that she had given him on the eve of their wedding. She said of the picture that "it speaks to me . . . and it says, 'Do not fear, my beloved, for God is *taking care of us both;* and though we are still separated for a little while, we shall meet again *at home* by-and-by."[7]

Susie believed that she would enjoy fellowship with Charles in heaven. She asserted, "I cannot imagine that God will omit from Heaven's blessedness the brightest and choicest benediction of our earthly life. It is my confident belief that I shall see and know my beloved again in glory, and that there, our earthly love, purified and sanctified, shall continue and maybe, increase in the perpetual light of the presence of our King and Saviour."[8] She requested that her readers pray for her that she would be a "partaker of that blessedness which my beloved now enjoys."[9]

Soon after Charles died, and prior to the transport of his body back to London, a memorial service was held at the Scotch Presbyterian Church in Mentone, where a year earlier he had preached for the opening of the church building.[10] Among the many flowers that were kindly sent for the service, Susie contributed palm branches, a symbol of her confidence that her beloved husband was now "before the throne, and before the Lamb" where he worshiped with the "great multitude," and she was confident that he was then declaring, "Salvation to our God which sitteth upon the throne, and unto the Lamb."[11] Susie was applying Revelation 7:10 to the new heavenly context of her husband. It was as natural as breathing for her to employ scriptural descriptors for whatever matter was at hand. Though she did not travel back to London to participate in the numerous memorial services held for Charles, she did send a note along that was attached to his casket.[12] It read, "With Christ, which is far better. I will follow thee, my husband. Undying love from 'the wife of thy youth.'"[13]

It is not known why Susie did not return to London but opted instead to remain near Mentone. The likely reason is that she was physically weakened from the last two weeks of Charles's life. She had felt the heavy blow of his death and, for one already somewhat frail, to make a thousand-mile journey again by train, boat, and carriage was more than she could bear, emotionally or physically. And it would have been difficult for her to find a moment of peace and rest in London. Throngs of people pressed into the week of services that were held in memory of Charles, and at least 100,000 people lined the streets as his casket made its way to the cemetery. There would have been no rest or healing for Susie in London.

Susie remained in France and Italy and enjoyed the hospitality of Sir Thomas Hanbury at his vast estate just a few miles from Mentone. Hanbury Gardens was the site for Sir Thomas's residence, La Mortola. The eighty-acre oasis with the pristine beauty of abounding gardens was a balm of healing to Susie's mind and body. While there she often meditated on the apostle Paul's words, "With Christ, which is far better," and in those words she found consolation for her grief and, as she remembered, "the comforting power of the assurance, that even though my precious husband had bidden adieu to the *best* that earth could give, his being *'with Christ'* was FAR BETTER."[14]

Hanbury collected a vast array of exotic plants and trees from around the world, and they filled the nooks and crannies of the sprawling estate that touched the shores of the Mediterranean Sea. Susie described the gardens:

> Imagine, dear reader, if you can, some eighty acres or more of land, sloping down to the sea, and filled with the products of almost every clime, but especially of tropical and sub-tropical countries; put into your imaginary picture a great variety of palm, olive, orange, lemon, citron, fig, carob, medlar, eucalyptus, acacia, camphor, pepper, pine, fir, evergreen, oak, and cypress trees, with magnificent specimens of flowering aloes, agaves, euphorbias, cacti, myrtles, etc., etc., and an almost endless profusion of flowers of every kind, which need thousands of bottles for the preservation of the seeds of a single year, and you have some idea of the place we are supposed to be visiting. No wonder that such a spot is a favourite resort for botanists, horticulturists, and lovers of the beautiful and curious handiwork of our great Creator.[15]

Of especial significance to Susie was the trellis-covered walkway on the property where just a month prior she had walked with Charles. As they had made their way down from the large patio of La Mortola for their walk, Charles had likely pointed out to Susie some lovely masterpiece of nature off in the distance, perhaps a fish jumping in the waters of the Mediterranean. *The Sword and the Trowel* reported, "The last time Mr. Spurgeon spent a day at the *Palazzo Orengo*, he rode in a bath chair[16] along this flower-bordered pathway, that from the far eastern end of the

pathway he might show his dear wife one of the most charming panora-
mas in the whole region—the valley of Latte, with Ventimiglia, basking
in the sunshine."[17]

This time, Susie walked alone down the same trellised pathway. Per-
haps memories of her healthier years, when she had hiked the Alps with
Charles, flooded her grieving heart. Still today, Hanbury Gardens are
stunningly beautiful, with its offering of lemon, olive, and grapefruit trees;
its array of flowers and plants; and its views of the mountains and the sea.
Susie referred to the gardens, located near Mentone on the French and
Italian border, as the "loveliest of all gardens" and considered that "even
Eden itself could scarcely have been fairer."[18]

❧❦❧

Susie returned to Westwood in March.[19] She described her home as
"beautiful but desolate" and "very dear to my beloved." She wondered what
God's plans were for her now that she was separated from Charles. She
steeled herself for the days ahead: "I found that to 'do the next thing' was
earnestly to set to work at the Book Fund." Money was still flowing into
the Fund and she confidently declared, "I fully believe that God constrained
me to the service, and strengthened me for it, in order to keep heart and
mind from dwelling too constantly upon my loneliness and grief."[20]

She credited God for using the Fund for her benefit, saying, "Many a
trial has been lightened by the uplifting of its sweet ministry; and many a
dark day has been made bright at eventide by the encouragement granted
to my loving efforts." She described the Fund as serving her "in the deepest
sorrow my life can ever know," pointing to "the consoling power of active
service for the Lord and His poor servants."[21]

After returning to London, Susie wrote about her experiences at Hanbury's lovely abode that also provides a glimpse at Susie's lovely writings.

I can see two pilgrims treading this highway of life together,
hand in hand,—heart linked to heart. True, they have had rivers

to ford, and mountains to cross, and fierce enemies to fight, and many dangers to go through; but their Guide was watchful, their Deliverer unfailing, and of them it might truly be said, "In all their affliction He was afflicted, and the Angel of His presence saved them; and He bare them, and carried them all the days of old."

Mostly, they went on their way singing; and for one of them, at least, there was no joy greater than to tell others of the grace and glory of the blessed King to whose land he was hastening. And when he thus spoke, the power of the Lord was seen, and the angels rejoiced over repenting sinners. But, at last, they came to a place on the road where two ways met; and here, amidst the terrors of a storm such as they had never before encountered, they parted company,—the one being caught up to the invisible glory,—the other, battered and bruised by the awful tempest, henceforth toiling along the road,—alone!

But the "goodness and mercy" which, for so many years, had followed the two travellers, did not leave the solitary one; rather did the tenderness of the Lord "lead on softly," and choose green pastures for the tired feet, and still waters for the solace and refreshment of His trembling child. He gave, moreover, into her hands a solemn charge,—to help fellow-pilgrims along the road, filling her life with blessed interest, and healing her own deep sorrow by giving her power to relieve and comfort others.[22]

A Lady of Letters

Every January brought "heartache" and "sad memories" to Susie, for it was the month of Charles's death. In 1899, she wrote, "The swiftly-passing years may mitigate the grievous pain of the wound God's hand gave me seven years ago, but they cannot heal it; only the same gracious hand can do that; and it seems to me He hath bound up the sore heart just enough to make life bearable, while His purposes are being unfolded." Though life was "bearable" for Susie, she frequently acknowledged that she had been "blessed among women" during her "husband's lovely life." She found that her loneliness without Charles tempted her to think of herself as empty.[1] Though Susie shed many tears after Charles's death, she was not paralyzed by her sadness, but instead she engaged herself again in the Book Fund and its auxiliary ministries.

A means that helped Susie maintain her equilibrium through sadness and suffering was writing. Thomas remembered his mother as having "rare literary gifts." He recounted her years as an author: "She began her career in this department before her marriage, when, at her lover's desire, she made selections from one of his favorite Puritans for a little book entitled, *Smooth Stones Taken From Ancient Brooks*. She was a constant and valued contributor, for many years, to the pages of *The Sword and the Trowel*, her 'Personal Notes on Texts' being specially prized, and she was responsible for the Magazine itself till recently. Her latest literary labour, and that which must have cost her most, was as joint-compiler with J. W. Harrald [Spurgeon's secretary, who also served at times as a pastor] of *C. H. Spurgeon's Autobiography*. How this task tugged at her heart-strings none can know."[2]

As Thomas noted, Susie first discovered the joys and trials of putting together a book in 1855, when she and Charles were engaged. Even after the significant labor of gathering material, her first publishing effort, *Smooth Stones Taken From Ancient Brooks,* did not even bear her name. That book, a collection of salient quotes by the Puritan preacher Thomas Brooks, carries only Charles's name as the compiler.

When the name Spurgeon, coupled with authorship, is considered, one's thoughts immediately race to the famous London preacher, not to his wife. Though not *as* prolific a writer as her famous husband, Susie Spurgeon was an imaginative and productive author in her own right. Though she didn't see herself as much of a writer,[3] she penned five books, numerous articles, and was a major contributor to, compiler of, and co-editor of the massive four-volume *Autobiography*.

Her written treasures have mostly been obscured beneath the mountain of material by and about her famous husband, and early editions of Susie's books are now difficult to obtain. Her literary contributions are beautiful in their prose and relevant to even modern readers. Her literary prolificacy was cultivated by her serious commitment to the Bible, her voracious reading of devotional literature, and her thirty-eight-year exposure to the example of Charles. Her writing is also steeped in God-centered theology and its practical outworking in her ministry.

Not only did she face internal doubts about her writing ability, her prodigious literary contributions mostly came from hands that trembled with pain. On one occasion, she wrote of constant pain of head and hand that hindered her from writing.[4] However, her suffering cast her more fully on the Lord she loved and provided an endearing connection with her readers. In 1884, in the first book that carries her name, *Ten Years of My Life in the Service of the Book Fund,* she wrote, "We are such old friends now, my dear readers and I—we have so long enjoyed familiar intercourse, and have been for so many years delightfully associated in Book Fund work—that we need no formal introduction to each other."[5]

Susie's writing is appealing, for she brings her readers into the thoughts of her heart, as if she has poured a cup of tea for her guests, invited them to draw near to the fire, and engaged them in conversation. She respected her readers, treating them as friends.

With ardent love, she expressed her desire to the "task of making the Book Fund, as far as lies in my power, as pleasant and beautiful a thing to read about as it is to direct and administer."[6] In that statement, Susie reveals something important about her writing. Her objective was not simply to get facts on paper to be bound and sold as a book; she wanted to write beautifully. Even her Book Fund reports were not simply the pragmatic ledgers that an accountant might employ; they were intimate narratives that connected her with her readers and transported them into the hearts and homes of distressed pastors and their families.

Though she sometimes apologized for her personal entries in the volumes, she nevertheless seemed to delight in providing her readers with glimpses into her home. Her readers appreciated her transparency, for such openness was somewhat rare in Victorian times. The first volume, *Ten Years of My Life in the Service of the Book Fund*, covers the years 1876–1885. *The Sword and the Trowel* considered this volume Susie's autobiography.[7]

Her second volume on the Book Fund is simply titled, *Ten Years After: A Sequel to Ten Years of My Life in the Service of the Book Fund.* This work covers the years 1886–1895. It is an important work not only because of Susie's narration of the Book Fund ministry and the collection of tender letters from pastors contained therein, but also because it accounts for the period of Charles's last six years of life and her first four years as a widow. Susie's own testimony of the book is that it "has in it an entry which invests it in a more sacred and solemn interest than the other,—in this garden there is a sepulcher, —and the shadow of a great grief lies on the latter half of the book." Rhetorically, she asks, "Should I therefore have withheld its blessed story? Nay, rather, it seems fit that all should know how God comforted me in my affliction, and in His wondrous pity and compassion uplifted me, from the sorrow of my loss, into the joyful hope of eternal re-union in the land that knows no death."[8] This is a theme that recurs in Susie's work; she writes about her suffering, not to evoke the pity of her readers but to display the comfort of God and *His* pity and compassion. Her aim is to glorify God, not to exalt her loneliness, physical sufferings, or emotional turmoil.

In the Book Fund narratives, "two delightful volumes," as Thomas described them, Susie "told the fascinating story of her work in a charming style peculiarly her own, but which has been not inaptly compared to her husband's."[9] Thomas makes a lofty yet accurate comparison when he places Susie's writings beside those of Charles's. Perhaps Susie's style was influenced by her husband's, developed prior to meeting him, or some mixture of the two.

Thomas accurately intimated that his mother's books have similarities with Charles's in writing style. First, her writing is picturesque in its descriptions, especially in her portrayals of nature. She writes of birds, flowers, water, bees, her lemon tree, and even a log in her fireplace that whistled as it warmed. Charles encouraged his students that if they kept their eyes open that they would "not see even a dog following his master, nor a mouse peeping up from his hole, nor will you hear even a gentle scratching behind the wainscot, without getting something to weave into your sermons if your faculties are on the alert."[10] Susie described Charles's love of the sights and sounds of Nightingale Lane: "The song of birds was sweetest music to him, and the commonest flowers gave him joy, because they both revealed to him the love of his Father's heart."[11]

Second, she writes from a biblical frame of reference. In a chapter from her devotional book, *A Cluster of Camphire*, she opens with Psalm 94:19, moves to the Song of Solomon, and then to the first chapter of 2 Corinthians.

Susie, versed in the whole of Scripture, was able to skillfully interact with passages of the Old and New Testaments. Of Psalm 94 she prays: "Blessed Lord, how sweet is this text in my mouth." She continues, "Give me grace, dear Master, to sit at Thy table, this morning, and eat and drink abundantly, as Thy beloved ones may do, of the divine dainties Thy love has here provided." Throughout, she looks to God for comfort: "Human comforters we may have had, and we blessed them for their kindness; but none can comfort like Thee, for Thou art 'the Father of mercies, and the God of all comfort.'"[12]

Third, she draws from the works of numerous authors, such as John Bunyan, Frances Havergal, Thomas Goodwin, John Milton, and Andrew Murray, and integrates quotations from their poetry and prose to illustrate her points. From the Puritan Thomas Goodwin she quotes, "Sermons preached are, for the most part, as showers of rain that water for the instant. . . . But *printed* sermons are as snow, that lies long on the earth, they are longer-lived, they preach when the author cannot, and—what is more—when he is not."[13]

Susie looked to her favorite authors for understanding into the human condition. She recognized that many Christians appeared to be unhappy and unfruitful, wandering, like Israel, in the desert. Susie understood that faith in Christ and obedience to His teaching was essential to enjoying the rest that He provides.

It was not just quotations that undergirded her work that she looked for in the writings of others, but she also offered poems and hymns that she felt would encourage her readers. Theodore Monde's hymn "The Changed Motto" is one such example:

Day by day His tender mercy
Healing, helping, full and free,
Sweet and strong, and oh! so patient,
Brought me lower while I whispered—
"Less of self, and more of Thee." [14]

As a pianist and singer of hymns, she was well acquainted with such collections, including *Our Own Hymn Book*, edited by her husband. Compiled in 1866, the hymnbook contains over two hundred psalms and over nine hundred hymns, a number of them written by Charles. [15]

Fourth, she writes theologically, not in a technical manner, but with her exegesis naturally woven into her text. Susie finds encouragement in God's grace, in the doctrines of election, preservation, providential care, omniscience, and love.

Fifth, the outgrowth of her doctrinal commitments is seen in her practical aim; she wants her readers to find comfort in the theology that she expounds. Commenting on Psalm 31:15, *My times are in Thy hand,* Susie recognized that the practical aim in the passage was to calm the reader and provide a foundation of peace. She asked: "Why then need I trouble or tremble?" Believing that almighty God ordered and kept her life and that His Word was trustworthy soothed her troubled heart. [16] She appealed to her readers to apply the doctrines of God's ordering of their lives, His power, and His care to "your present circumstances, however dark or difficult they may be." [17]

Like her husband before her, Susie was a Calvinistic Baptist; that is, she believed, embraced, and found comfort in the doctrines of God's sovereign grace. For her, the doctrine of election was not a topic to debate but a truth designed to "comfort our hearts" and to give us "good hope through grace." [18] For Susie, the place for biblical theology was not just the ivory tower of academia but primarily the heart, hands, and feet of the child of God. For example, she wanted Christians to respond to doctrine by faith. She urged, "If we would trust Him for the keeping, as we do for the saving, our lives would be far holier and happier than they are."[19]

Seventh, she writes beautifully. One example will suffice: "This truth has been running through the fields of previous thought, as a silver stream-let glides through the meadows; —here, it should deepen and expand to a broad and fathomless ocean, had I the power to speak of its height, and depth, and length, and breadth, and to tell of the love of Christ, which passeth knowledge."[20] Susie could have simply declared that God's love was obvious in all the other doctrines that she expounds in her chapter. However, she chose a more pictorial method to her script. Even with such descriptive language, she felt that her pen was wholly inadequate to depict the beauty of God.

Ten Years After provides further detail into her book ministry with reports, letters from pastors, an account of the growth of the Fund with its branches—The Pastor's Aid Fund, The Foreign Workers Fund, The Auxiliary Book Fund—and Susie's analysis on every aspect of the Fund. She also provides a more detailed glimpse into her suffering than she did in *Ten Years*, but more importantly, she pointed out how God comforted her in "the terrors of a storm,"[21] as she navigated life alone. Yet, she wanted her reader to know that she was not really alone: "But the 'goodness and mercy' which, for so many years, had followed the two travelers, did not leave the solitary one; rather did the tenderness of the Lord 'lead on softly,' and choose green pastures for the tired feet, and still waters for the solace and refreshment of His trembling child."[22]

Though Charles was dead, Susie grasped that God was not yet done with her, but He left with her a "solemn charge—to help fellow-pilgrims along the road, filling her life with blessed interest, and healing her own deep sorrow by giving her power to relieve and comfort others."[23] It was Susie's aim that her readers might see "how unspeakably good the Lord has been to me" and, therefore, that they might "be led to love Him more, and serve Him better, and trust Him more fully."[24] Part of the service that she envisioned for her readers was to love, pray for, and find ways to support poor pastors and their families.

H. T. Spufford penned a tribute to Susie in December of 1903. He said of *Ten Years After* that it was "one of the most touching books of the closing period of the 19th century."[25]

The Sword and the Trowel, December 1895, imagined that Charles would have been pleased with the release of the sequel from the pen of his "long-invalid wife." "How surprised and how rejoiced the dear 'Master of Westwood' would be if he could see the book . . . relating the rise and progress of the many *new* branches of holy service which have been originated since the first volume was issued."[26] *Ten Years After* faithfully documented the Book Fund enterprise, but it also served as a memorial volume to Charles, considered so lovely because the "bereaved one who knew him best and loved him most" wrote it.[27] Further, the review surmised that the "personal reminiscences, never previously published" will "moisten many an eye, and move many a heart to send off to the beloved worker tangible tokens of sympathy and help in her life-work."[28]

Susie's descriptive style of writing is not often imitated in modern days. Some might consider her sentences too flowery, more poetry than prose. Her manner of speech is, in part, a product of the literature that she read, the era in which she lived, and the husband that God had provided her. Again, like Charles, Susie believed that the world was a conservatory, endless in meaning and awaiting an artist or author to paint, sing, and write of God's glory evident in all things. Charles mused, "When I go into my garden, I have a choir around me in the trees. They do not wear surplices, for their song is not artificial and official. Some of them are clothed in glossy black, but they carol like little angels; they sing the sun up, and wake me at break of day; and they warble on till the last red ray of the sun has departed, still singing out from bush and tree the praises of their God."[29]

Charles and Susie perceived messages in flowers, gentle flowing water, the cool breeze on a fall morning, and in the parting of trees that allow glimpses of the blue sky above. Nature provided sermons and stories, readily employable as descriptors of Christ, the gospel, and the Christian life. When Susie looked at the Book of Nature, she read warnings against sin to be heeded, promises to be embraced, and encouragements to walk faithfully before God. In May of 1881, she pondered,

> We have open-air concerts day and night now at "Westwood;" for the songs of a multitude of feathered choristers round the house give us constant and delightful entertainment. During the day, blackbirds, thrushes, and a host of sweet-voiced finches, keep up a succession of chorales and concerted pieces with amazing zest and energy; but as night draws on, and the moon sheds her soft light over the landscape, our listening ears are charmed by the still more delicious music of the nightingales, who sing their lovely solos and duets from the covert of a bosky little coppice at the foot of the hill.

Susie especially loved the nightingale's love song.[30] Her birds sang a "symphony of praise" to God, and she was challenged to join with them in thanksgiving for His provision. Susie's feathered friends stirred up memories of the previous "fourteen or fifteen" years of her life.[31] Those memories both predated and followed her surgery of 1869. Therefore, she had learned to praise God in seasons of relative health and in times of great pain. Her description also lends credence to the consideration that Susie's suffering was intensifying much earlier than her surgery, probably around 1867. And, she hinted at the severity of her physical challenges by describing her hardships as a "narrow winding valley, where pain and weakness made the walking rough and difficult, and where sometimes the Shadow of Death fell across my very feet."[32] Susie let her readers in on her personal suffering as a means to help them to see how she found comfort in God:

> Yet no terror reigned there, for it was a prosperous and fertile place, as valleys often are; the dew of heaven lingered in its

depths, nourishing many sweet flowers of faith and patience, which perchance might have dropped in a sunnier spot, while now and again the weary traveller found "quiet and resting places," provided with such abundant compensating delights, that in their enjoyment the toil and trial of the way were well-nigh forgotten. And now even this exceeding goodness is exceeded for by the power and love of the Lord, the "valley has been exalted," the season for constant suffering has given place to a brighter experience, and though health and vigour are very far from being perfect, there are times when so much of life's purest pleasures can be enjoyed, that one feels every song should be a psalm, and every breath should bear a burden of praise. Verily, God hath been very gracious to me; He hath brought me out into a "large place," and given me a "goodly heritage," where I can

> "With the sunlight on my forehead
> Stand upon the mountain brow,"

and, gazing far below, see all the way by which He hath led me, and wonder at and admire the love and wisdom of His guiding hand. Oh, for the power to shout forth His praise.[33]

Susie's poetic musings are from her Book Fund report. She diligently disclosed numbers of people served with books, provided examples of correspondence from pastors, and she appealed for help to support the work; however, she did not hold back from sharing her personal pain and God's faithfulness to care for her. Perhaps this, in part, was the secret of Susie and one reason that so many people loved her. She *let* people see her weaknesses, struggles, and hardships. She was like her readers in more ways than perhaps they had imagined. Though she was married to a very famous pastor who had the ear of everyone from the simple merchant to the prime minister, she felt pain, sadness, loneliness, and discouragement. Through her books and articles, she welcomed her readers to see her as she was. And it was not only her sorrows that she drew attention to; she addressed the pains and disappointments of her readers directly.

> Beloved Friends, —it may be that, for some of you, the New Year opens in sadness and silence, without the merry crash of bells, and the welcoming cheers which celebrate its advent, and signify its joy to so many other hearts. Your trials are heavy, your comforts are few, earthly sorrows weigh you down, and hinder the glad mounting of your spirit to Heavenly places in Christ Jesus. The prospect of incessant toil and weariness oppresses you, or the retrospect of sorrow and suffering has benumbed you, and you do not feel you can heartily respond to the usual salutation of friend to friend, "I wish you a Happy New Year," —you would rather have done with earth, and that God gave you the wings of a dove, that you might fly away and be at rest.[34]

There are many literary devices that Susie might have employed in crafting those sentences and, in doing so, communicated more simply and directly. Yet she wrote imaginatively as she addressed the hearts of her readers. Her unpretentious words created an atmosphere where she might have been sitting beside her readers, holding their hands, and looking at them with comforting eyes as she said:

> I quite understand your feelings, I have fellowship with you in your fear and faintness of heart; but I bring afresh to you, today, the sweet and comforting assurance that your blessed Lord knows all your sorrows, sees all your sufferings, is watching over you with a Divine love and care which knows no cessation, and will, in His own good time, either relieve or release you.[35]

When Susie penned those words, she was a widow, feeling the burdens of a widow's sorrow. Though Charles had left behind sufficient money and help for Susie, she grieved him. And beyond the unique sufferings that most widows encounter, her physical maladies continued. Susie missed her family as her sons were engaged in their various ministries. Her servants, though they brought her much joy and help, especially her dear friend Elizabeth Thorne, were no substitute for the laughter of Charles or the voices of her sons. However, she found her refuge in God, her hope in His Word, and she enjoyed the comforts and experiences in the everyday things of life. She was honest about her loneliness, sufferings, and joys as she dipped her quill in ink and described Christ as she saw Him in the Bible, in nature, and in the circumstances of her life.

Her writing was Christ-centered, saturated with Scripture, seasoned by years of joys and sorrows, and embraced all of life—lemon trees, New Year's bells, and memories of her marriage to Charles. Letters arriving at her doorstep often brought with them encouragement in the way of funds for her ministries and by the comforting words contained therein. Her spirits were lifted when she received letters of thanks for the books she had written. Many such letters remain, and they provide insight into Susie as an author.

> Sometimes, when I am weary and dispirited, mostly from physical causes, the Lord sends me a gracious uplifting, by the pen or the word of a friend, which causes me to take heart again, and believe that my labour has not been in vain, or without the seal of His approval. A month or two ago, during a season of heart-drought, I received the following letter, which dropped like dew on my soul. "Dear Mrs. Spurgeon, I feel I must write a few lines to you, now that I am sending my usual contribution to the Lord's work in your hands. I cannot tell you all the consolation your *Carillon of Bells* has brought to me. It seems to me as if, when writing the book, you knew all about my troubles, and I

find great comfort in reading some portion of it every day. God will bless you for your kindness in sending forth such words of cheer and help. I have the *Cluster of Camphire,* too, and am equally charmed with its contents."[36]

In her devotional books, Susie interacted with passages of Scripture in ways that were designed to honor the character of God and administer gospel help to her readers. She published three devotionals: *A Carillon of Bells* (1896), *A Cluster of Camphire* (1898), and *A Basket of Summer Fruit* (1901). Her devotional writing is saturated in Scripture and warmly applied to her readers.

Commenting on Mark 6:48, "*He saw them toiling in rowing,*" Susie visualized the brief passage, "Do you see that small ship on a wind-swept lake? Storm and darkness are fast gathering their forces together, the sea is tossing and raging in passionate response to the war-cry of the tempest, and serious danger is menacing the men in the frail vessel." She then portrays the disciples as "straining every nerve and muscle to make for the opposite shore, they labour at the oars with almost superhuman strength but they are no match against the tremendous force of the wind and wave which beats them back continually, and threatens to engulf them." Then she turns to her readers: "Your heart fails you as you look on their perilous position, and you expect every moment that the sea will swallow up its prey."[37]

Just as easily she could have written that their ship encountered a storm, and that they were greatly afraid. But her pen places her readers on the boat where they are allowed to see that the ship is small; the lake is "wind-swept" and darkness so deepens that it joins forces with a "tossing sea." The tempest does not simply howl; it screams with a "war-cry," and the men are not simply in trouble but "serious danger is menacing" them. They are not only sailing on a boat, but they are tossed in a "frail vessel." It is man against sea, and sea laughs at the fragility of the manly disciples who are frightened out of their wits. Yet they were "straining every nerve and muscle" as they made their way to the shore, and they draw up almost "superhuman strength" as they fought against the waves and rowed into the wind; however, "they are no match against the tremendous force of the wind and wave." They make a bit of progress only to be beaten "back continually."

And it is not only the sailors who are overmatched and whose hearts sink in fear. Susie's readers are invited to feel the strain of rowing and the effect of water splashing upon the disciples' weathered faces as they encountered deathly trouble and realized their utter helplessness. Susie's word pictures allowed her readers to experience the disciples' hearts fail as they anticipated that "the sea will swallow up its prey." The men are now prey on the paper from which Susie Spurgeon employed her skill as a master wordsmith. However, she does not leave the men or those who are attentive to their story lost at sea:

> But now turn your gaze land-wards. On the bow of an adjacent
> hill stands a solitary, but majestic Man. He is intently watching
> the rowers in that trembling, storm-tossed bark. Not a danger is
> over-looked, not an effort is unnoticed, not a fear in their hearts
> that does not thrill His soul with pity, and appeal to His tender-
> est love. He is going to save them, and in the manner of their
> deliverance will gloriously manifest His own Divine power and
> goodness. He will presently tread under His feet the waves of
> that turbulent sea, and compel those fierce gales to quail before
> Him in silent homage.[38]

For Susie, it was always the gospel, always Jesus. Man is at sea, tossed, helpless, and facing certain death. But there is a "majestic Man." He is not unaware of the hopeless condition of His people. He is watching. He is the Savior who "will tread under His feet the waves of that turbulent sea" and subdue its dangers as He rescues those whom He so graciously redeems. Such was the writing of Susie Spurgeon.

Susie was insecure in her skill as an author and wanted nothing published that had not been examined by the eyes of her "director in chief," her "dear Editor."[39] She affirmed, "To him I run in search of counsel, comfort, or wise advice, and need I say I always find it?"[40] Though doubts about proficiency as an author plagued Susie, her aim was clearly set; it was her chief desire in her writing to glorify God.[41]

Susie's writings are most remembered today by her contributions to *C. H. Spurgeon's Autobiography*. This colossal work, originally produced in four volumes, is a repository of biographical narrative. It is the starting point for anyone interested in learning more about Charles and Susie Spurgeon.

Volume one of the *Autobiography* appeared in 1897, volume two was published in 1898, with volume three following in 1899, and volume four in 1900.[42] At times, Susie found it difficult to work on the *Autobiography* because so many memories of her beloved husband came rushing back to her mind and dampened her emotions. In the opening chapters of volume two, she deals with the subject of Charles and their courtship, marriage, and wedded life. She recognized that no other biographer could do justice to that chapter. However, she felt ill equipped for such an important task.

Recalling the memories of her years with Charles and inking them to paper for the world to read was no doubt painful. She reflected, "Many a time, I feel I must lay down my pen, and give it all up; for in reading and transcribing my husband's letters, and living, as it were, over again those days of precious sweetness and sympathy, the inexpressible loss I have sustained is recalled . . ."[43] While writing the early chapters in volume two, she felt lonely and needy for God's help in ascending "again into the high-lands of sweet content with God's will, and gladness (for my dear one's sake) . . ." She asked her friends to pray for her.[44] As expected, the *Autobiography*, much anticipated, was well received both in England and around the world. A "Special Lecturer on Missions and Ethics of the Ministry, in the great summer Bible School of Baylor University" wrote to Mrs. Spurgeon expressing thanksgiving for volume one.[45]

Of volume two, the Baylor lecturer mentioned that it had just appeared (January of 1899) in America and that he was "eagerly expecting his copy." He planned to develop a lecture on Spurgeon's life, he said: "For, when I read the book (Vol. I), my tears flowed so spontaneously and my heart burned so within me to be a more worthy ambassador of Christ, that I doubt not a true account of his life will urge thousands of brethren to a more earnest and efficient ministry."[46] Susie could have dreamed of nothing more wonderful than her husband's story motivating others to a life of faithful service to Jesus. However, not everyone was so pleased with the *Autobiography*. Some, Susie lamented, were bothered that she delayed sharing in earlier volumes information that she planned for the later volumes. Others criticized her for not revealing more about Charles. Most people received the volumes very warmly.[47]

A full examination of all Susie's writings is beyond the scope of this book. Yet, take a moment to consider her literary output. Susie's widowhood allowed her more time for writing and most of her literary contributions occur *after* Charles's death. As a widow, she publishes five stand-alone books, numerous pieces for *The Sword and the Trowel*, and is heavily involved in the "translation and dissemination" of Charles's sermons. From about 1873 until her death in 1903, she also provided the texts for "Spurgeon's Illustrated Almanack."[48] As well, she penned numerous other passages concerning the Book Fund and opined about other subjects, including a booklet (*A Protest Against Bazaars*) regarding how churches raise funds.

Susie's prolificacy as a writer and her management of the Book Fund required a formidable effort; she would be celebrated for her faithfulness if she did little more. Susie, however, was not one to casually shirk opportunities for ministry, especially if they were ministries that Charles had prioritized in his own work. Perhaps then it should not be surprising that the sickly and lonely widow took up the role of a church planter.

CHAPTER 14

Planting a Final Seed

C an you tell us where to find the Baptist meeting-place, if you please?"
     "Don't know, mum: never 'eard of no such people as Baptises 'ere."
Such was Susie's conversation with a local resident at Bexhill-on-Sea.[1] It was the spring of 1895, Susie Spurgeon was sixty-three, a widow for three years, and she had suffered physically for at least twenty-eight years. She likely imagined that she would live out her days serving God by administering the Book Fund from her home, Westwood. Susie labored diligently in her ministries, refusing to lazily watch the days pass while she bided her time. By 1895, she was an accomplished author; her first book, *Ten Years of My Life in the Service of the Book Fund*, had been well received. Her next book, *Ten Years After*, newly released in 1895, had already received much attention.

Susie managed a busy household that bustled with activities; she received guests, used her property as a centerpiece of ministry, and she was heavily invested in advancing Spurgeon's gospel legacy. The widow, busy about many eternally significant ministries, would soon embrace a task that no one could have expected. Susie Spurgeon was about to help launch a new church.

Westwood was undergoing repair, and Susie chose to visit the coast for a couple of weeks for a change of scenery. Her health had improved somewhat since 1892, and she was able to travel more frequently. Susie found Bexhill to be "finely situated, and very healthful."[2] However, the seaside village was in the midst of a building boom and somewhat disordered as businesses and hotels were springing up to meet the growing influx of tourists and convalescents.[3] Bexhill, like other such towns during the Victorian era, was sought out not only because of its beauty and proximity to the sea but also, according to the conventional thinking of that time, because it fostered environmental conditions conducive to healing. Susie was familiar with nearby towns and the general area.

The town of Eastbourne, stunningly beautiful with its seven white cliffs (known as the Seven Sisters), was just a few miles away, and it was a special place for Susie; she had traveled there with Charles in early October of 1891, just prior to his final trip to Mentone. And Brighton, the place of Susie's surgery and where sons Thomas and Charles had received a good part of their early education, was just over twenty miles away.

Susie desired to worship with a Baptist church on that Lord's Day morning when she had sought directions from the stranger, but she was disappointed upon discovering that no such place existed. People of Baptist conviction lived in Bexhill, and there had been attempts over the years to establish a church, but nothing had lasted. Unable to find a group of Baptists to worship with, Susie and her friends attended the Wesleyan Chapel but she couldn't relieve her mind of the thought that there was no Baptist chapel at Bexhill-on-Sea.[4]

After Susie returned home to London, she spent a good part of a year praying for and pondering the situation at Bexhill. During that time, her friends, Pastor J. S. Hockey and his wife, visited her at Westwood. In 1880, Hockey was accepted as a student at Spurgeon's Pastors' College, during which, and following his time at the school, he had also served as a pastor. When he arrived at Westwood, he had recently resigned his church and was in search of a new ministry. Though opportunities presented themselves on occasion, nothing panned out for him. Susie believed that the "Lord had shut every door" even though, she said, "he is a man much beloved, and has long been a faithful servant of God." Susie prayed that God would provide a place of service for Pastor and Mrs. Hockey. While praying, Susie was surprised as, "there flashed upon my mind the thought, 'God would have him go to Bexhill, and raise a cause there to His glory.' My heart at once responded, 'Yes, Lord, so may it be' and from that moment I did not doubt but it would come to pass."[5] Susie believed that the "olden days of open vision and prophecy" were over. However, she asked, "Does not our loving Father, even now, though in gentler fashion, sometimes speak to His children by what they *see*, as certainly and truly as if a voice had reached their outward ears?"[6]

Susie then related an incident from a few days prior, waking up just after midnight. She felt compelled to leave her bed and open the curtains. She "obeyed the impulse, and was rewarded by a sight, common though it may be, but so fraught with spiritual meaning to my soul, that it will be photographed on my mind while life lasts." It was a dark and starless night; in the distance, she could barely see a few village lights. On the horizon, there was a narrow parting of the clouds, and "along this passage-way the moon was sailing, a ship of silver passing through a river of light, while the cloud-banks on either side were luminous with celestial radiance."

Striking to her was the contrast between the deep black sky and "the brilliance of the rifted clouds." It seemed to her as if "Heaven's pearly gates were opened, and through them came streaming the light of that city that 'had no need of the sun, neither of the moon to shine in it; for the glory of God did lighten it, and the Lamb is the light thereof.'" Describing the effect of her experience, she pondered that the "midnight scene" was "more spiritual than anything I had before witnessed. It seemed to have *God* in it, and the place whereon I stood was holy ground."[7]

Fully confident in the reliability of the Scripture, Susie believed that the canon of Scripture was closed. Yet, like Charles before her, she believed in the active ministry of the Holy Spirit in leading His people. Her midnight experience was not a vision, but, as she described it, it was "common enough." She believed that God used the common view of the midnight sky in an uncommon way. Susie felt that God was leading her to see His glory in that night sky, and she believed that God also gave her the thought about Hockey going to Bexhill.

Eventually, Susie disclosed her idea to her friend. Her creative and brutally honest proposal to him certainly could not have been mistaken for a sales pitch. She said, "It was no path of roses in which I propose that my friends should travel; it is no easy matter to go to a strange place, where you do not know a single soul, and introduce yourself as a probable pastor for a non-existent church!"[8] No easy matter indeed. Though there was no smooth road ahead of Pastor Hockey, he embraced Susie's proposal, and she supplied him with her full confidence and support. Susie's persistence was impressive. Not only had she determined that a Baptist church was needed at Bexhill, she also decided that Hockey was to be its pastor. Her determination and decision making were not isolated from prayer; they came from her biblical conviction that God leads Christians through prayerful dependency on Him.

After arriving at Bexhill, Hockey gathered a group of Baptists from the area who were *also* eager for the establishment of a chapel. Soon after, a plot of land was secured where a "School-Chapel" was to be built. With stunning faith, Susie voiced that she had no doubt about the future success of the endeavor. She wrote, "Then, when the little flock have a fold of their own in which to meet, they will grow and prosper until they are strong enough to undertake the building of a large house for the worship of God and the honor of His name."[9] Her confidence was inspiring; for she had no doubt that the church would be successful.

Initially, the fledgling congregation rented a facility while their projected building was planned and built. Susie had definite views concerning how a building was to be obtained. First, no debt would be incurred. Charles and Susie had been committed to no debt at home and no debt for their church throughout their marriage. Susie personally committed to giving all that she could to support the work, and she conveyed to the people her faith that God could be trusted to provide the rest. Second, she required that no "worldly" means be employed to raise money. She and the little congregation would tell their needs to God and share them with fellow believers, giving them an opportunity to support the work. She asserted:

> I am going to give all I possibly can to it, and trust in my rich
> Father to send me the remainder. He knows how much will be
> needed; and if He inclines the hearts of any dear friends to help
> me in this new work for Him I shall very gratefully accept their
> assistance. But I shall "beg" only of Him, and there will be no
> Concerts, or Bazaars, or worldly entertainments of any sort to
> share in the erection of Beulah Baptist Chapel, Bexhill-on-Sea.[10]

At the time of the Bexhill project, Susie was not a young, energetic, and healthy church-planting visionary; she was a widow with physical limitations. And yet, it doesn't seem that she gave much attention to any obstacles that might stand in her way. She focused on the matter ahead and, without resources in hand, she had faith that God had led her and that He would provide for the establishment of the church.

As 1896 ended, the first building, the school-chapel, just a few blocks north of the shoreline, was opened in a special ceremony led by Susie's son Thomas.[11] Susie was unable to attend this service. Charles and Thomas laid the foundation stones for this first building with silver trowels given to them by their mother, which were rich in significance regarding their father's ministry. The trowel employed by Charles had been used by his mother in 1868 in laying the first stone of the College House for the Stockwell Orphanage. She had also used it in 1880 to lay the stone for the girls' house.[12] It had also been recently employed to lay the memorial stones of the Chiswick Baptist Chapel, another memorial chapel to Charles H. Spurgeon.[13] Thomas Spurgeon also had a trowel from his mother; it was the one that his father used for the foundation stone of the Pastors' College in 1873. Both trowels were employed for the Beulah Baptist Chapel.[14] These words were engraved thereon:

These foundation stones were laid,
August 11, 1896,
to the glory of God,
and in tender memory of that prince of preachers,
C. H. Spurgeon,
by his twin sons, Charles and Thomas,
on behalf of their beloved mother.
Shewing to the generation to come the praises of the Lord. Psalm lxxviii
verse 4.[15]

The Sword and the Trowel recorded that Pastor Hockey gave praise to God and he communicated his thanksgiving to "dear Mrs. Spurgeon" for her help. It also reported that "Pastors Charles and Thomas equally shared the duties of stone-laying, and the elder of the twin-brothers preached in the evening from the words 'Jesus Christ and Him crucified.'"[16]

The evening service was held at the Wesleyan Chapel,[17] the very place where Susie had attended when she could not locate a Baptist congregation. Sharing Susie's Christian spirit of brotherly love, the Wesleyans were amenable to the Bexhill church plant effort led by Mrs. Spurgeon, and they were of one mind with her on the authority of the Bible. Though Susie was unable to attend the opening of the "School-Chapel," she sent a telegram that read, "This is the Lord's doing; it is marvelous in our eyes. I am with you in spirit, blessing and praising our gracious God."[18] A framed reply was forwarded to Mrs. Spurgeon at Westwood. It read:

Am desired by large and enthusiastic company of Baptists and
other friends at stone laying to send you loving greetings, and
offer warm gratitude for your generous interest. They praise
God that your heart has so fully responded to His call to raise
a building to His glory, and they are thankful for the strength
of threefold cord of mother's love, father's memory, and sons'
loyalty today demonstrated.[19]

Love of Susie and Charles Spurgeon was still widespread in England
and across the world in 1896. Friends, many who lived far from Bexhill,
provided money for the first phase of the building project. However, it
was Susie's expectation that the growing congregation would join more
fully in the financing of the next phase of the building plan, the "House
of Prayer," as Susie referred to it. However, even with more local support,
Susie realized that the fledgling congregation didn't have the resources to
fully support the building, pastor, and other ministries that were required.
Therefore, outside help remained an important concern. Consistent with
Susie's rules for building, no debt had been accrued and no "worldly
means" had been employed to raise money for the building. And a third
requirement was also honored: "The Building in its whole or parts was not
to be called 'C. H. Spurgeon Memorial Chapel.'"[20] This also represented
Charles's own attitude about his life and ministry. For example, after the
Down-Grade Controversy, Charles was aware that some people wanted
to create a Spurgeon denomination; Charles vigorously opposed such a
plan. Though the building was not to be named after Spurgeon, it was
a memorial to him and, like the Metropolitan Tabernacle, it would be a
place of gospel preaching.

As 1896 progressed, Susie rejoiced in the early success of the Bexhill
ministry and the faithfulness of Pastor Hockey. She saw the church as
"a beacon lighted in Bexhill, which shall never be extinguished."[21] She
declared: "The old, old gospel preached by the Lord's servant has lost
none of its ancient fire and power." She challenged the people to, by God's

grace, "rally around the preacher [as] a gracious, praying, believing people, steadfast in the old truths, watchful over the old landmarks, faithful to sound doctrine, and 'full of faith and of the Holy Ghost.'" If they did that, then she believed a great future was in store for Beulah Baptist Chapel. For Susie, the church would flourish "by the preaching of the Word."[22] It should be noted here that Beulah Baptist Church remains today as an evangelical witness to Bexhill-on-Sea and surrounding areas.[23]

Susie had faith, she was committed to sound doctrine, and she believed in the importance of the ministry of the Holy Spirit and the need of the congregants to support their faithful pastor. Support of one's pastor was a particular passion of Susie's throughout her married life, and it continued to be a focus of her concern as a widow. Working to improve the situation of pastors never waned as she grew older.

With the start of 1897 and the school chapel open free of debt, void of questionable fundraising, and remembering but not named after Spurgeon, funds came in for the next phase of the building project. On January 31, the church was formally constituted with forty members.[24] Susie thought much on that day, for just five years prior, her "dearly-beloved" had died.

Though she sometimes wondered if life would be possible without him, she was able to offer a positive testimony to the faithfulness of God. She lovingly declared, "But what pitiful tenderness hath God shown to me in my widowhood and loneliness. Though he has taken away the sun from the sky, He has made the evening star exceeding bright; and as faith looks up with longing eyes to Heaven, clusters of radiant promise-lights are visible, which cheer and direct the weary traveler on the journey home."[25] Certainly Susie was cheered as she contemplated how pleased Charles would be to know that a fervent gospel witness was developing at Bexhill.

Susie attended worship services at Bexhill on Sunday, April 11, and was overcome with emotion and thanksgiving. Reflecting on the service she said, "Do you think, dear friends, that I had a Sabbath day at Bexhill which will be remembered by me till I come to the gate of Heaven?"[26]

The Sword and the Trowel reported that on April 12, 1897, "Mrs. C. H. Spurgeon cut the first sod, and so began the preparation of the ground for the new Chapel."[27] As she turned the soil, there is little doubt that her mind was on Charles and his over forty years of gospel ministry. Susie was described as resembling Queen Victoria that day,[28] and to those who knew her best, admired her devotion, and benefited from her ministry, she was a queen.

Pastor Hockey remarked that "there would not have been a Baptist Chapel at all in Bexhill had it not been for her, and certainly they would not have the larger edifice about to be erected had it not been for her splendid generosity."[29]

At the groundbreaking ceremony for the larger building, Susie spoke to the gathered crowd:

> I would like, dear friends, to say just a few words, I am not going to make a speech. God has not bestowed upon me the gift of utterance, and my son will speak on my behalf, but I want to tell you how delighted I was yesterday to hear your dear Pastor preach the pure and simple gospel in that little Chapel we have just left. You cannot imagine how dear this place is to me. All the tenderest emotions of my heart are touched by the sight of this "little Beulah" of yours,—and mine. It has been built to the glory of God, first and foremost, and He has already come and taken possession of it, and made it His own house, by "receiving sinners" there. He has filled it with His glory! But it also enshrines the precious memory of my dear one who has gone with Him, and therefore it has a peculiar sacredness for me. This cutting of the first sod is a small beginning of what I am sure will have a great and glorious ending, for the work is of the Lord all the way through, and He never does things by halfs.[30]

Following Mrs. Spurgeon's speech outside the chapel, the group returned inside, where son Charles spoke of how his father would approve of the good work at Bexhill. After Charles spoke, pastor W. H. Harris of Eastbourne rejoiced at his opportunity of meeting Mrs. Spurgeon and declared, how "from the bereaved home at 'Westwood' a most gracious ministry was still being exercised. The present school-chapel, and the larger one about to be built were the results of that ministry."[31] Perhaps somewhat surprising, Susie agreed to be photographed, and for prints of her to be sold with purchases benefitting the building fund of Beulah Baptist Chapel. Prior to this announcement, *The Sword and the Trowel* had received a groundswell of interest in such a photograph.

That May, Susie wrote a lovely piece about Bexhill.

I have been to Bexhill. I have seen my "beautiful little Zion," I have heard the gospel in all its fullness and simplicity proclaimed within its walls, I have worshipped the Lord with a grateful heart, and sung His high praises in the assembly of His people, and I have sat with them at His table, and remembered His love, and His death. Verily, that day I came to Elim with its wells and palm trees, and my soul encamped there with great joy by the waters.[32]

As Susie contemplated the ministry at Bexhill, she said "a great awe fell upon me, and I could have wished that every brick, and stone, and rafter, and every blade of grass growing in the field, had had a voice to shame my silent tongue, while they sang the praises of Him who has done such great things for us!"[33]

Just three months later, July of 1897, Beulah Baptist Chapel was making progress on their new facility. On the seventh of the month, a day Susie referred to as a "perfect day," Charles, Thomas, and close family friend Pastor Archibald Brown, addressed the crowd that gathered at Bexhill for the laying of another foundation stone. Susie laid the "sparkling block of marble," the foundation stone of the larger chapel. She declared:

> God was giving me one of the greatest desires of my solitary life in thus seeing the successful commencement of the larger House of Prayer to be built, first for His honour and glory and then in undying memory of my beloved, who still lives in the hearts of thousands in this and other lands, not by remembrance only, but by those wonderful gospel utterances which even now seem to leap from his living lips, and are made "the power of God unto salvation to every one that believeth." It was the joy and aim of his life to preach the pure and simple gospel, and point poor sinners to a pardoning Saviour, and, as that same blessed work is being carried on in Beulah Chapel, and the truths for which he lived and died are fully and fearlessly proclaimed there. . . . Small wonder that the placing of that memorial stone, the gathering together to celebrate God's goodness to us, and the uprearing of fresh Ebenezers to His praise, should be almost overwhelming joy to one so deeply interested in the work.[34]

Charlie referred to July 7, 1897, as "a gold letter day for Bexhill Baptists and the many friends who gathered with them to witness the laying, by Mrs. C. H. Spurgeon, of the memorial stone of the larger Chapel now in course of erection."[35] Concluding the ceremony, Susie addressed the crowd:

> Dear Friends,
>
> I have great pleasure in declaring that this stone is well and truly laid and as for the present moment it represents to us the large edifice which is, we hope, to rise here, we very solemnly dedicate it to the glory of God, and His worship, and to the

sweet memory of His dear servant, C. H. Spurgeon. I want to thank you all for coming here today, and I wish to express double thanks to the dear Tabernacle people; it is so good of them to come. I feel your sympathy and help very much indeed, and I pray you to accept the assurance of my deep gratitude. I bid you a most hearty welcome, both in my own name, and in that of the dear friends at "Beulah."[36]

The inscription on the foundation stone read:

> This stone was laid 7th July 1897,
> By
> Mrs. C. H. Spurgeon,
> to the glory of God,
> and in perpetual remembrance of
> her beloved husband's blameless life,
> 40 years' public ministry,
> and still-continued proclamation of the gospel
> by his printed sermons.

I have hallowed this house, which thou hast built to put My name there forever; and Mine eyes and Mine heart shall be there perpetually. I Kings ix.3

Resta W. Moore,	John S. Hockey,	Charles Thomas,
Architect.	Pastor.	Builder.

Both Charles and Thomas spoke, and referenced their father's gospel ministry and the contributions of their beloved mother. Thomas compared his mother to Queen Victoria: "I suppose that if we were loyal, and only loyal, we would have to say, 'We have no Queen but Victoria.' I yield to none in loyalty to Queen Victoria, but I am bound to say I have another Queen, and she sits upon the platform now. Have we not been favoured with Queen's weather, for the sun shines his brightest on this glad occasion?" Thomas went on to speak of the long and faithful ministry of his father and the tinge of sadness that they felt as well as the "glad joy . . . of our somewhat mournful memories."[37] He recalled his father's love of church planting and then he turned his attention to his mother:

> I venture also to say that I think I see in this marble a symbol
> of my precious mother; she will pardon what I say about her,
> the words shall be very few. You will see in this marble the
> marks of fire it has undergone, processes which in themselves
> were terrible, but which were necessary for the bringing forth
> of such fine-grained stone capable of receiving so high a polish.
> Very few of you can know how my dear mother has suffered
> in her person, and in the bereavement which we cannot forget
> just now. I am sorry to say that, only last week, she has been in
> the fires of pain again, so much so that I almost began to fear
> whether she would be able to be present with us here. But God,
> through the process of trial has brought her to us and to the
> Church what we could not otherwise possess, the fineness of
> her disposition and the polish of her character, you can see it in
> her writings—all this is through the fire of the furnace through
> which the Lord has caused her to pass. I need not tell you I love
> my mother, and I want to renew to her in your hearing and be-
> fore God the pledge of my unfaltering affection. . . . I am as sure
> of her love for me as of mine for her. She had the start of me,
> in fact, but I loved her as soon as I was able to love. Whenever
> I look upon this stone, I shall think lovingly and prayerfully of
> her, and I beg you to do the same.[38]

In keeping with Susie's earnest commitment, "The church was opened on 17th August 1898, free of debt; a local church of England member gave Pastor Hockey a blank cheque to complete the transaction."[39]

Between 700 to 800 people crowded into the new chapel by three o'clock in the afternoon, and "just before the hour for commencing the service, Mrs. Spurgeon entered, leaning upon the arm of her son Charles; and the large congregation spontaneously rose in token of gratitude that she was able to be present on the memorable occasion, and in sympathy with her at the remembrance of her beloved husband, whose name is inseparably associated with the new sanctuary."[40] A "book board made from part of a charred beam in the first Metropolitan Tabernacle" was given to the church to hold the pulpit Bible.[41] The church still today has the board on display. The pulpit itself was a gift from Mr. and Mrs. R. A. Torrey (of the United States), who were friends of Charles and Susie. Torrey ministered with D. L. Moody.[42]

A year after Susie died, the Bexhill church recorded her death in the "Church Minute book on October 22, 1903. A memorial tablet on the north-east wall of the Church to her memory was unveiled on March 16, 1904, by her son, Pastor Charles Spurgeon."[43]

The tablet's inscription reads as follows.

This Tablet is Erected
By
The Church and Congregation Meeting Here
In Grateful Memory Of
Mrs. C. H. Spurgeon,
Who Entered Glory October 22, 1903.
Through Her Initiative Under God
This Church Was Founded
And Largely By Her Liberality
These Buildings Were Erected.
"She hath been a succourer of many." *Romans 16:13.*[44]

In 1899, Mrs. Spurgeon thanked the many people who had helped at Bexhill with the chapel and the manse. Waxing eloquent, she said:

No one standing opposite the Clifford Road, where the two ways meet, and looking upon the block of beautiful buildings which stretch down the street, free from the burden of debt, and dedicated to the glory of God and the extension of the Kingdom of the Lord Jesus Christ, could refuse to see His hand in it all, or refrain from saying, "What hath God wrought!"[45]

Indeed, God did a great work in the planting and establishing of the church at Bexhill, and He did it in large part through a widow. That the church is still vibrant today is a testimony to the vision of Susie Spurgeon.

CHAPTER 15

Seeing the King and His Glory

At the February 10, 1892, memorial service for Charles Spurgeon, held at the Metropolitan Tabernacle, a telegram Susie sent from Mentone was read: "My heart bleeds with yours, but our beloved's joy is full. We shall see him again, and our hearts shall rejoice. Death shall be swallowed up in victory, and the Lord God will wipe away tears from off all faces."[1] Susie fully expected that she, along with the congregants of the Metropolitan Tabernacle, would enjoy fellowship with Charles again and that there was a future day of rejoicing with him in heaven still to come.

Charles had shared Susie's conviction. His "Love Song" to her, penned many years earlier, included a stanza that illustrates a heavenly vision of marriage.

All earthborn love must sleep in the grave,
To its native dust return;
What God hath kindled shall death outbrave,
And in heaven itself shall burn.

Though He who chose us all worlds before
Must reign in our hearts alone,
We fondly believe that we shall adore,
Together before His throne.[2]

In 1895, three years after the death of Charles, Susie wrote, "God comforted me in my affliction, and in His wondrous pity and compassion uplifted me, from the sorrow of my loss, into the joyful hope of eternal reunion in the land that knows no death."[3] She described her life's journey with Charles as "two pilgrims treading this highway of life together, hand in hand,—heart linked to heart."[4] She remembered their trials together as "rivers to ford, and mountains to cross, and fierce enemies to fight, and many dangers to go through."[5] Though in the midst of their challenges, she said that "their Guide was watchful, their Deliverer unfailing."

Their journey was one of mostly "singing." But, eventually,

They came to a place on the road where two ways met; and here, amidst the terrors of a storm such as they had never before encountered, they parted company.[6]

Susie, though, knew that God was her helper:

But the "goodness and mercy" which, for so many years had followed the two travelers, did not leave the solitary one [but rather] the Lord "lead on softly," and chose green pastures for the tired feet, and still waters for the solace and refreshment of His trembling child.[7]

When Charles "parted company" with Susie as he was "caught up to the invisible glory," she felt "battered" and "alone." She later recalled: "On that memorable night, desolate and sorely stricken, I, like Hezekiah, turned my face to the wall, and wept, and cried to the Lord in my distress, and the answer was whispered to my soul in the words of the above text, 'Fear thou not: for I am with thee.'"[8]

The widow years of Susie Spurgeon were a mixture of joy, grief, suffering, and productivity. Along with other ministries that she led, she was faithful to pray for and support the Metropolitan Tabernacle where Charles had invested so much of his heart, energy, and money.

Newspapers in both England and America provided regular updates on Susie, her activities, and her health. *The Brooklyn Daily Eagle* included a somewhat humorous report that, nevertheless, is indicative of the interest in which Susie was held in America.

> The miniature lake in the beautiful grounds at Westwood, Mrs. C. H. Spurgeon's home, always contained, until quite recently, at least one graceful swan. Reading in the papers that the King was reducing his stock of *royal birds*, Mrs. Spurgeon wrote asking whether she would be allowed to purchase one of them. Sir Francis Knollys, in reply, inquired whether his correspondent was Mrs. C. H. Spurgeon of the Metropolitan Tabernacle, and on receiving an affirmative answer, said the King would be pleased to present Mrs. Spurgeon with a bird if she would accept one. The gracious offer, it is unnecessary to say, was accepted, and in due course a letter of thanks was sent. The king once again replied, saying he was glad to have given Mrs. Spurgeon pleasure. The bird, which is a very fine one, has been appropriately named, His Majesty.[9]

The multi-columned Greek architecture of the Tabernacle building stood as one of Charles's greatest achievements, testifying to his enduring ministry among the people of London. And though it would be mostly devastated by fire in April of 1898, Susie was a key reason that the great building rose again from its ashes. Charles would have been proud to know that his son Thomas had taken leadership of the church soon after his death.

On January 1, 1899, nine months after the fire, the Tabernacle basement was reopened for congregational worship, though still disordered from ongoing work. The total cost for rebuilding the Tabernacle was £44,550, of which £16,000 was still needed. Thomas followed in the steps of his father, and he honored the sentiment of his mother in opposing church debt; therefore, the building would only be rebuilt as sufficient funds were at hand.

Thomas and his mother devised a plan to help in the fundraising efforts. Susie imagined that, perhaps, due to the deep love for her husband that remained throughout the great city and around the world, many people might be more inclined to support the Tabernacle's rebuilding effort if she hosted a reception and was present to receive donations. Thomas sent out an advertisement announcing, "My beloved mother (Mrs. C. H. Spurgeon), has most kindly consented to receive gifts at the Tabernacle on the afternoon of Wednesday, February 8th." Furthermore, he said, "The reception will last from 3 till 9 o'clock. Mrs. C. H. Spurgeon herself, on account of her weak state of health, cannot promise beyond 5 o'clock." Thomas, knowing his mother's wishes, continued, "What joy it will give her to be assured that loyalty to Christ and love for her late dear husband will ensure the re-construction (free of debt) of the House of Prayer in which C. H. Spurgeon so long exercised his unique ministry."[10]

Susie penned a letter in support of the effort: "Of all the memorials raised to the dear memory of my beloved husband, this one should have the pre-eminence in our affections." She urged the people to do all that they could and included her address so that they could mail funds directly to her.[11]

After Susie's death, Thomas wrote that she was a contributor to the rebuilding fund of the Tabernacle and that she "delighted us all and rendered invaluable service to the cause, by holding a Reception in the basement of the Tabernacle, on Wednesday February 8th, 1899. At that one sitting, she received not less than £6,367, a record collection, surely, in the annals of Dissent at least."[12] The money raised during those two hours of Susie's presence was equal to about $30,000.00 in American currency in 1899, which is about $100,000.00 valuation today. The ability of Susie to raise so significant an amount of money in short order indicates how highly she was regarded and how deeply people loved and remembered Charles some seven years after his death.

For thirty-six years, Susie was the happy wife of Charles Haddon Spurgeon. After Charles's death, Susie remained faithful to God through her service in the Book Fund, by writing, and through her diligence in the extension of the godly legacy that Charles had left behind. However, her loneliness was sometimes rather acute. On occasion, she sought relief at one of England's seashores. In 1899, Susie traveled to a southeastern coastal town "hoping for restoration of mental and physical strength." She had been there with Charles in early October of 1891. Charles had then written, "Mrs. Spurgeon's company here makes me feel very happy..."[13] This time her companion was her longtime friend Elizabeth.

Day after day, sitting by the shore and watching the waves roll in, she felt depressed and nervous over the work that she had to do with the Book Fund and its auxiliary ministries. She seemed particularly concerned about her son Thomas and his challenging work as the pastor of the Metropolitan Tabernacle. Charles, during his pastorate there, had led in the starting of many ministries, and his presence proved to be essential to their sustenance. After his death, it was difficult to keep the ministries funded. As long as Charles was on the scene, money flowed into the church more freely. After his death and some measure of controversy over who would be the next pastor, the Tabernacle's receipts declined.[14]

The skies appeared like a canvas of bright blue as Susie walked to the end of the pier and planned to spend the morning reading, pondering, responding to correspondence, and taking in the sunshine and fresh air. She was playful after a time and made tiny boats from envelopes and tossed them into the sea. For a little while, she forgot about her anxieties and enjoyed the beauty of creation and the strength that she felt that morning.

As she reached the bottom of her bag of letters, she discovered a gift of £100 to be used as she saw fit in her various ministry pursuits. She turned to her companion Elizabeth and shared the good news. Elizabeth responded, "What an answer to prayer, how beautiful!" and then they joined together in singing the Doxology.

How sweet was the sound of the two aging saints, friends for almost forty years, singing to the wind and the sea of God's rich blessings. Susie imagined God saying to her, "So you thought that I had forgotten you, faithless one; how could you be so foolish and ungrateful? The thousands of pounds which are needed to rebuild My House of Prayer are but the 'small dust' of the treasures of which I am owner and Master!"[15] The "House of Prayer" this time was not Beulah Baptist Chapel at Bexhill, but instead it was the Metropolitan Tabernacle.

As Susie and Elizabeth sang on the pier that spring day in 1899 while the water lapped at the posts below, they were celebrating the faithfulness of God in sending the gift of £100. Susie rebuked herself for worrying as she recounted God's faithfulness in providing for the Tabernacle over the years. It was as if God spoke to her, "Have I not graciously helped and sustained you these many years, and are you going to doubt My pity and My power now?"[16]

Susie then walked along the pier and through a door with a sign over its entrance that read: "Licensed for music, singing, and dancing." She asked herself, "Had not the Lord given me a full and free license and right to be merry at heart that morning? So I went in (the room was, of course, quite empty), and there and then my soul indulged itself in all three symbols of sacred mirth and triumph, for He had put a new song in my mouth, and music into my life, and given wings to the feet of my service!" Susie danced around the room and then walked over to the piano and played a tune while singing at the top of her lungs. She felt as if the very "waves danced for joy, the boisterous wind caught up the notes of my praise, the sea-gulls echoed it as they circled round and round." She sat in the empty music room "happy, humbled, overwhelmed by a sense of the undeserved goodness of the Lord."[17] This was Susie's testimony time and again as she had witnessed God's care and provision throughout her life.

༚༅༚

When the Metropolitan Tabernacle was reopened, September 1900, the *Los Angeles Times* carried a headline: "Spurgeon's Church. It Has Risen from Its Ashes and Will Be Reopened This Week—A Half-burned Bible and a Widow's Devotion." The story was of a Bible that was recovered in the ashes of the Tabernacle and offered detail about Susie's fundraising effort in 1899.

A good portion of the new Tabernacle found its funds in a rather peculiar reception that this devoted old lady held in the unfinished Tabernacle one afternoon last February. In the first place her physician absolutely forbade it, but that made no difference. She proposed to see her congregation—for she considered that the congregation belonged to her as much as to her son, the present pastor—and see them she did, doctor or no doctor.

She was placed in a chair on the platform, the swarming workmen were cleared out for a time and the congregation came in. Shopkeepers shut up shop to be present, and city clerks got a rare half-holiday. One by one the great crowd filed by the old pastor's widow, whose simple black dress made her look more pale and frail than ever, and each one shook her hand and gave her a sealed envelope.

That procession continued for two hours, and when it was over there was $30,000, mostly in small sums, piled up beside Mrs. Spurgeon, and $6,500 more came by mail. She had been an invalid for twenty-five years, and how she managed to stand the emotional and physical strain of that afternoon, no one knows. She says it was an answer to prayer.[18]

It was an answer to prayer indeed. The regard for the memory of Charles and love for Susie was evident in that shops had closed, clerks were let off of work early, and numerous people from across the city had lined up to give Susie money for the support of the Tabernacle. The paper also included a sad note: "It is not thought probable that Mrs. Spurgeon will ever be able to see, in its finished state, the edifice that she did so much to rebuild." The paper furthermore reported, "At Westwood . . . is the air of a place whose owner lies ill, a nurse tells you that Mrs. Spurgeon cannot be seen, and in the entry there stands an invalid's chair that has been used seldom indeed of late."[19]

Physically and emotionally, for the rest of her life, Susie experienced a number of low points, and often she was confined to her bedroom, though not always to her bed. During those times, she felt significant pain and weakness. She received letters from near and far and she was appreciative of the sympathetic expressions that found their way to her bedside.[20]

In the late winter of 1900, Susie underwent another surgery, and, like her first one from 1868, its nature was not revealed. *The Sword and the Trowel* noted:

> Our readers will rejoice to know that Mrs. C. H. Spurgeon's doctor believes that he has discovered and removed the cause of her recent severe suffering. The operation was successfully performed on Monday, February 12, by Dr. Bunn, of Upper Norwood, assisted by his partner, Dr. Rutherford; and each day since, up to the time of making up these "Notes," the doctor has been able to report that his patient has been going on "satisfactorily." This gives additional reason for blending thanksgiving with the supplications which many are offering on Mrs. Spurgeon's behalf.[21]

However, by March, her improvement stalled, and her pain increased.[22] In the months that followed, she made progress and enjoyed some seasons of relief, only to be cast back into the bed of affliction again.

In May of 1901, Susie wrote, "Dear Friends, I have longed, oh! so intensely, for the time to come when I might again speak in these pages of the Lord's loving dealings with me, and let you know how, throughout a long and trying time of suffering, His grace has been sufficient for me." She continued, "Sometimes I have prayed, 'Do, dear Lord, enable me to write, if only a brief paragraph, just to tell of all Thy mercy and loving-kindness to me; let me praise Thee from 'out of the depths' into which Thou didst bring me!'" She lamented, "But I found that His will for me was that I should be silent; He locked up thoughts and words, restrained all mental activity, and brought me so low that a sense of absolute powerlessness bound both body and spirit." Her aim in writing that note was not to burden her readers with further details of her sufferings but that they would help her to "honour my Lord by praising Him for the 'grace abounding.'" She also had hoped to help her readers: "I would fain comfort dear afflicted friends with the comfort wherewith I myself am comforted of God. Perhaps He will permit this at a distant day; but, for the present, weakness still cripples my pen, and I can say no more."[23]

Often as she rested at Westwood, she reflected on her earlier travels with Charles. "Ah! 'tender grace of a day that is dead,' thy joy is not lessened by distance, nor lost by separation; rather is it stored both in Heaven and in my heart's deepest chambers, and some day, when that casket is broken, it will 'come back to me,' not here, but in that happy land where the days die not, where 'the touch of a vanished hand' shall be felt again, and 'the sound of a voice that is still' shall again make music in my ravished ears!"[24]

When Charles died in 1892, she envisioned joining him in heaven and singing praises around God's throne. Prior to his death, Susie considered faithful Christians who had died and who were with Christ. Though confident in their eternal security in Christ, Susie nevertheless grieved the loss of Christian loved ones, friends, and people connected to her church and the Book Fund. With every death, she knew that "in the homes of our friends, dark shadows had gathered over hearts left desolate, and with sympathetic grief we could feel the chilling gloom of the fatal messenger's presence, though he had but *passed our door*."[25]

In October of 1903, the "messenger" did not pass Susie's door; he tarried.

On one of the last days of her life, Susie summoned Thomas to her bedside (October 17, 1903) and blessed him. Thomas said that the "parting benediction from her dear lips" would "echo in my grateful heart till I also hear the Master's call." It was the blessing of "Christiana's farewell blessing on her children: —'THE BLESSING—THE DOUBLE BLESSING OF YOUR FATHER'S GOD BE UPON YOU, AND UPON YOUR BROTHER FOR EVER AND EVER! AMEN.'"[26] A little later she added, "GOOD-BYE, DEAR TOM, THE LORD BLESS YOU FOR EVER AND EVER! AMEN."[27]

On the previous day, Susie had engaged in joyful conversation with her "faithful friend and companion, Miss Thorne." Thomas remarked that Elizabeth had "nursed her in this last illness with a devotion that could be born only of deep affection." Susie asked her friend, "Whom shall I see next?" Elizabeth replied, "Whom would you like to see, darling?" Thomas recounted, "Then, with a face all a-flame with the joy of blest anticipation, the exile, so soon to be brought home, she exclaimed, 'MY HUSBAND!'"[28]

Charles Ray noted that Susie, at the end her life, manifested "strong faith in the God whom she had trusted for so long." She was able to muster the strength to declare, "Though he slay me, yet will I trust in him" (Job 13:15). Confidently she asserted, "His love in times past forbids me to think, He'll leave me at last in trouble to sink." She requested that those in the room with her "complete the verse."[29] Near the very end she testified, "Blessed Jesus! Blessed Jesus! I can see the King in his glory."[30] Susie Spurgeon died on Thursday, October 22, 1903, and was later buried alongside her beloved husband.

The Baptist reported that a notice was posted outside of the Tabernacle on the morning of Susie's death that simply read: "Mrs. C. H. Spurgeon entered Heaven at 8:30 this morning."[31]

Thomas Spurgeon summarized his mother's remarkable life:

At half-past eight on the morning of Thursday, October 22nd, 1903, "My Mother" was not, for God took her. There had been much suffering during the last illness, but the end itself was peace. When the world was waking, she was falling on sleep, to wake in the brighter world on high. Such was the passing of a truly remarkable woman, —good, gifted, gracious; a succourer of many, especially of the struggling servants of the King. They in their thousands rise up, with her sorrowing sons, to call her blessed. Who can tell the joys that now entrance her ransomed soul? Ah, mother mine, the "happy land" you sang about to your little boys, the dear Redeemer to whom you pointed them, the loving husband, for another sight of whom your heart has yearned so long, the holy service, and the sacred rest of which you wrote so sweetly, —all these are yours for evermore! "Amen, so let it be!"[32]

Thomas wrote of her devotion to her family:

It would be difficult to say what the faithful wife did not do for her toiling husband during these happy early years. She consoled him in his sorrows and disappointments; she succoured him, "as an angel of God," when men spake all manner of evil against him falsely, she nursed him in his sicknesses, she entertained his guests, and accompanied him on his foreign travels. She even reproduced for him a sermon he had delivered in his sleep from a text which he had failed to expound satisfactorily before he retired to rest.

On September 20th, 1856, two boys were given of God to crown with joy the wedded hearts; and henceforth, she lived and laboured for her sons as well as her husband. In the old home at

Nightingale Lane she was both wife and mother, and a model of what each should be. She had the joy of seeing her sons grow up to fear God, and to preach the Gospel of His grace; and she knew full well that her patient training had much to do with this. I trace my early conversion directly to her earnest pleading and bright example. She denied herself the pleasure of attending Sunday evening services that she might minister the Word of Life to her household. There she taught me to sing, but to mean it first,

> "I do believe, I will believe,
> That Jesus died for me;
> That, on the cross, He shed His blood
> From sin to set me free."

My dear brother was brought to Christ through the pointed word of a missionary; but he, too, gladly owns that mother's influence and teaching had their part in the matter. These made the soil ready for a later sowing. So that each of us can say,

> "And if I e'er in Heaven appear,
> A mother's holy prayer,
> A mother's hand and gentle tear,
> That pointed to a Saviour dear
> Have led the wandered there."[33]

On Tuesday, October 27 at 11:30 a.m., relatives and friends of Susie Spurgeon gathered in the library at Westwood. Her coffin, draped with flowers, was the focal point in the room. A memorial service was held, led by Pastors W. Fuller Gooch and J. S. Hockey. The song chosen for the service was "Art thou weary?"

The October 30, 1903, edition of *The Baptist* published a detailed report of Susie's funeral service that was held at Chatsworth Road Baptist

Chapel, not far from Westwood and a five-minute walk from the West Norwood Cemetery where she was to be buried beside Charles. The headline in large bold print read:

THE
HOME-GOING OF MRS. C. H. SPURGEON.
LARGE ASSEMBLY AT FUNERAL SERVICE
PATHETIC SCENES AT THE GRAVESIDE.[34]

The Baptist reported that the funeral service was set for one o'clock, but many mourners arrived by noon. By the time the procession arrived, the chapel seats were filled and a number of students from the Pastors' College had to stand. The majority of the congregation was made up of women, dressed in black. Twenty girls from the Stockwell Orphanage sang, and the organist played peaceful music.

> At five minutes past one Pastor Archibald Brown and Mr. C. B. Sawday met the coffin at the doors, and the large congregation rose. Slowly, very slowly, the oak casket, hidden in lovely wreaths, was carried down the aisle, and when placed within the communion rail, was surrounded by palms and fronted by a bed of white flowers on black velvet, bearing the word "Rest."

Thomas and Charles Spurgeon walked together down the aisle with Thomas's son Harold just behind them. Following them was Susie's cousin and longtime friend Susannah Olney, and other members from the Spurgeon family—brother, nephew, and three sisters of Charles Spurgeon along with other family and friends. Included in the family procession were the servants and gardeners from Westwood, who were very much like family.

Charles and Susie's longtime friend and pastor of the church, Archibald Brown, who had presided at Charles's funeral, brought the sermon. Pastor G. Turner and C. B. Sawday assisted. Surrounding the coffin were many flowers from the "Societies at the Tabernacle, its Elders, its Deacons, and its Stewards, while not a few other Churches sent their tributes too, with the Orphans and the Students."[35]

⁂

The Baptist recounted the re-formation of the procession to make its way to the West Norwood Cemetery and to "the crest of the hill where stands the beautiful monument covering the vault in which has hitherto lain the mortal remains of the great preacher. The congregation toiled up the slopes through drizzling rain, and when Mr. Archibald Brown read the final sentences his hearers' faces were hidden under a crown of umbrellas."

Following Pastor Brown's concluding remarks, the students of the Pastors' College began the final song: William Cowper's hymn, "There Is a Fountain."

> E'er since, by faith, I saw the stream
> Thy flowing wounds supply,
> Redeeming love has been my theme, and shall be till I die:
> And shall be till I die, and shall be till I die.[36]

The crowd joined the Pastors' College students in singing as the great hymn of God's redeeming love filled the skies at the West Norwood Cemetery.[37]

As the crowd dispersed and the reporter, along with Rev. Hobbs, looked over the flowers that draped the ground near the large vault, it was noted: "With us stood the young pastor of Beulah, Thornton Heath, of which Mrs. Spurgeon has been a member since 1889. The church had sent a wreath, as had the stewards of the Tabernacle, and the church at Greenwich." Church records of Beulah, Thornton Heath reveal in their official minutes that indeed Susie had joined their church in 1889.[38] The church was a very short walk or drive from Westwood and Susie was able to attend on occasion, something she could not have done if she had attempted the longer drive to the Tabernacle.

Church records at the Metropolitan Tabernacle indicate that Susie remained on *its* membership roll until her death. The most likely scenario is that Susie never requested that her membership be removed from the Tabernacle, and yet she was also allowed to join the Beulah Church because it was near to her home and, in her sickly condition, she was able to attend on occasion. However, after Susie's death, the Metropolitan Tabernacle denied that Susie had ever been a member of Beulah. While a member at Beulah, Susie made donations to the church's ministries and gave encouragement to the church in her correspondence. Surprisingly, she even donated their first organ—to be used for the glory of God and not for any entertainment purposes. Surprising, because Charles did not employ musical instruments at the Metropolitan Tabernacle. Regardless, Charles had been instrumental in planting Beulah Baptist, Thornton Heath, and his secretary, Harrald, had served as the church's first pastor.

One of the guests at the funeral and graveside service for Susie was Pastor Thomas L. Johnson. Johnson was a former slave from Virginia who, after the American Civil War, had made his way to England, and had sought out Charles Spurgeon. Charles, hearing his testimony, admitted Johnson to the Pastors' College (entering the school at age forty). It was during his enslavement that Johnson had first heard of Spurgeon from his slaveholder; and the more Johnson heard, the more he wanted to know about him.

Never did he imagine making a journey to England to meet the famous preacher.[39] After his first meeting with Charles, Johnson said, "His first words set me at ease, but his sympathetic kindness was beyond my highest hope. He took me by the hand, asked me a few questions, and wished me success."[40]

After his time at the college, Johnson left for Africa with the Baptist Missionary Society to serve his native land. While there, he wrote to Susie and sent her a verse from a song. She recorded a portion of his note in her book *Ten Years of My Life*. "A quaint message comes to me today across the sea from Africa. It stirs pleasant memories and well fulfills the loving commission given to encourage and strengthen my heart. Thus it runs: 'Tell dear Mrs. Spurgeon to "Keep inching along, Jesus Christ'll come by-an-by.""[41]

After a year in Africa, Johnson's wife was stricken by sickness and soon died. Johnson's own health was poor, and it was recommended that he return to America for medical care.[42] Susie mailed him a box of books, and Charles enclosed ten pounds. During the war, Charles had entered the fray and taken a strong stand against slavery. His stand was costly. Though Charles was often invited to preach in America during the years of the Civil War, he was threatened that he would be beaten or worse if he were to accept such an offer. Spurgeon's sermons were burned in Alabama. One scholar notes: "Anti-Spurgeon bonfires illuminated jail yards, plantations, bookstores, and courthouses throughout the Southern states."[43] That said, Charles and Susie's regard for all men, regardless of race, was notable in their friendship with and their love for Johnson. Charles and Susie were not ones to test the wind's direction to determine their convictions. They simply sought to be faithful to Christ.

Johnson returned to England from America in November of 1891, and in February of 1892, he attended Charles's funeral in London. In the summer, he and his second wife moved near to Susie at Sydenham, the location of the Crystal Palace. He then traveled to Plymouth for missions work and later returned to London where, due to his sickness, it was decided that he could not return to Africa. Johnson preached at Bournemouth and in various places across the Continent. *The Baptist* stated, "He has received constant kindness at the hands of Mrs. Spurgeon, and has had the melancholy satisfaction of being present at both funeral services [Charles and Susie's]."

Charles and Susie Spurgeon had helped bring the gospel to thousands and helped transform hearts for Christ. What Susie wrote after the death of Charles could now be said about both of them: To those who knew them best, and therefore loved them most, their precious memory grows dearer and sweeter every day. There was no one like them in all the world. "What an attraction Heaven now presents!" The Lord Jesus is there, and Charles and Susie with him.

On that October morning in 1903, Susie met the Savior who she had long trusted and was rejoined in fellowship with Charles whom she had long loved.

Johnson's writing about Susie's passing is a testament to the love of Charles and Susie Spurgeon, to the grace and goodness of the God they loved, and to the legacy of Susie, herself:

On October 22nd, 1903, dear Mrs. Spurgeon passed to her rest, and by her departure I lost one of my most kind and helpful friends. I attended the funeral at Norwood. In February 1892, I was present at the funeral of Mr. Spurgeon, at Norwood. There was a similar manifestation of sorrow on this occasion, but also the same triumphant Christian sentiments expressed. Here is a little hymn I composed at that time:

GONE HOME.
IN MEMORY OF OUR DEAR MRS. C. H. SPURGEON.

"Because I live, ye shall live also." John XIV.19.

God's promise of covenant love,
Which links us to the Home above.
Gone home to live with Jesus,
Our Prophet, Priest, and King;
And in His blessed presence,
Redemption's song to sing.
Gone home to live with Jesus,
The ever loving One:

Who left His home in Glory
That sinners might be won.

Gone home to live with Jesus,
To share that Heavenly Rest:
And with her own beloved,
To be forever blest.[44]

The Legacy of Susannah Spurgeon

Susie Spurgeon is mostly tucked away beneath the truths and legends of her famous husband. Students know her primarily as Charles Spurgeon's wife; they are aware that she donated books to poor pastors and that she was an invalid, but not much more.

Although Susie's accomplishments were not as mountainous as were her famous husband's, they are significant. On the one hand, we should not cast her in marble and pay any homage to her that is due only to God. After all, she struggled with sin, was fearful at times, and dealt with loneliness. On the other hand, we should give her the honor that is due her name.

As she would no doubt agree, we should avoid the sort of entrance that Richard Day gave to her in his biography of Spurgeon, "Enter the heroine," but we should nevertheless appreciate her for who she was. And though we can't accomplish the same things in the same ways that Susie did, we can certainly glean principles from her life that are worthy of our consideration and imitation. If Susie Spurgeon remained faithful to God, even beneath the presses of affliction, and instead of complaining served God, then, by God's grace, we can also.

SUSIE LOOKED TO JESUS

"Look unto me, and be ye saved, all the ends of the earth: for I am God, and there is none else." Those words from Isaiah 45:22 were often on the lips of Charles Spurgeon. It was in a small chapel on a snowy Sunday morning when the message of looking to Christ sped to his heart from the lips of an uneducated lay preacher who preached from that same passage. Spurgeon looked to Christ and was saved.

Rev. S. B. Bergene preached from Romans chapter 10 at the Poultry Chapel of London. Susie looked to Christ and was saved. Later, when she penned her Christian testimony for Charles as a part of the church membership process at the New Park Street Chapel, he responded that though he was amazed at the depth of her Christian testimony, "I could not imagine that you had *seen* (emp.) such great sights, and were so thoroughly versed in soul-knowledge."[1]

Susie later wrote:

Eyes and heart are both sorely aching with grief at the sight of the sin, and selfishness, and sorrow, which are within and around me; but help me, dear Lord, to look up, enable me to 'lift up mine eyes unto the hills, from whence cometh mine help." As travellers on the great mountains refrain from looking down the steep precipices, keeping their eyes fixed on the heights above lest a sudden vertigo should overcome them, so may I look unto the Lord with humble, steadfast gaze, and receive courage and strength to press onward and upward in the path he has marked out for me![2]

Susie's life and message says to us, "Look to Jesus." This message she offered to non-Christians and Christians alike. She would say to every

Christian grieving over, fighting against, and hating their sin, or suffering through physical or emotional pain to look to Christ for help.

SUSIE TRAINED HER CHILDREN IN THE WAYS OF THE LORD

It is widely believed that it was due to Susie's serious health problems that she was unable to give birth to more children. Regardless, she was faithful to train her twin sons in the gospel. Charles was often in faraway cities and villages preaching, but, even so, he had no concerns as to the spiritual training of his sons. Similarly, Charles's own father had often been away from home for ministry, and, therefore, much of Charles's spiritual instruction in his childhood and youth was left to his mother.

One evening, while en route to a preaching engagement, Charles's father, John Spurgeon, was troubled over feelings of guilt for not spending sufficient time with his children. He turned back home, and, upon arriving, overheard his wife "pleading most earnestly for the salvation of all her children, and specifically for Charles, her first-born and strong-willed son." Hearing her prayers gave John confidence that his family was in good hands while he was away. Charles wrote, "My father felt that he might safely go about his Master's business while his dear wife was caring so well for the spiritual interests of the boys and girls at home, so he did not disturb her, but proceeded at once to fulfill his preaching engagement."[3]

Charles Ray recalled of Susie, "Although so weak and ailing and confined to her bedroom for such long periods of time, Mrs. Spurgeon was a faithful trainer of her twin sons in the Christian doctrine, and she had the joy of seeing them both brought to Christ at an early age."[4] Both boys were baptized on September 21, 1874, and Mrs. Spurgeon was able to attend the services, something rare for her at that time due to her health.

The church honored Charles and Susie at the service:

On that occasion she was presented by the church with an illuminated address, in which hearty thanks were expressed "to

Almighty God for calling so early in life to the fellowship of the saints the two sons of our beloved and honoured pastor," and praising "our gracious Lord that it should have pleased Him to use so greatly the pious teachings and example of our dear sister, Mrs. Spurgeon, to the quickening and fostering of the divine life in the hearts of her twin sons, and we earnestly pray that amidst her long-continued sufferings she may ever be consoled with all spiritual comfort and by the growing devoutness of those who are thus twice given to her in the Lord."[5]

Susie read the Bible, prayed, and sang with her boys around the piano—all the while teaching them the importance of integrity in their profession of faith. Both Thomas and Charles became gospel ministers, and they served admirably. After Charles's death, Thomas was eventually called as pastor of the Metropolitan Tabernacle. When Susie died, her son Charles said of her, "Far too little has been heard of the surpassing wealth of blessing and the unrivalled sweetness of the influence, exerted by the dear sufferer whose home-going we mourn."[6]

SUSIE LOVED AND TREASURED THE BIBLE AND READ MANY BOOKS

Susie's habit was to read through the Bible every year and also to meditate on a small portion of Scripture each day. Similarly, Charles was well acquainted with the Scripture, but he said that his preference was to

lay my soul asoak [sic] in half a dozen verses all day than rinse my hand in several chapters. Oh, to be bathed in a text of Scripture, and to let it be sucked up into your very soul, till it saturates your heart! Set your heart upon God's Word! Let your whole nature be plunged into it as cloth into a dye![7]

Even a cursory reading of Susie's published works reveals a lady who was well steeped in the Bible *and* who drank deeply from the well of other authors. Books were essential to Susie and Charles's relationship. One of Susie's first gifts to Charles was a full set of John Calvin's commentaries. Charles inscribed the following in volume one:

The volumes making up a complete set of Calvin were a gift to me from my own dear, tender wife. Blessed may she be among women. How much of comfort and strength she has ministered unto me it is not in my power to estimate. She has been to me God's best earthly gift, and not a little even of heavenly treasure has come to me by her means. She has often been as an angel of God unto me.[8]

Susie read widely from a variety of authors whom she deemed loved Christ. She esteemed Frances Havergal's works and considered them "royal books." After Havergal died, Susie spoke of her hymns as "heavenly music" and her songs as "angelic." Of her books, Susie commended her treatise *Kept for the Master's Use* because of its teaching on consecration. She said that it was—

her swan-like death song, the sweetest and best of all. I intend, as long as I can afford it, to put this pearl of books, as an *extra* blessing, into every parcel I send out from the Book Fund, and may the Lord grant that through its sweet influence many may be led to consecrate body, soul, and spirit anew to His service and His cause.[9]

Susie's appreciation of books was, in part, due to the example of Charles.

My love for the Book Fund work is frequently stimulated by noting the tender regard my husband has for his books, and the constant and patient use he makes of them; and a glance at the well-filled shelves at home sets my heart a-longing to introduce like blessings into the scantily-furnished studies of our needy brethren.[10]

SUSIE LOVED PASTORS AND THEIR FAMILIES

Susie was committed to helping pastors, especially those who were associated with the Pastors' College and those who struggled in poverty. For the annual Pastors' College Conference, her gift of a book to each student was one of the highlights of the event. Susie's appreciation of the pastoral office began when as a youth she attended the services of Pastor James Smith at the Metropolitan Tabernacle. Over time she increasingly valued the pastoral office, gave priority to Spurgeon's ministry in her marriage, encouraged him in his reading and study, and longed for other pastors to enjoy the benefits that he enjoyed in owning and reading books. Her two books on the Book Fund are a treasury of compassionate interaction between her and pastors.

Charles once asked:

What must ministries become if their [pastors] minds are starved? Is it not a duty to relieve the famine which is raging in many a manse? Is it not a prudential measure, worthy of attention of all who wish to see the masses influenced by religion, that the preachers who occupy our pulpits should be kept well furnished with material for thought?[11]

And Susie answered.

In Victorian England, the more refined congregations valued the polished pulpiteer. Charles, though teeming with old-fashioned Puritanism, could nevertheless fill any building in England to overflow at a moment's notice (once preaching to well over twenty-thousand people at the Crystal Palace). But most of England's pastors did not preach to large crowds; they served much smaller congregations of very meager means and, therefore, the pastor was often insufficiently paid. These pastors were often married with several children who were only barely fed and clothed. Therefore, though books would have greatly benefited both pastor and church, a godly pastor prioritized the physical needs of his family over and beyond his own needs.

Empty bookshelves came at a great price to both pastor and congregation. Susie understood that—she loved pastors, and she loved their churches. She knew that to invest in a pastor was to invest in the church, the gospel, and the spread of God's kingdom. She argued, "Books are not *luxuries* to the under-paid and over-worked pastor, but simply indispensable tools for his labour."[12] Charles believed that "to build cathedrals is little compared with building up preachers." Loving pastors was at the heart of both Charles and Susie; they invested in ministers through the Pastors' College, the Book Fund, the Pastor's Aid Fund, and in innumerable other ways. Susie's legacy is cast in love for pastors. Beyond the books, she often ministered financial aid and supplied clothing and other resources.

Susie wrote, "Somebody said to me once in a letter—'Three empty things often keep company: an empty bookshelf, an empty head, and an empty chapel.'" She could readily recall "scores of instances in which the empty pocket and the empty cupboards were actually responsible for the three former 'empties.'. . . It is usually a lack of liberal ministration *from the people to the pastor* which results in the famishing of the whole community." She continued,

> Keep your minister's table well provided, and you shall be fed
> with the finest of the wheat; see that his earthly cares do not
> press on him painfully, and your own hearts' burdens will be

lifted by his heavenly teachings; supply him with this world's needful comforts and he will not fail to bring you solace and consolation in your time of extremity. If he has sown unto you spiritual things, is it a great thing that he shall reap carnal things?[13]

She recognized that there were some churches that were so poor that they could do no more; therefore, she believed that larger churches should come to the aid of the poorer congregations to help support their pastor and ministry.

One year after her death, the August 1904 edition of *The Sword and the Trowel* published an appeal that speaks to the longevity of Susie's work. "Miss E. H. Thorne, to whom Mrs. C. H. Spurgeon bequeathed her Book and Pastor's Aid Funds, would be very grateful for donations and parcels of clothing for these Funds. Address, —'Westwood,' Beulah Hill, Upper Norwood, London, S.E."[14]

In 1903, Charles Ray completed his biography of Susie. He desired that the Book Fund not lack for money or effort. "The work must not flag for lack of funds, and as the demand has always been so much greater than the supply, the wherewithal to provide the books cannot be received too quickly."[15]

Charles and Susie were generous with their money while they were alive, and in God's bountiful provision, they enjoyed a lifestyle that allowed them the ability to support others.

When Charles died, he left a significant enough estate to care for Susie for the remainder of her days. She had sufficient funds, servants to assist her, and relationships to sustain her. As well, her two sons ministered near to her home. Therefore, it is no surprise that Susie continued her benevolence in supporting others and in leaving money behind to help further support and advance the Book Ministry. Ray writes, "That the devoted woman who originated the Fund, who conducted it with such splendid success for so long, and who gave so generously in her lifetime of her services and substance, has left some money for the Fund will doubtless only act as an incentive to other 'stewards of the Lord' to give liberally, so that this important effort may more and more cope with the need which led to its institution."[16]

Elizabeth Thorne's oversight of Mrs. Spurgeon's Book Fund continued until 1913, after which there is no known record of its continuation as a formal ministry. However, Susie's example had already spun many other such works that gave away, loaned, or provided in some other way books, clothes, and support for impoverished pastors and their families.

One modern example of how Susie's book distribution ministry lives on can be found in the Banner of Truth Book Fund that "supplies ministers, missionaries, colleges and seminaries, and needy individuals all around the world with books either free of charge or at heavily subsidized prices." This fund was inspired around 1960 "by the story of Mrs. Spurgeon's Book Fund." The result, "hundreds of thousands of books have been sent out all over the world."[17]

SUSIE LOOKED FOR THE BEAUTY OF GOD IN ALL THINGS—AND FOUND CREATIVE WAYS TO COMMUNICATE HIS BEAUTY TO OTHERS

Susie remembered an evening stroll along the grounds of Westwood to "gather roses—to preserve their perfumed leaves." She described how her roses had stood up to the "fervid glances of the sun, and the hot kisses of the South wind" and yet, in the midst of such a trial, she found them "blooming in clusters of unusual beauty . . . apparently as fresh, and cool, and invigorated as if the blessed rain for which we had prayed had already fallen." As she gathered the roses, she caught a bloom that was falling to the ground. She noticed that it was "besprinkled with water." She then perceived that the "shake of the rose" had brought forth water from its "inmost recesses." The reservoir of water, contained within *all* of Susannah's roses, had strengthened them "against the heat of the day" and refreshed them with water from within.[18] She applied her discovery to Christians struggling under the "heat and burden of the day":

> Think a moment on my roses and how tenderly God has provided for their need. Could He be less thoughtful for thine? Has He made such wonderful provision for their sustenance and refreshment during the days of drought, and "forgotten to be gracious" to thee? Ah, no! Thou well knowest it is not so.[19]

Susie's books reflect the beauty of God as displayed in creation and in all of life. With the stroke of her pen she uncovers lessons, in beautiful prose, from birds, trees, mountains, rivers, and the moon and stars. Susie didn't simply see water on roses and turn away; she described the water and the roses, and she looked deeper and recognized God's provision for his creation. Like Charles, she rejected a false spirituality that closed its eyes to the beauty of the world around her. She embraced beauty and described beautiful things in ways that drew attention to the glory of God and her own enjoyment. It is not just nature in which she savored beauty; she described items in her home, Spurgeon's pens, his books, and a chair in his study descriptively.

SUSIE FACED HARDSHIPS WITH FAITH AND SERVICE

Susie was a great sufferer; however, she was not a great complainer. One of the endearing qualities about her is that she did not suffer in complete privacy; some of that was by choice, but other was due to the interest that so many people had in her. Her experiences were printed in newspapers around the world. She saw her trials as a means to depend on God and to give Him glory. Her stories of suffering led others to pray for her and help them to see the trustworthiness of God in the midst of their own suffering.

Her son Charles wrote:

Sick saints are fair lilies surrounded by the thickets of their wants, that they may be for Christ alone; such a lily was my dear mother, shut up in the prison-house of pain so that she might shed a fragrant influence through her Book Fund, and thereby perfume the hearts and homes of many, and make the Church of God redolent with the aroma of a consecrated life.

He continued by quoting Susie's own words:

When the storms come, and our trees of delight are bare and leafless, when He strips us of the comforts to which His love has accustomed us—or more painful still,—when He leaves us alone in the world, to mourn the absence of the chief desire of our heart;—to sing to Him *then*, to bless and praise and laud His dear name *then*, this is the work of His free grace only.[20]

What is striking about Susie in reference to her trials is that her most significant suffering began so early in her life and marriage, when she was but thirty-five years old, maybe younger. Charles was exchanging letters with her surgeon by 1867. In July of 1869, Spurgeon writes to his father, "My poor wifey gets weaker and weaker tis always full of pain. However, all must be well."[21]

Susie's faith, perseverance, and hard work in the midst of her sufferings were remarkable. The Book Fund began in 1875, and she managed it until her death. Her first book was published in 1886; she became the editor of *The Sword and the Trowel* after Charles died and continued for several years. Her church planting efforts began in 1896, and by 1900, she had completed the publication of all four large volumes of the *Autobiography* of Spurgeon. She had raised $30,000.00 in two hours on a cold February day in 1899 to help rebuild the fire-destroyed Tabernacle. She answered hundreds of letters, and even near the end of her life, she still was managing the Book Fund.

Her son Charles wrote, "Most indefatigable in her work, she to the end laboured for the Lord, and even when the mind was weary, and the body exceedingly weak, she would persist in selecting some more texts, as was her wont, for the Illustrated Almanack; and constantly displayed her anxiety lest some poor minister be forgotten, and be kept waiting for his long-looked-for prize of books."[22] She did all these things while suffering greatly. Someone had sent Susie a quotation that she framed and hung in her sick room: "God never makes a mistake." She trusted God and believed that His ways are always right. Such an attitude kept her going when her energy was drained.

Susie did all that she could for as long as she could. She is also honored for her simple acts of service at the New Park Street Chapel and the Metropolitan Tabernacle. Thomas Spurgeon remembered that "in all the good works of the ever-growing Church, Mrs. C. H. Spurgeon took her proper part, and one of her tenderest ministries was attending to and exhorting the female candidates for baptism. How many greet me, to this day, with such glad words as these, 'She led me to the baptismal pool, you know, and I shall never forget her loving words to me.'"[23]

SUSIE ADVANCED HER HUSBAND'S LEGACY

Susie's greatest legacy was not through the Book Fund, nor was it her church planting, nor the various other church ministries that she was engaged in, nor was it the books that she authored. Her greatest legacy is her ministry to and love for her beloved husband and her advocacy of his writings and ministry.

Susie's marriage to Charles was truly a lifelong romance. Charles could not have met the demands of his ministry, have written so prolifically, and have left such an indelible mark on history without the encouragement of Susie. She read to him when he was depressed, prayed diligently for him when he was away from home, wept with him in his trials, and cared for him in his sicknesses. She even had a term of endearment for him: "Tirshatha," meaning, "Your Reverence."[24]

Charles, because he enjoyed the love of such a godly woman, felt free to express his joys and his sorrows with her. And though she felt stinging pain when he was slandered in the press, she thanked God that "he lived to be honoured above most men for his uprightness and fidelity."[25] Charles responded to the respect that he received from Susie with many sincere displays of love. He understood the importance of his beloved's encouragement to his life and ministry. In a letter dated March 18, 1856, to his mother, Spurgeon gushed with thanksgiving:

> Susie is a blessed creature and does not attempt to keep me
> from the Lord's work but on the contrary she is willing to deny
> herself for the Lord's sake. How sweetly she cheers me when
> I think I have not preached well and she bids me go on again
> and whispers, "What—you, unbelieving? At such unexampled
> success—what, you doubt?"[26]

It was much easier for Spurgeon to preach, write, and lead in ministry because of the encouragement and cheers of his "precious love." Susie's preferential encouragement of Charles was an investment in him but also an investment in the spread of the gospel. It is largely because of her support that Charles is so widely read and benefited from today.

After Charles's death, Susie spent the rest of her life promoting the gospel that he loved through her work of preserving his story in the *Autobiography* and through the translation and dissemination of his books and sermons around the world. Susan Barker writes, "During the 28 years that Susannah Spurgeon was in charge of the Book Fund nearly 200,000 books were placed into the hands of over 25,000 ministers and many hundreds of thousands of sermons were sent throughout the world. . . . As a result, Charles Haddon Spurgeon's name became known, not just because he was a powerful preacher, but because his books and sermons were distributed widely in Britain, and, indeed, throughout the world by 'Mrs. Spurgeon's Book Fund.'"[27]

Susie often wrote about her "Work Abroad." A few of the countries where missionaries and others received parcels from her fund included New Zealand, China, Congo, and India. Through Susie's influence, the fame of Charles Spurgeon increased and spread long after he had gone to be with Christ. Charles lived on in Susie's heart, and though she remained faithful in service until she died, she also longed to be reunited with her dear husband in heaven.

Pastor Archibald Brown said of Susie: "Our sister is done with days, and months, and passing seasons. It is all eternal Sabbath. With her beloved, and ours, she sees the King. The two have now met. She, who watched his last breath on earth, has breathed her last, and that last breath has re-united them forever."[28]

❦

Charles Ray surmised, "If greatness depends on the amount of good which one does in the world, if it is only another name for unselfish devotion in the service of others—and surely true greatness is all this—then Mrs. C. H. Spurgeon will go down to posterity as one of the greatest women of her time."[29]

Susie never thought of herself as a great woman, and certainly not as one of the greatest women of all time. She felt the weight of her sin. She was anxious when Charles was away from home. She was quick to admit and repent of her sins, and was honest with her friends and readers about her struggles, and she lived hopefully by remembering that all she had experienced was because God loved her.

What would Susie say if she could speak to us now from heaven? Her son Thomas imagined such an occurrence: "Methinks she would press upon us, even more earnestly and sweetly than before, the preciousness of the Word, and our duty to hide it in our hearts. She would bid us prize and plead the promises. She would charge us to cling to the Cross and to cleave to that which is good. She would implore the unsaved at once to trust the finished work of Jesus."[30]

She would as well challenge us to be active in good works for Jesus. At the memorial service held at Westwood, pastor W. Fuller Gooch challenged those in the room to "loving imitation."

> The dear departed one will be sorely missed, and sorely wanted. Who shall fill the vacant place she has left? There may be some in this room, to whom her memory shall be a stimulus to redoubled effort, and loving care for others. As we think of her self-sacrificing, patient toil for those whom she loved for their Master's sake, let us be stirred to follow, as far as in us lies, the example she has set. Our working days on earth will soon be done; God grant that we may be anointed as with fresh oil, and go forth to labour for our Lord until we also hear the summons, "Come up hither," and go where we shall see the Saviour who loved us, and be reunited with all the dear ones who have gone before![31]

The question remains: Who shall take up the Lord's work with greater fervor because of Susie's example? Susie had the same question.

> I do not know that I ought to be anxious, either for the present or future of my work. It belongs to the Lord so manifestly; He gave it, He has supported it, He has smiled upon it ever since. Surely I need have no care as to what shall become of it when I leave it. No: yet sometimes the thought will intrude into quiet moments, "Who shall carry this on?"... Ah, foolish heart! What needless vexation and anxiety these questions give thee, and how much of vanity and self-sufficiency do they reveal?... Why, the Lord has hundreds of servants, ready and waiting to do His bidding, and to do *thy* work ... Hush thee, then! wait, and watch, and work; "rest in the Lord, and wait patiently for Him."[32]

Archibald Brown, at the grave of Susie Spurgeon, concluded his message:

Farewell, sister! We praise God for thee. For the help thou didst bring thy husband in his ceaseless toil and hard-fought battle, we are grateful. For thy ministry of love to the poor of our Lord's servants, hundreds of hearts enshrine thy memory. Among the sincerest of thy mourners, this day, are humble workers unknown to fame. Many a pastor's wife, weary of her struggle with poverty, has received thy loving aid, and now calls thee "blessed." . . . Thy sons survive thee; they follow the hallowed footprints left; and, with one heart, we pray, "Thou God of father and mother, be Thou their glorious all-sufficiency, and let Thy benediction descend upon their children, and their children's children, until Jesus come, and all are gathered to the Eternal Home!"[33]

❧

Two miles from Westwood and just down the hill from the site of the Crystal Palace is the West Norwood Cemetery. Soon after entering the Gothic style inner cemetery gates, and to the right and left up the hill, is a monument that houses the caskets of both Charles and Susie Spurgeon. Carved into the granite on the left side of the monument are some of the last words ever spoken by Susie, lyrics from the pen of the author of "Amazing Grace." The lyrics are a perpetual reminder that for Christians, there is no need to worry but to, "Hush, thee, then! wait and watch, and work: 'rest in the Lord, and wait patiently on Him.'"[34]

> In Loving Memory of Susannah Spurgeon
> Born Jan. 15, 1832. Died October 22, 1903
>
> His love in time past forbids me to think,
> He'll leave me at last in trouble to sink;

Each sweet Ebenezer I have in review,
Confirms His good pleasure to help me quite through.

Since all that I meet shall work for my good,
The bitter is sweet, the medicine is food;
Though painful at present, wilt cease before long,
And then, O! how pleasant, the conqueror's song.[35]

Afterword

I grew up in Dublin, Ireland, where very few people have heard the name Spurgeon, and even fewer know anything about Charles or Susie. I had little regard for my ancestors while I was young, and my parents did not speak of them often. When they were spoken about, it was just in passing, or if someone visiting our church found out that there were "Spurgeons" in the congregation. I certainly did not give them much thought.

I remember being asked by a friend of mine, who had read a lot of Charles Spurgeon's writings, what book of his I liked the best. I felt ashamed to say that I had read none of his books. This happened at a time in my life when God was growing my own faith, as I had spent much of my life not really paying a lot of attention to God. So, I picked up Spurgeon's "Morning and Evening" devotional and started reading. I thought that the writing would be boring and difficult to understand because it had been written so long ago. On the contrary, to my surprise, I found that Spurgeon's writings brought Jesus alive in a simple yet profound way. God used the words of my great-great-grandfather, along with the Bible and other writings, to open my eyes to my need of Him. Charles's love and devotion to his Saviour was all throughout his writings, and, quite often, something I would read would strike deep in my heart.

Having read *Susie*, I find myself surprised again by another of my ancestors. It has shown me more of the depths of Susie's faith. I find myself wanting to have a good chat with her about her walk with God. I think I could have really related to her had I known her personally. I know, though, that she would not have been the amazing lady she was if she had not first trusted God and all His promises to her. She was rooted in Christ, she abided in Him, and she made sure she went to Him in all situations. When there were good times, she gave Him the praise, and when there were trials, she fell on her knees before Him. Again and again she went to the Fountain of Living Water and drank deeply from it. Then, and only then, was she able to do all she did in her life. I find myself encouraged to do the same, to have Jesus as everything I need in my life, to abide in Him day after day, and then glorify Him in whatever tasks He brings.

As Ray has pointed out, Susie and Charles were also fully committed to passing on the gospel message to their sons, Charles and Thomas (my great grandfather). I also know that they prayed for their descendants. C. H. himself wrote in the *Cheque Book of the Bank of Faith* on August 1, "I pray for my descendants throughout all generations. Be thou their God as thou art mine. My highest honour is that thou has permitted me to serve thee; may my offspring serve thee in all years to come."

Our God is such a generous and giving God, because He has answered this prayer so far. My grandfather, Harold (Thomas's son), lived for the glory of Jesus; my dad (David) also followed Him; and God has opened my brother's (Richard) and my eyes to the glory of Christ and given us a desire for Him. I intend to bring my children up in the faith, and by God's grace, this prayer will continue to be answered for generations to come, to the glory of God.

SUSIE SPURGEON COCHRANE
Great-great-granddaughter of Susie Spurgeon

Acknowledgments

In November 1892, the widow Susie Spurgeon mailed her husband Charles Spurgeon's pulpit Bible to Northfield, Massachusetts, where her friends D. L. and Emma Moody resided. Inside the Bible, Susie wrote: "This Bible has been used by my precious husband and is now given with my unfeigned pleasure to one in whose hands its blessed service will be continued and extended."[1]

Susie was confident in the ministry of D. L. Moody, and her confidence was obviously well placed, evident in Moody's establishment of the Chicago Evangelization Society (later renamed Moody Bible Institute) and the Bible Institute Colportage Association (BICA), today Moody Publishers. The first book ever published by the BICA was Charles Spurgeon's classic, *All of Grace*, in 1894. It is fitting that Moody is now publishing a biography of Susie Spurgeon on the 115th anniversary of her death and almost 125 years since publishing *All of Grace*.

I wish to thank the fantastic team at Moody. Thank you, Randall Payleitner, for receiving my book proposal and not stopping me at the gate; Ingrid Beck, for your contagious excitement about *Susie*, your guidance, and for cheering this project onward; Amanda Cleary Eastep, for your kindness, patience, and sense of humor, and for making *Susie* a much better book; Ashley Torres, for your energetic work in marketing; Erik Peterson, for your lovely work as the creative director; and Connor Sterchi, for your concise, clear, and thoughtful communication with me and for moving the book forward. To all at Moody who participated in this project—from the editorial team and proofreaders, to the design and marketing staff—thank you!

It is an inestimable blessing to me for my longtime friend *and* one of my modern heroes of the faith, R. Albert Mohler Jr., to have written the foreword to *Susie*. His wide-reaching ministry, including his tireless leadership of The Southern Baptist Theological Seminary (SBTS) is a model of excellence. Al and his wife, Mary, are wonderful examples to my family.

I am indebted to my friend Chris Reese who was the first person in the publishing world to embrace Susie's story. Chris's encouragement included introducing me to the folks at Moody. He has a heart befitting a servant of our Savior.

Thank you to other friends who brought discerning eyes to the text along with research help: Jessica Roberson, Susan DeLand, George Scondras, Scott Williams, Maureen Gardner, Wes Hammock, Katelyn Hammock, Hannah Rhodes, and Mary Rhodes.

I first met William (Bill) and Maureen Gardner at SBTS; they were visiting America for the first time from London. After I told them about an upcoming trip to London, Bill offered to pick me up from the airport. Such was the beginning of a wonderful friendship. Bill and Maureen chauffeured my wife, Lori, and me around London and embarked on numerous research trips on my behalf. *Susie* would not have happened without them.

Through Bill and Maureen, I met Susannah (Susie) Spurgeon Cochrane, the great-great-granddaughter of Charles and Susie. She and her husband, Tim, welcomed Lori and me into their home. Susie also provided an endorsement and wrote a beautiful Afterword; her great-great-grand-parents would be proud. Susie's lovely mother, Hilary Spurgeon, also kindly answered a number of questions for me and provided a wonderful photograph of Thomas Spurgeon and family.

My friend Christian George challenged me to write this biography. During his time as curator of the Spurgeon Library, Christian provided me with unlimited access to the resources there. He also introduced me to his excellent team of Spurgeon scholars, led by Phillip Ort. Phillip is now the director of the Spurgeon Library and has been supportive throughout this project.

Thanks to president Jason Allen, and all at Midwestern Baptist Theo-logial Seminary (MBTS), who assisted me in research. The Spurgeon Library at MBTS is stunningly beautiful and the center of the world for Spurgeon research.

Thanks to Donald S. Whitney, my friend of almost thirty years. Don served as my doctoral supervisor at SBTS. He is an excellent writer and teacher, a godly example, and a friend and mentor who shepherded me through the doctoral program.

Numerous other professors and leaders at SBTS gave me valuable counsel including: Michael Haykin, Tom Nettles, Joe Harrod, Coleman Ford, and Jeff Robinson. These men are dear friends.

The *Susie* project has introduced me to many new friends including Donnie Fox, Shannon Benefield, and Michael DeLand of Clear Creek Baptist Bible College in Pineville, Kentucky. They provided me extended stays and hospitality on their campus to write. Idyllic!

While in England for research, I was warmly received and assisted by numerous people. Hannah Wyncoll (daughter of Peter Masters, longtime pastor of the Metropolitan Tabernacle [MT]) made church archives available to me. The MT enjoys a thriving ministry with a thou-sand people in attendance each Sunday. Peter Morden warmly received me to Spurgeon's College, and librarian Annabel Haycraft, provided answers to questions as well as digital resources. Others assisting me in England include:

- Malcolm and Ruth Lane of the Artillery Street Evangelical Church, Colchester, England (where Charles Spurgeon was converted)

- Eileen Hori, administrator, St. Andrew's Street Baptist Church, Cambridge (where Charles was a member)

- Emma Walsh, college librarian, Regent's Park College/Angus Library, University of Oxford

- Former pastor of Beulah Baptist Church, Bexhill-on-Sea, Graham Holliday and his wife Christine; associate pastor David Lockwood and wife Caroline; and church staff and members Erika James, Susan Matthews, and Ron Edwards

- Martin and Angela Ensell (Martin is pastor of Waterbeach Baptist Church, where Charles Spurgeon first served as pastor)

- Gary Aves, who owns the property bordering the River Lark where Spurgeon was baptized

- Pastor John Clevely of Beulah Family Church in Thornton Heath, London, who provided me digital copies of church records

- Gizlé Landman, Head of Academy, Harris Academy (HA), Upper Norwood, London; Rebecca Higgs and other staff from HA

I was granted access to several research libraries including the archives and special collections at the James P. Boyce Centennial Library; The Southern Baptist Theological Seminary, where I conducted much of my research (thanks to Adam Winters and staff); the Spurgeon Library, Midwestern Baptist Theological Seminary, Kansas City; the Library of the SHFP (French Protestant Historical Society), Paris; and the John T.

Christian Library, New Orleans Baptist Theological Seminary (thanks to Jeff Griffin and Ky St. Amant).

Many thanks to those who endorsed this book (too many to mention). Your sacrifice of time, energy, and effort in reading and commenting on the manuscript is much appreciated. Thank you to Lee Dodd, a faithful pastor who manages the @CHSpurgeon Twitter account of almost 90,000 followers. Lee signed on early to help promote *Susie* to his vast social media network. Thanks, Lee.

Special thanks to my mother, Dorothy, and my father- and mother-in-law, Rodney and Lou Webb. They have been supportive of this project from the beginning. As well, my late father, Ray, never failed to be proud of my educational and literary pursuits.

Hearty thanks to friends Cory Pitts, Eric James, and David Bailey for their input and to the staff at the Legacy Hotel (who reserved my chair for me).

Special thanks to Grace Community Church of North Georgia (GCC). It would have been impossible to have engaged in a work of this magnitude without the leadership of my fellow elder Kevin Jarrard; Europe trip-planners Scott and Bonney Williams; and our deacons Paul Turner, Josh O'Neil, and Adrian Rink. Thanks to the entire GCC congregation for supporting my research and writing. Thank you for your generosity in funds, time, and encouragement. I love you!

And last, because they are first: To my beautiful wife, Lori, and our six daughters Rachel, Hannah, Sarah, Mary, Lydia, and Abigail, sons-in-law Adrian and Caleb, and four grandchildren—Susannah, Josiah, Caleb, and Eden Rose—you have sacrificed the most. Thank you for loving me, praying for me, supporting me, and for providing me quiet space at home and time away from home to work. I love you more than I am able to adequately express.

My six-year-old daughter Abigail asked for her name to be on the cover of the book. I treasure the hours that Abigail spent with me in my office. Often, I asked her: "Abigail, what are you doing today?" Her response: "I am working on Susannah Spurgeon." She is the youngest, finest, and loveliest Spurgeon scholar anywhere. Thank you, sweet Abigail.

Finally, praise be to my great God and Savior for His mercy and grace, providing all that I needed and much more, to study and write about the beautiful Susie Spurgeon.

Two are better than one, because they have a good reward for their toil. For if they fall, one will lift up his fellow. . . . a threefold cord is not quickly broken (Eccl. 4:9–10, 12b esv).

Notes

Susie, Herself: An Introduction

1. Mrs. C. H. Spurgeon, *Ten Years After!: A Sequel to "Ten Years of My Life in the Service of the Book Fund"* (London: Passmore & Alabaster, 1895), 206.

2. Ibid., 221.

3. Ibid., 185.

4. Ibid., 171.

5. Ibid.

6. Ibid., 172.

7. C. H. Spurgeon, *C. H. Spurgeon's Autobiography: Compiled from His Diary, Letters, and Records, by His Wife, and His Private Secretary* (London: Passmore and Alabaster, 1897–99; repr., Pasadena, TX: Pilgrim Publications, 1992), 4:371.

8. Mrs. C. H. Spurgeon, *Ten Years of My Life in the Service of the Book Fund: A Grateful Record of My Experience of the Lord's Ways, and Work, and Wages* (London: Passmore & Alabaster, 1887), 79.

9. Mrs. C. H. Spurgeon, *Ten Years After!*, 213–14.

10. Duncan Ferguson, "The Bible and Protestant Orthodoxy: The Hermeneutics of Charles Spurgeon," *Journal of the Evangelical Theological Society* 25, no. 4 (1982): 457.

11. Richard Ellsworth Day, *The Shadow of the Broad Brim: The Life Story of Charles Haddon Spurgeon; Heir of the Puritans* (Philadelphia: The Judson Press, 1934), 105.

12. Mrs. C. H. Spurgeon, *Ten Years After!*, 194.

13. *The Sword and the Trowel: A Record of Combat with Sin & Labour for the Lord* (London: Passmore and Alabaster), December 1903, 606.

14. Charles Ray, *The Life of Susannah Spurgeon.* In *Free Grace and Dying Love* (1903; repr., Edinburgh: The Banner of Truth Trust, 2013), 123–24.

Chapter 1: Formation and Family

1. In this section and through the remainder of the book, numerous references to birth, baptism, marriage, family, land, and death records are derived from census, newspaper, land, and other such legal reports. These reports are copies of originals that are stored at such sites as ancestor.com, findmypast.com, newspapers.com, and nationalarchives .gov.uk. In some cases, legal documents, such as death certificates, have been ordered. I compared legal reports with the written biographical records and newspaper reports to arrive at my conclusions. General historical information, considered common knowledge, is not specifically cited every time.

2. See *Ten Years*, 333, for one example. Mrs. C. H. Spurgeon, *Ten Years of My Life in the Service of the Book Fund: A Grateful Record of My Experience of the Lord's Ways, and Work, and Wages* (London: Passmore & Alabaster, 1887).

3. Tyler Duke, "Outbreak of 1853–1854," London Pulse Projects, n.d., https://londonspulse .org/outbreak-of-1853-1854/.

4. Charles Dickens, *A Tale of Two Cities* (London: Chapman & Hall, 1864), 1. Spurgeon's own copy, held at The Spurgeon Library, Midwestern Baptist Theological Seminary, Kansas City, Missouri.

5. *The British Banner*, Vol. III—No. 155, 1. Wednesday, December 18, 1850.

6. C. H. Spurgeon, *C. H. Spurgeon's Autobiography: Compiled from His Diary, Letters, and Records, by His Wife, and His Private Secretary* (London: Passmore and Alabaster, 1897–99; repr., Pasadena, TX: Pilgrim Publications, 1992), 2:176.

7. Ibid.

8. Henry Clay Fish, *Pulpit Eloquence of the Nineteenth Century: The German, French, American, English, Scotch, Irish, and Welsh Pulpit* (1858), 218, Discourse XVII on J. J. Audebez, https://books.google.com.

9. Charles Tylor, ed. *Memoir and Diary of John Yeardley, Minister of the Gospel* (Philadelphia: Henry Longstreth, 1860), 222–23.

10. Mrs. C. H. Spurgeon, *Ten Years*, 227.

11. H. I. Wayland, *Charles H. Spurgeon: His Faith and Words* (Philadelphia: American Baptist Publication Society, 1892), 27.

12. *The Sword and the Trowel: A Record of Combat with Sin & Labour for the Lord* (London: Passmore & Alabaster, August 1897), 439.

13. Jardim Formoso, "Sir Francis Cook DNB" (March, 2009), http://jardimformoso.blog spot.com/2009/03/sir-francis-cook-dnb.html. See also *The West Briton and Cornwall Advertiser*, October 9, 1873.

14. "Cook, Son, and Co.," Wikipedia, https://en.wikipedia.org/wiki/Cook,_Son_%26_Co.

15. Sally Mitchell, *Daily Life in Victorian England* (London: Greenwood Press, 1966), 5.

16. *The Morning Advertiser*, London, October 25, 1842.

17. Mitchell, *Daily Life*, 6.

18. Ibid., 7–8.

19. C. H. Spurgeon, *Autobiography*, 1:211.

20. Mitchell, *Daily Life*, 7. The ruins of the Crystal Palace, centerpiece of the Great Exhibition, remain at Sydenham Hill, London. The Crystal Palace burned in 1836 and was not rebuilt. Winston Churchill referred to the destruction of the Palace as "the end of an era." https://londonfirejournal.blogspot.com/2005/07/crystal-palace-1936.html.

21. Mitchell, *Daily Life*, 7.

22. Susie's home, number 7, was destroyed during World War II. However, housing still exists in the remaining structure (houses were connected) that survived the bombing. When facing the structure, the house on the far left would have been similar to Susie's home, which was on the far right. A photograph of Susie's house can be found in *Autobiography*, 2:14.

23. C. H. Spurgeon, *Autobiography*, 2:6.

24. Ibid., 2:4.

25. Ibid., 1:303–20.

26. Ibid., 2:3.

27. Charles Ray, *The Life of Susannah Spurgeon*. In *Free Grace and Dying Love: Morning Devotions* by Susannah Spurgeon (1903; repr., Edinburgh: The Banner of Truth Trust, 2013), 127.

28. Susannah Spurgeon, *Free Grace and Dying Love: Morning Devotions* (repr., Edinburgh: The Banner of Truth Trust, 2013), 18.

29. Timothy Larsen, *A People of One Book: The Bible and the Victorians* (Oxford: Oxford University Press, 2012), 1.

30. Ibid., 2–4.

31. Ibid., 6.

32. *The Sword and the Trowel*, November 1903, 550.

33. Robert seems to already have had a residence and/or a business here. Falcon Square is the location that most Spurgeon biographers place Robert, and they introduce him as R. B. Thompson of Falcon Square.

34. *The Observer* (London, England), April 21, 1862, 8.

35. Letter held by the Angus Library at Regent's Park College, Oxford, England. Used by permission.

36. C. H. Spurgeon, *Autobiography*, 3:187.

37. The 1871 census wrongly records Robert Bennett Thompson as Richard. However, the record is correct that his most recent occupation was that of wine merchant, for this was the employment that he listed on his marriage certificate in 1870 and his death certificate in 1873. By comparing R. B.'s signature from his marriage license in 1831 to his marriage license in 1870, it is clear that the signatures are the same. By considering the marriage license, census reports, and address listed on R. B.'s obituary, it is clear that the 1871 census mistakenly records Robert as "Richard." Therefore, "Richard" is Robert Bennett Thomson, Susie's father and Spurgeon's father-in-law.

38. Certified Copy of an Entry of Death: Given at the General Register Office, Penzance, Cornwall. Registered on October 6, 1873 by John James, Registrar.

39. The legal record indicates that his effects were less than £400. This would have been a very modest amount of money. In a later legal record, his effects are listed as less than £45. This discrepancy is either a misprint or a corrected record. At issue is that R. B. seems to be in debt at the time of his death, and, perhaps, after all of the legal proceedings, his remaining assets were only £45.

40. Lewis Drummond, *Spurgeon: Prince of Preachers* (Grand Rapids: Kregle, 1992), 573.

Chapter 2: A Progressing Pilgrim

1. "City Temple, London," Wikipedia, https://en.wikipedia.org/wiki/City_Temple,_London.

2. Albert Dawson, *Joseph Parker, D.D., His Life and Ministry: Minister of the City Tabernacle, London* (London: S.W. Partridge & Co., 1901), 66.

3. C. H. Spurgeon, *C. H. Spurgeon's Autobiography: Compiled from His Diary, Letters, and Records, by His Wife, and His Private Secretary* (London: Passmore and Alabaster, 1897–99; repr., Pasadena, TX: Pilgrim Publications, 1992), 2:5–6. The specific date of Susie's conversion is unknown. She writes that the service was "about a year before Mr. Spurgeon came to London" (*Autobiography*, 2:5). Spurgeon preached at New Park Street, for the first time, on December 18, 1853. Thomas Spurgeon believed her conversion was in 1852.

4. Ibid., 2:6.

5. Ibid., 2:5.

6. Ibid., 2:4.

7. Ibid.

8. Ibid., 2:4. Susannah referred to Thomas Olney as "Father Olney."

9. Ibid., 2:3–4.

10. Ibid., 2:5.

11. Ibid. Spurgeon's second sermon was on Sunday evening, December 18, 1853.

12. Ibid.

13. Ibid.

14. Ibid, 2:6.

15. Ibid., 1:340. New Park Street Chapel was not the only Baptist congregation facing challenges; many of the Baptist Union churches were in decline.

16. Ibid., 1:35. Emphasis in original.

17. Ibid., 1:353.

18. Though it seems unusual that New Park Street, with their prominent history of esteemed pastors, would call a nineteen-year-old to serve as their pastor, it was not without precedent in the history of the church. Patricia Kruppa notes, "Two of his famous predecessors, John Gill and John Rippon, had also been only nineteen when called to preach to the congregation, so Spurgeon's youth was not a great deterrent, and may have tempted some to hope that history would repeat itself. Spurgeon confided to his father that many had 'expressed their belief that my originality, or even eccentricity, was the very thing to draw a London audience.' It seems likely that the congregation at the New Park Street Chapel decided to gamble on Spurgeon, hoping that his fresh manner and unconventional sermons might revive their sagging fortunes" (Patricia Stallings Kruppa, *A Preacher's Progress* [New York: Garland, 1982], 70).

19. C. H. Spurgeon, *Autobiography*, 2:6–7. Susie referred to William Olney as "a true Mr. Greatheart" (2:6). "Greatheart" is a character from *Pilgrim's Progress*. Tom Nettles, commenting on Spurgeon's love for *Pilgrim's Progress*, writes, "At the top of the Puritan standard for spirituality, creativity, and practical knowledge—the book that rendered all mere novelists as pretenders to literary art—was Pilgrim's Progress by the tinker from Bedford, John Bunyan. Throughout Spurgeon's life he 'sought to review every edition' of Pilgrim's 'and, if possible, commended it for a particular audience appropriate to the binding, type-press, and price'" (Tom Nettles, *Living by Revealed Truth: The Life and Pastoral Theology of Charles Haddon Spurgeon* [Fearn, Scotland: Christian Focus, 2013], 443).

20. Ibid., 2:7.

21. C. H. Spurgeon, *Pictures from Pilgrim's Progress: A Commentary on Portions of John Bunyan's Immortal Allegory* (Pasadena, TX: Pilgrim, 1992; Bellingham, WA: Logos Bible Software, 2009), 4.

22. Ibid.

23. Peter Morden, *Communion with Christ and His People: The Spirituality of C. H. Spurgeon* (Eugene, OR: Pickwick, 2013), 29. Morden's book includes a detailed account of Bunyan's influence on Spurgeon (26–30). He also notes the importance of *Foxe's Book of Martyrs* to Spurgeon but argues that the writings of John Bunyan "were of greater significance" with *Pilgrim's Progress* having "the greatest impact" (26).

24. C. H. Spurgeon, *Autobiography*, 2:7.

25. C. H. Spurgeon, *Pictures from Pilgrim's Progress*, 5–6.

26. Ibid., 11.

27. *The Sword and the Trowel: A Record of Combat with Sin & Labour for the Lord* (London: Passmore & Alabaster), February 1898, 50.

28. Ibid.

29. Susannah Spurgeon, *Free Grace and Dying Love* (repr., Edinburgh: The Banner of Truth Trust, 2013), 64.

30. George Stevenson, *Sketch of the Life and Ministry of the Rev. C. H. Spurgeon* (New York: Sheldon and Company, 1859), 22.

31. C. H. Spurgeon, *Autobiography*, 1:299.

Chapter 3: Hearts United at the Crystal Palace

1. "AD Classics: The Crystal Palace/Joseph Paxton," http://www.archdaily.com/397949/ad-classic-the-crystal-palace-joseph-paxton/.

2. M. F. Tupper, *The Poetical Works of Martin Tupper: Including Proverbial Philosophy, A Thousand Lines, Hactenus, Geraldine, and Other Poems*, series 1, Proverbial Philosophy, *"Of Marriage"* (New York: John Wilen, 1859), 156.

3. C. H. Spurgeon, *C.H. Spurgeon's Autobiography: Compiled from His Diary, Letters, and Records, by His Wife, and His Private Secretary* (London: Passmore and Alabaster, 1897–99; repr., Pasadena, TX: Pilgrim Publications, 1992), 2:8.

4. Ibid.

5. Ibid.

6. Ibid.

7. Ibid., 2:13.

8. Though we cannot say with full assurance, discerning from census data, it is almost certain that the garden of Susie and Charles's engagement was her grandfather Sampson Knott's garden.

9. C. H. Spurgeon, *Autobiography*, 2:8.

10. Ibid., 2:8–9.

11. Ibid., 2:9.

12. Ibid.

13. Ibid.

14. Ibid.

15. Ibid., 2:13–14.

16. Ibid.

17. Ibid., 2:13.

18. Ibid., 2:14.

19. Ibid., 2:15.

20. Ibid., 2:16.

21. Ibid.

22. Ibid.

23. Susie described the volume by Thomas Brooks as a "rusty-looking book." Charles asked her to "go carefully through *this* volume" (emphasis added). He wanted Susie to find edifying statements in the book and mark them. From Susie's markings, Charles later published *Smooth Stones Taken from Ancient Brooks*. I did a brief survey of some of the statements in *Smooth Stones* and found that the quotes came from a variety of Brooks's writings.

24. C. H. Spurgeon, *Autobiography*, 2:19.

25. Ibid.

26. Ibid. *Smooth Stones* was first published in 1855 during Charles and Susie's engagement.

27. Susie's membership records are held at the Metropolitan Tabernacle in London.

28. Charles Ray, *The Life of Susannah Spurgeon*. In *Free Grace and Dying Love* (1903; repr., Edinburgh: The Banner of Truth Trust, 2013), 143–44.

29. Iain Murray, *Letters of Charles Haddon Spurgeon* (Edinburgh: The Banner of Truth Trust, 1992), 54.

30. John Bunyan, *The Pilgrim's Progress* (1865; repr., Edinburgh: The Banner of Truth Trust, 1977), 134.

31. Ibid.

32. Ray, *The Life of Susannah Spurgeon*, 144.

33. Murray, *Letters*, 55.

34. C. H. Spurgeon, *Autobiography*, 2:9.

35. Ibid., 2:17.

36. Letter held at the Metropolitan Tabernacle, London.

37. C. H. Spurgeon, *Autobiography*, 2:17.

38. Ibid., 2:18.

39. Ibid.

40. Ibid., 2:19.

41. Ibid., 2:18.

42. Ibid., 2:1. Susie described the tension she felt in determining how much to write of their love story. She believed she had two options: "The one, to conceal, as gracefully as possible, under conventional phraseology and common-place details, the tender truth and sweetness of our mutual love-story; —the other, to write out of the fullness of my very soul, and suffer my pen to describe the fair visions of the past as, one by one, they grew again before my eyes into living and loving realities" (2:1). She chose the latter: "I felt compelled to do so. My hand has but obeyed the dictates of my heart, and, I trust also, the guidance of the unerring Spirit" (2:1). Let the reader rejoice that Susie revealed as much as she did about their love story.

43. Ibid., 2:24.

44. Ibid., 2:23.

45. Ibid., 2:23–24.

46. Ibid., 2:24.

47. Ibid. From a letter to his father, June 19, 1855, Spurgeon wrote about missing Susannah: "I am happy, but had rather be home again; —you will guess the reason. I only want that one person to make the trip a very fine one; —but patience" (C. H. Spurgeon, *The Letters of Charles Haddon Spurgeon*, comp. Charles Spurgeon [London: Marshall Brothers, 1923; Bellingham, WA: Logos Bible Software, 2009]).

48. Steven J. Lawson, *The Gospel Focus of Charles Spurgeon* (Orlando, FL: Reformation Trust, 2012), xix.

49. C. H. Spurgeon, *Autobiography*, 2:24.

50. Ibid.

51. Ibid.

52. Ibid.

53. Ibid. Along with his letters to Susannah, it is estimated that Spurgeon wrote approximately 500 letters each week: C. H. Spurgeon, *Autobiography: The Full Harvest*, rev. ed. (Edinburgh: The Banner of Truth, 1995), 2:192.

54. C. H. Spurgeon, *Autobiography*, 2:26.

55. Ibid.

56. Ibid., 2:27.

57. Ibid.

58. Ibid., 1:4.

59. Ibid.

Chapter 4: A Marriage Made *for* Heaven

1. C. H. Spurgeon, *C.H. Spurgeon's Autobiography: Compiled from His Diary, Letters, and Records, by His Wife, and His Private Secretary* (London: Passmore and Alabaster, 1897–99; repr., Pasadena, TX: Pilgrim Publications, 1992), 2:28.

2. Lewis Drummond, *Spurgeon: Prince of Preachers* (Grand Rapids: Kregel, 1992), 229.

3. C. H. Spurgeon, *Autobiography*, 2:28. The order of the marriage ceremony and other details of the Spurgeons' wedding day may be found in *Autobiography*, 2:28–31.

4. Ibid., 2:28.

5. Ibid.

6. Tom Nettles, *Living by Revealed Truth: The Life and Pastoral Theology of Charles Haddon Spurgeon* (Fearn, Scotland: Christian Focus, 2013), 85–86.

7. C. H. Spurgeon, *Autobiography*, 2:29.

8. Ibid., 2:30.

9. *The Sword and the Trowel: A Record of Combat with Sin & Labour for the Lord* (London: Passmore & Alabaster, 1865–1904), November 1903, 551.

10. Ibid.

11. Mrs. C. H. Spurgeon, *Ten Years After!: A Sequel to "Ten Years of My Life in the Service of the Book Fund"* (London: Passmore and Alabaster, 1895), 63.

12. Ibid.

13. C. H. Spurgeon, *Autobiography*, 2:16.

14. Ibid., 2:17.

15. Drummond, *Spurgeon*, 245.

16. C. H. Spurgeon, *Autobiography*, 2:28.

17. Ibid., 2:30.

18. Ibid., 2:17.

19. Russell H. Conwell, *Life of Charles H. Spurgeon: The World's Great Preacher* (Philadelphia: Edgewood, 1892), 233–34.

20. Ibid., 235.

21. Patricia Stallings Kruppa, *Charles Haddon Spurgeon: A Preacher's Progress* (New York: Garland, 1982), 110.

22. Anne Vogt-Bordure, Pauline Thomann, Hotel Le Meurice, n.d. 4. This document is produced by the Hotel Le Meurice.

23. Ibid.

24. Ibid., 6.

25. C. H. Spurgeon, *Autobiography*, 2:176.

26. Ibid.

27. Ibid., 2:177.

28. Ibid., 2:176–77.

29. *The Sword and the Trowel*, February 1867, 73.

30. C. H. Spurgeon, *Autobiography,* 2:180.

31. Ibid., 2:176.

32. *The Sword and the Trowel,* January 1872, 5.

33. C. H. Spurgeon, *Autobiography*, 2:180.

34. Ibid.

35. Ibid., 2:28.

36. Ibid., 2:182.

37. Ibid.

38. Ibid., 2:183.

39. Ibid.

40. Ibid., 2:184.

41. Mrs. C. H. Spurgeon, *Ten Years of My Life In the Service of the Book Fund: A Grateful Record of My Experience of the Lord's Ways, and Work, and Wages* (London: Passmore & Alabaster, 1887), 377–78.

42. C. H. Spurgeon, *The Metropolitan Tabernacle Pulpit: Sermons Preached and Revised by C. H. Spurgeon,* vols. 1-63 (Pasadena, TX: Pilgrim Publications, 1970–2006), 16:642. Volumes 1–6 are referred to as the New Park Street Pulpit; volumes 7–63 are associated with The Metropolitan Tabernacle.

43. C. H. Spurgeon, *Autobiography,* 2:185.

44. C. H. Spurgeon, *The Metropolitan Tabernacle Pulpit,* 16:640.

45. Ibid.

46. C. H. Spurgeon, *Autobiography,* 2:189.

47. Ibid.

48. Ibid., 2:190.

Chapter 5: The New Parents

1. G. Holden Pike, *James Archer Spurgeon* (London: Alexander & Shepheard, 1894), 20.

2. Arnold Dallimore, *C. H. Spurgeon: The New Biography* (Chicago: Moody, 1984), 125–130.

3. A. Cunningham Burley, *Spurgeon and His Friendships* (London: Epworth, 1933), 29.

4. W. Y. Fullerton, *Thomas Spurgeon: A Biography* (London: Hodder and Stoughton, 1919), 34.

5. Burley, *Spurgeon and His Friendships,* 30.

6. Ibid., 31.

7. Ibid., 32.

8. Manton Smith, *The Essex Lad Who Became England's Greatest Preacher: Life of C. H. Spurgeon for Young People* (London: Passmore and Alabaster, 1892), 7.

9. Burley, *Spurgeon and His Friendships,* 32.

10. Ibid., 33.

11. Charles Ray, *The Life of Susannah Spurgeon.* In *Free Grace and Dying Love* (1903; repr., Edinburgh: The Banner of Truth Trust, 2013), 191–92.

12. Fullerton, *Thomas Spurgeon,* 32.

13. Ibid.

14. Ibid.

15. Ibid., 39.

16. Ibid., 36.

17. Ibid.

18. The Pastors' College began with only one student soon after Charles and Susie were married. W. Y. Fullerton, *C. H. Spurgeon: A Biography* (London: Williams and Norgate, 1920), 227. Spurgeon referred to the college as "his first-born and best beloved" (227). The college had its roots in the conversion and subsequent preaching of Thomas Medhurst. Medhurst met with Spurgeon for several hours each week, beginning in 1855 (229). Spurgeon's students grew in number through the years. Fullerton notes, "It was clearly understood that the College did not exist to make ministers, but to train them" (231). Initially the college met at the Tabernacle and in 1873 moved to a more permanent location (232). Fullerton writes, "In the College the great event of the week was the Friday afternoon lecture by the President" (233).

19. C. H. Spurgeon, *Lectures to My Students* (1875–1894; repr., Edinburgh: The Banner of Truth, 2008), 237.

20. C. H. Spurgeon, *Metropolitan Tabernacle Pulpit: Sermons Preached and Revised by C. H. Spurgeon* (Pasadena, TX: Pilgrim, 1970–2006), 11:253. Spurgeon's text was from Ephesians 5:25–27: "Husbands, love your wives, even as Christ also loved the church, and gave himself for it; that he might sanctify and cleanse it with the washing of water by the word, that he might present it to himself a glorious church, not having spot, or wrinkle, or any such thing; but that it should be holy and without blemish."

21. Ibid., 54:367.

22. William Williams, *Charles Haddon Spurgeon: Personal Reminiscences*, rev. and ed. Marguerite Williams (London: The Religious Tract Society, n.d.), 36. Westwood was the name of Spurgeon's last home in London.

23. Ibid., 33.

24. C. H. Spurgeon, *Autobiography*, 3:103.

25. C. H. Spurgeon, *Metropolitan Tabernacle Pulpit*, 54:363.

26. C. H. Spurgeon, *Autobiography*, 4:64.

27. Fullerton, *Thomas Spurgeon*, 40.

28. Ibid.

29. Ibid., 40–41.

30. Ibid., 41. Charles Haddon Spurgeon also had a touch of the artist's gift. See Christian George, https://www.spurgeon.org/resource-library/blog-entries/spurgeons-enduring-ministry-an-interview-with-christian-george.

31. Ibid., 42.

32. Ibid., 43.

33. Ibid., 44.

34. Ibid.

35. Ibid., 45.

36. Ibid., 46.

37. Ibid., 48.

38. Burley, *Spurgeon and His Friendships*, 35.

39. C. H. Spurgeon, *The Letters of Charles Haddon Spurgeon* (Collected and Collated by His Son Charles Spurgeon), (London; Edinburgh; New York: Marshall Brothers, Limited, 1923), 93–94, Logos Software.

40. *The Sword and the Trowel: A Record of Combat with Sin & Labour for the Lord* (London: Passmore and Alabaster, November 1903), 552.

Chapter 6: The Shadow of Sorrow: Tragedy and Faith

1. *The Observer*, October 26, 1856, 2.

2. *The Manchester Guardian*, October 21, 1856, 3.

3. *The Observer*, November 9, 1856, 6.

4. Large churches with popular pastors were not uncommon in London. Ian Randall referred to Spurgeon as "the most outstanding preacher of the Victorian era." He described the era of Spurgeon as "marked by great pulpiteers who attracted large congregations" (Ian M. Randall, *A School of the Prophets: 150 Years of Spurgeon's College* [London: Spurgeon's College, 2005], 1). One of London's popular preachers was Joseph Parker. Whereas Spurgeon addressed over five thousand people each Lord's Day at the Metropolitan Tabernacle, Joseph Parker preached to three to four thousand (A. Cunningham Burley, *Spurgeon and His Friendships* [London: Epworth, 1933], 47. See also G. Holden Pike, *Dr. Parker and His Friends* [London: T. Fisher, 1904]).

5. Spurgeon's sons were born September 20, 1856.

6. Charles Ray, *The Life of Susannah Spurgeon*. In *Free Grace and Dying Love* (1903; repr., Edinburgh: The Banner of Truth Trust, 2013), 164.

7. Ibid.

8. W. Y. Fullerton, *C. H. Spurgeon: A Biography* (London: Williams and Norgate, 1920), 91.

9. C. H. Spurgeon, *C.H. Spurgeon's Autobiography: Compiled from His Diary, Letters, and Records, by His Wife, and His Private Secretary* (London: Passmore and Alabaster, 1897–99; repr., Pasadena, TX: Pilgrim Publications, 1992), 2:202.

10. *The Observer*, October 26, 1856, 3.

11. Ibid.

12. *The Manchester Weekly Times and Examiner*, October 25, 1856, 11.

13. *The London Guardian*, October 27, 1856, 4.

14. C. H. Spurgeon, *Autobiography*, 2:207.

15. Ibid., 2:191.

16. Mark Hopkins, *Nonconformity's Romantic Generation* (Eugene, OR: Wipf and Stock, 2006), 128.

17. Ray, *The Life of Susannah Spurgeon*, 165.

18. C. H. Spurgeon, *Autobiography*, 2:192.

19. Ray, *The Life of Susannah Spurgeon*, 166.

20. Ibid.

21. This letter is kept at the Metropolitan Tabernacle in London. I had an opportunity to view a number of Spurgeon's letters during a visit to the Tabernacle in May 2015. This letter to his mother, in contrast to other letters I viewed, is written with poor handwriting, whereas Spurgeon's penmanship was normally excellent. His son Charles reflected, "In early days it [Spurgeon's penmanship] was like copper-plate, and to the end of his life, unless deformed by pain, it was always singularly chaste and clear." Spurgeon, *The Letters*, 7. It is possible that the poor handwriting, reflected in this letter, was due to physical pain, but his problems with gout came later in his life. Therefore, it is more likely that his poor handwriting was due to the distress caused by the Music Hall disaster. The letter includes very few periods; instead Spurgeon uses dashes to separate one sentence from the other. I was unable to discern at least one word and, therefore, inserted a line. In a couple of other cases, where I could reasonably guess the word, I filled it in. There are also water stains on the letter, which could be evidence that Spurgeon shed tears while writing to his mother. Used by permission.

22. Though I was unable to determine the exact timing of the revival, it seems to have been just before Spurgeon returned to the pulpit on November 2, 1856.

23. Ray, *The Life of Susannah Spurgeon*, 167.

24. See Christian George, "Spurgeon Almost Quit," *B&H Academic Blog*, May 6, 2015, http://www.bhacademicblog.com/spurgeon-almost-quit/.

25. Ray, *The Life of Susannah Spurgeon*, 167.

26. C. H. Spurgeon, *Autobiography*, 2:193.

27. Ibid., 2:213.

28. Ibid.

29. C. H. Spurgeon, *The New Park Street Pulpit: Containing Sermons Preached and Revised by the Rev. C. H. Spurgeon, Minister of the Chapel*, 6 vols. (Pasadena, TX: Pilgrim Publications, 1970–2006), 2:377.

30. Ibid.

31. Ibid.

32. Ibid.

33. Ibid., 377–84.

34. Ibid. 377.

35. Ibid., 401.

36. C. H. Spurgeon, *Autobiography*, 2:193.

37. Ibid., 2:219–20.

38. Ibid., 2:220. Spurgeon died at age 57 on January 31, 1892.

39. Ray, *The Life of Susannah Spurgeon*, 168–69.

40. Darrell W. Amundsen, "The Anguish and Agonies of Charles Spurgeon," Christian History and Biography, January 1, 1991, 23, https://www.christianitytoday.com/history/issues/issue-29/anguish-and-agonies-of-charles-spurgeon.html.

41. C. H. Spurgeon, *Autobiography*, 2:193.

42. Mrs. C. H. Spurgeon, *A Cluster of Camphire: Words of Cheer & Comfort to Sick and Sorrowful Souls* (London: Passmore and Alabaster, 1898; repr., Springfield, MO: Particular Baptist Press, 2009), 40.

43. Ibid., 41.

44. J. C. Carlile, *C. H. Spurgeon: An Interpretative Biography* (London: The Religious Tract Society, 1933), 189.

45. George Herbert, *Herbert Poems*, "Affliction 5" (New York: Alfred A. Knopf, 2004), 109.

46. Carlile, *C. H. Spurgeon: An Interpretative Biography*, 189. The "pastor's pastor" in the quote refers to Richard Baxter.

47. C. H. Spurgeon, *Autobiography*, 2:186.

48. Ibid.

49. Ernest Bacon, *Spurgeon: Heir of the Puritans* (Arlington Heights, IL: Christian Liberty Press, 1967), 39.

50. C. H. Spurgeon, *Autobiography*, 2:187.

51. Ibid.

52. Spurgeon, quoted in Hopkins, *Nonconformity's Romantic Generation*, 130.

53. Ibid.

54. Mrs. C. H. Spurgeon, *A Cluster of Camphire*, 32.

55. C. H. Spurgeon, *Autobiography*, 2:175.

56. Mrs. C. H. Spurgeon, *Ten Years of My Life in the Service of the Book Fund: A Grateful Record of My Experience of the Lord's Ways, and Work, and Wages* (London: Passmore & Alabaster, 1887), 26.

57. H. L. Wayland, *Charles H. Spurgeon: His Faith and Works* (Philadelphia: American Baptist Publication Society, 1892), 226.

58. C. H. Spurgeon, *The Metropolitan Tabernacle Pulpit: Sermons Preached and Revised by C. H. Spurgeon* (Pasadena, TX: Pilgrim Publications, 1970–2006), 53:196.

Chapter 7: Hand in Hand at Home and Abroad

1. When the Nightingale Lane home was being rebuilt in the late 1860s the Spurgeon family moved temporarily to Brighton. However, it seems that Spurgeon mostly remained in London.

2. "Angel of the House" is a Victorian-era phrase referring to the wife and/or mother. It is reflective of the idealistic perspective of the wife/mother as a homemaker that was prominent in the nineteenth century. In Susannah's case, she was an angelic wife and mother. Spurgeon referred to her as an "angel of God" to him.

3. G. Holden Pike, *The Life and Work of C.H. Spurgeon*, 6 vols. (London: Cassell and Company, 1892), 2:221–23.

4. Ibid., 226.

5. Arnold Dallimore, *C. H. Spurgeon: The New Biography* (Chicago: Moody, 1984), 142.

6. For an analysis of Spurgeon's income and expenditures, see Christian George, "4 Reasons Spurgeon Died Poor" October 10, 2016: https://www.spurgeon.org/resource-library/blog-entries/4-reasons-spurgeon-died-poor. The article indicates that Susie reported to a newspaper that Spurgeon left her £2,000. Perhaps she meant liquid assets as Spurgeon's will has his effects at more than £10,000. If the paper accurately quoted Susie, the £2,000 translates into a quarter of a million dollars in today's terms. The value of Spurgeon's estate, though, was well over a million dollars and Susannah was able to maintain a reasonably high manner of living. She retained servants after Spurgeon died, traveled, and was never in financial need. And beyond her own needs, she donated money to her Book Fund and its various auxiliary ministries and to other worthy causes, including the church that she helped to plant.

7. C. H. Spurgeon, *C.H. Spurgeon's Autobiography: Compiled from His Diary, Letters, and Records, by His Wife, and His Private Secretary* (London: Passmore and Alabaster, 1897–99; repr., Pasadena, TX: Pilgrim Publications, 1992), 2:146.

8. Ibid., 2:183.

9. Ibid.

10. Ibid., 2:284.

11. Ibid., 2:286.

12. Ibid., 2:291–92.

13. Ibid., 2:292.

14. Ibid., 3:100–101.

15. C. H. Spurgeon, *Autobiography*, 3:98–100.

16. Mrs. C. H. Spurgeon, *Ten Years of My Life in the Service of the Book Fund: A Grateful Record of My Experience of the Lord's Ways, and Work, and Wages* (London: Passmore & Alabaster, 1887), 22.

17. C. H. Spurgeon, *Autobiography*, 3:98.

18. Ibid.

19. Ibid., 3:97.

20. Ibid., 3:101.

21. C. H. Spurgeon, *The Cheque Book of the Bank of Faith* (New York: A. C. Armstrong & Son, 1892), 315.

22. C. H. Spurgeon, *Autobiography*, 2:295–96.

23. Ibid., 2:296.

24. Ibid., 2:296–7.

25. These books and other similar titles are housed at the Spurgeon Library, Midwestern Baptist Theological Seminary, Kansas City, Missouri.

Chapter 8: The Great Sufferer

1. *The Sword and the Trowel: A Record of Combat with Sin & Labour for the Lord* (London: Passmore and Alabaster, 1865–1904), November 1903, 553.

2. Ibid.

3. Christian George, https://www.spurgeon.org/resource-library/blog-entries/spurgeons-enduring-ministry-an-interview-with-christian-george.

4. H. I. Wayland, *Charles H. Spurgeon: His Faith and Works* (Philadelphia: American Baptist Publications, 1892), 228.

5. *The Sword and the Trowel*, November 1903, 553.

6. Charles Ray, *The Life of Susannah Spurgeon*. In *Free Grace and Dying Love* (1903; repr., Edinburgh: The Banner of Truth Trust, 2013), 185.

7. C. H. Spurgeon, *The Cheque Book of the Bank of Faith* (New York: A. C. Armstrong & Son, 1892), 240.

8. Mrs. C. H. Spurgeon, *Ten Years of My Life in the Service of the Book Fund: A Grateful Record of My Experience of the Lord's Ways, and Work, and Wages* (London: Passmore & Alabaster, 1887), 275.

9. C. H. Spurgeon, *C.H. Spurgeon's Autobiography: Compiled from His Diary, Letters, and Records, by His Wife, and His Private Secretary* (London: Passmore and Alabaster, 1897–99; repr., Pasadena, TX: Pilgrim Publications, 1992), 3:184.

10. Ray, *Susannah Spurgeon*, 185.

11. No literature is available that indicates she was pregnant again but miscarried.

12. Peter Masters, *Men of Destiny* (London: The Wakeman Trust, 2008), 46.

13. Ibid., 35–36.

14. Ibid., 36.

15. Ibid., 37.

16. Ibid., 39.

17. Ibid., 41.

18. "Spurgeon and Simpson," *The Baptist Quarterly,* https://biblicalstudies.org.uk/pdf/bq/20 -8_365.pdf.

19. Masters, *Men of Destiny*, 45.

20. "Sir James Young Simpson (1811–1870), https://christianheritageedinburgh.org .uk/2016/08/23/sir-james-young-simpson-1811-1870/.

21. "Spurgeon and Simpson," 366.

22. Ibid.

23. Ibid.

24. Ibid.

25. Ibid, 366–67.

26. Ibid, 367.

27. J. Drife, "The History of Obstetrics," *BMJ Journals*, http://pmj.bmj.com/content/ 78/919/311.

28. Ibid.

29. Susan Valerie Barker (2017) "Susannah and the Lemon Tree": *Mrs C.H. Spurgeon's Book Fund, Baptist Quarterly,* 48:4, 159–67, DOI: 10.1080/0005576X.2017.1376536 , 160, n5.

30. "History of Endometriosis," http://nezhat.org/endometriosis-treatment/history-of-endometriosis.

31. James Henry Bennet, *A Practical Treatise of Inflammation of the Uterus, Its Cervix and Appendages, and Its Connection with Other Uterine Diseases* (London: Churchill, 1861). I was able to read from the book at the Spurgeon Library at Midwestern Baptist Theological Seminary, which is home to approximately six thousand volumes that were in Spurgeon's library when he died. Spurgeon collected a wide variety of titles on topics from theology to birds. His library contains books of humor, poetry, and medical works. However, Bennet's book on cervical problems is indeed out of place even among the other health and medical books in the library. Therefore, Kruppa's argument is valid. Also see William Brian Albert, "As the Wind Blows Cold: The Spirituality of Suffering and Depression in the Life and Ministry of Charles Spurgeon" (Ph.D. diss., The Southern Baptist Theological Seminary, 2015), 147 n4.

32. Patricia Stallings Kruppa, *Charles Haddon Spurgeon: A Preacher's Progress* (New York: Garland, 1982), 108 n67.

33. Ibid.

34. *The Sword and the Trowel*, June 1870, 270.

35. C. H. Spurgeon, *Autobiography*, 2:292.

36. Mrs. C. H. Spurgeon, *A Cluster of Camphire: Words of Cheer & Comfort to Sick and Sorrowful Souls* (London: Passmore and Alabaster, 1898; repr., Springfield, MO: Particular Baptist Press, 2009), 116.

37. Kruppa, *Charles Haddon Spurgeon*, 108.

38. Ibid., 110.

39. W. Y. Fullerton, *Thomas Spurgeon: A Biography* (London: Hodder and Stoughton, 1919), 129.

40. Lewis Drummond, *Spurgeon: Prince of Preachers* (Grand Rapids: Kregel, 1992), 462.

41. Ibid., 461.

42. C. H. Spurgeon, *The Cheque Book of the Bank of Faith* (New York: A. C. Armstrong & Son, 1892), vi.

43. Susannah Spurgeon, *Free Grace and Dying Love: Morning Devotions* (1896; repr., Edinburgh: The Banner of Truth Trust, 2013), 18.

44. Mrs. C. H. Spurgeon, *Ten Years After!: A Sequel to "Ten Years of My Life in the Service of the Book Fund"* (London: Passmore & Alabaster, 1895), 238.

45. Ibid., 270.

46. Mrs. C. H. Spurgeon, *Ten Years of my Life*, 218.

47. Records held at the Metropolitan Tabernacle, London.

48. Mrs. C. H. Spurgeon, *Ten Years of My Life,* 219.

49. Ibid.

50. Ibid.

51. Ibid., 219–20.

52. C. H. Spurgeon, *Till He Come* (London: Marshall Brothers, n.d.), 135–36.

53. Mrs. C. H. Spurgeon, *Ten Years After*, 280.

54. Mrs. C. H. Spurgeon, *Ten Years of My Life*, 34.

55. H. L. Wayland, *Charles H. Spurgeon: His Faith and Works* (Philadelphia: American Baptist Publication Society, 1892), 229.

56. Iain Murray, *Letters of Charles Haddon Spurgeon* (Edinburgh: The Banner of Truth Trust, 1992), 163–64.

57. C. H. Spurgeon, *Lectures to My Students* (1875–1894; repr., Edinburgh: The Banner of Truth, 2008), 605.

Chapter 9: Mrs. Spurgeon's Book Fund

1. *The Sword and the Trowel: A Record of Combat with Sin & Labour for the Lord* (London: Passmore and Alabaster, 1865–1904), November 1903, 553.

2. Mrs. C. H. Spurgeon, *Ten Years of My Life in the Service of the Book Fund* (London: Passmore & Alabaster: 1887), 7. Charles Spurgeon noted, "We have named the work, 'Mrs. Spurgeon's Book Fund,' and we believe that it will not soon come to an end, but will do great work." The Book Fund continued for several years after Susie's death.

3. Ibid., 28.

4. Ibid.

5. Charles Ray, *The Life of Susannah Spurgeon*. In *Free Grace and Dying Love* (1903; repr., Edinburgh: The Banner of Truth Trust, 2013), 196–97.

6. Mrs. C. H. Spurgeon, *Ten Years*, 5.

7. Ibid., 69.

8. Letter held by the Metropolitan Tabernacle, London.

9. Susan Valerie Barker (2017) "Susannah and the Lemon Tree": *Mrs C. H. Spurgeon's Book Fund, Baptist Quarterly,* 48:4, 159–67, DOI: 10.1080/0005576X.2017.1376536.

10. Mrs. C. H. Spurgeon, *Ten Years*, 327.

11. Ibid., 220.

12. Ibid.

13. Ibid., 327–28.

14. Ibid., 5–6.

15. Ibid., 6.

16. Ibid., iii.

17. Ibid., 33–34.

18. Ibid., iii.

19. Ibid.

20. Ibid., iv.

21. Ibid., iii.

22. Ibid., iv.

23. Mrs. C. H. Spurgeon, *Ten Years After!: A Sequel to "Ten Years of My Life in the Service of the Book Fund"* (London: Passmore & Alabaster, 1895), 98.

24. Mrs. C. H. Spurgeon, *Ten Years*, 27.

25. Ibid., 126–27.

26. Ibid., iv.

27. Ibid., 260.

28. Ibid., 131–32.

29. Quoted in Tom Nettles, *Living by Revealed Truth: The Life and Pastoral Theology of Charles Haddon Spurgeon* (Fearn, Scotland: Christian Focus, 2013), 14.

30. Mrs. C. H. Spurgeon, *Ten Years*, 27.

31. Ibid., 153–54.

32. Ibid., 422.

33. Ibid., 417.

34. Ibid., 244.

35. Ibid., 29.

36. Ibid., 30.

37. Ibid.

38. Mrs. C. H. Spurgeon, *Ten Years,* 150.

39. Spurgeon's sermon "Baptismal Regeneration" was preached in June of 1864. In it Spurgeon strongly rejected the Church of England's sacramental/regenerative view of infant baptism. It was one of his most controversial sermons. However, by the end of his life, Spurgeon was warmly regarded by many in the Church of England.

40. Mrs. C. H. Spurgeon, *Ten Years,* 151.

41. Ibid.

42. Ibid., 152.

43. *Tobacco Talk and Smokers' Gossip* (London: George Redway, n.d.), 31. Spurgeon had a copy of this book in his library.

44. Mrs. C. H. Spurgeon, *Ten Years,* 153.

45. Ibid., 224.

46. Ibid., 155.

47. Ibid., 429.

Chapter 10: The Move to Westwood: The Book Fund Continues

1. Mrs. C. H. Spurgeon, *Ten Years of My Life in the Service of the Book Fund: A Grateful Record of My Experience of the Lord's Ways, and Work, and Wages* (London: Passmore & Alabaster, 1887), 123–24.

2. H. L. Wayland, *Charles H. Spurgeon: His Faith and Works* (Philadelphia: American Baptist Publications: 1892), 227.

3. Ibid.

4. Mrs. C. H. Spurgeon, *Ten Years,* 227.

5. John Bunyan, *The Pilgrim's Progress* (repr., John C. Nimmo, Ltd, 1895; Edinburgh: The Banner of Truth Trust, 1977), 178.

6. Mrs. C. H. Spurgeon, *Ten Years*, 148.

7. Ibid.

8. Ibid., iii.

9. Ibid., 70.

10. Ibid.

11. Mrs. C. H. Spurgeon, *Ten Years After!: A Sequel to "Ten Years of My Life in the Service of the Book Fund"* (London: Passmore & Alabaster, 1895), 26.

12. Ibid.

13. Ibid., 27.

14. Ibid.

15. Ibid.

16. Ibid.

17. Ibid., 77–78.

18. Iain H. Murray, *The Forgotten Spurgeon* (1966; repr., Edinburgh: The Banner of Truth Trust, 2012), 152. For a detailed account of the Controversy, see chapters 6–8.

19. Mrs. C. H. Spurgeon, *Ten Years*, 355–56.

20. Ibid., 357.

21. C. H. Spurgeon, *The Letters of Charles Haddon Spurgeon* (Collected and Collated by His Son Charles Spurgeon), (London; Edinburgh; New York: Marshall Brothers, Limited, 1923), 90, Logos Software.

22. C. H. Spurgeon, *Autobiography,* 2:193.

23. Ibid.

24. W. Y. Fullerton, *Thomas Spurgeon: A Biography* (London: Hodder and Stoughton, 1920), 131–32.

25. Ibid., 132.

26. Mrs. C. H. Spurgeon, *Ten Years,* 357.

27. H. L. Wayland, *Charles H. Spurgeon: His Faith and Works* (Philadelphia: American Baptist Publication Society, 1892), 230.

28. Ibid., 233.

29. Ibid., 234.

30. Ibid.

31. Ibid., 237.

32. Ibid., 239.

33. Jesse Page, *C.H. Spurgeon: His Life and Ministry* (London: S.W. Partridge & Co., n.d.), 96–97.

34. Wayland, *Charles H. Spurgeon,* 228.

Chapter 11: Mentone: Happiness and a Sad Goodbye

1. Nigel Faithfull, "Spurgeon at Menton," *Evangelical Times*, August 2003, https://www.evangelical-times.org/27818/spurgeon-at-menton/.

2. Ian M. Randall, "C. H. Spurgeon (1834–1892): A Lover of France," *European Journal of Theology* 24, no. 1 (2015): 57–65. This article considers Spurgeon's love of France from his introduction to Paris by Susie in 1856 through his preaching trips, his travel with Susie, and his visits to Mentone from 1872 until his death at Mentone in 1892. Spurgeon had numerous books on health and medicine in his library, including: Alfred Schofield, *Health At Home Tracts* (London: The Religious Tract Society, 1890). The first tract is titled: "How to Avoid Dying before the Time," 1–16. Though the author admits, "No one ever dies until his time comes," he also argues that such a sentiment "is too often used as a cover for our own carelessness in a way which is little short of criminal." To not care for one's body is to end one's own life "indirectly." 1. Spurgeon's death at 57 might be attributed to depression, Bright's disease, gout, overwork, being overweight, the stress he felt as he battled through various controversies, or more likely, a combination of factors.

3. James Henry Bennet, *Winter and Spring on the Shores of the Mediterranean* (London: J. A. Churchill, 1875), vii. This is the fifth edition. Bennet's health declined in 1859 and Spurgeon was familiar with earlier editions of this work.

4. Ibid.

5. Ibid., vii–viii.

6. Don Theobald, *Susannah Spurgeon* (Springfield, MO: Particular Baptist Press, 2016), 167–73. This biographical sketch of Susannah is part of the reprint of her book *A Cluster of Camphire*, by Particular Baptist Press.

7. *The Sword and the Trowel: A Record of Combat with Sin & Labour for the Lord* (London: Passmore and Alabaster, 1865–1904), January 1892, 17.

8. Ibid.

9. Faithfull, "Spurgeon at Menton."

10. Ibid.

11. Ibid.

12. C. H. Spurgeon, *Autobiography*, 4:258.

13. Ibid.

14. Ibid.

15. Ibid., 4:259.

16. Ibid., 4:260.

17. Ibid., 4:261.

18. C. H. Spurgeon, *The Cheque Book of the Bank of Faith* (New York: A. C. Armstrong & Son, 1892), vi–vii.

19. C. H. Spurgeon, *Till He Come* (London: Marshall Brothers, n.d.), 57.

20. Ibid., 160.

21. C. H. Spurgeon, *Autobiography*, 4:348.

22. Ibid., 4:342.

23. Ibid., 4:356–57.

24. Ibid., 4:365.

25. *The Sword and the Trowel,* January 1890, 13.

26. Ibid., February 1890, 61.

27. Ibid., January 1890, 13.

28. C. H. Spurgeon, *Autobiography,* 4:365.

29. *The Sword and the Trowel,* March 1892, 114.

30. Mrs. C. H. Spurgeon, *Ten Years After!: A Sequel to "Ten Years of My Life in the Service of the Book Fund"* (London: Passmore & Alabaster, 1895), 163.

31. Ibid., 164.

32. *The Sword and the Trowel,* March 1892, 110–11.

33. Mrs. C. H. Spurgeon, *Ten Years After*, 168.

34. Ibid., 168–69.

35. *The Sword and the Trowel,* March 1892, 124.

36. C. H. Spurgeon, *Commentary on Matthew: The Gospel of the Kingdom* (1893; repr., Edinburgh: The Banner of Truth Trust, 2010), ix–x.

37. Ibid., x n2, states that Joseph Harrald was the friend who completed *The Gospel of the Kingdom.*

38. Ibid., ix.

39. *The Sword and the Trowel,* March 1892, 110.

40. C. H. Spurgeon, *Autobiography,* 4:370.

41. Ibid., 4:371.

42. Ibid.

43. Mrs. C. H. Spurgeon, *Ten Years After*, 164.

44. Ibid., 167.

45. *The Sword and the Trowel,* March 1892, 127.

46. Mrs. C. H. Spurgeon, *Ten Years After*, 167.

47. C. H. Spurgeon, *Autobiography,* 2:187–88.

48. *The Sword and the Trowel,* March 1892, 109.

49. Ibid., 110.

50. Ibid., 110–11.

Chapter 12: With Christ, Which Is Far Better

1. Robert Shindler, *From the Pulpit to the Palm-Branch* (New York: Gospel Publishing House, n.d.), 27. This edition is in a large volume containing two books from Shindler.

2. Ibid., 111.

3. Ibid., 40.

4. C. H. Spurgeon, *C .H. Spurgeon's Autobiography: Compiled from His Diary, Letters, and Records, by His Wife, and His Private Secretary* (London: Passmore and Alabaster, 1897–99; repr., Pasadena, TX: Pilgrim Publications, 1992), 4:371.

5. Shindler, *From the Pulpit to the Palm-Branch*, 112–13.

6. Ibid., 113.

7. C. H. Spurgeon, *Autobiography*, 1:4.

8. *The Sword and the Trowel: A Record of Combat with Sin & Labour for the Lord* (London: Passmore and Alabaster, 1865–1904), January 1897, 9.

9. Ibid., 10.

10. Shindler, *From the Pulpit to the Palm-Branch*, 50.

11. Ibid., 51.

12. Ibid., 96. Susie remained in Mentone and surrounding areas for a few months. She sent a letter for A. T. Pierson to read at the February 10, 1892, service for the members of the Metropolitan Tabernacle. Pierson was not the formal pastor of the Metropolitan Tabernacle but supplied the pulpit for an extended period during Spurgeon's last prolonged illness and after his death. Pierson stated, "I must unburden myself of the last message at hand from dear Mrs. Spurgeon, who cannot be here today, and from whom, perhaps without design on her part, I have only this morning received a beautiful, tender, and sisterly letter, a portion of which certainly belongs to you" (102). He then read the parts of the letter that were directed to the church. Susie penned the letter a week after Spurgeon died. She looked to Scripture and wrote, "'He is not here; he is risen,' is as true of my beloved as of my beloved's Lord. Today he has been a week in heaven. Oh, the bliss, the rapture, of seeing his Saviour's face! Oh, the welcome home which awaited him as he left this sad earth! Not for a moment do I wish him back, though he was dearer to me than tongue can tell. I shall pray much for you all during the week of grief. I feel myself like a shipwrecked mariner who has with difficulty reached the shore, and now looks with streaming eyes and fainting heart on others still struggling through those awful waves of sorrow. With Christian love and in intensest sympathy, Your grateful friend, Susie Spurgeon" (103).

13. Ibid., 96.

14. Mrs. C. H. Spurgeon, *Ten Years After*, 167.

15. *The Sword and the Trowel*, May 1892, 247.

16. A chair with three wheels, designed for the elderly or invalid, with a steering mechanism. The chair was either pulled from the front or pushed from the rear. Therefore, someone would have accompanied Mr. and Mrs. Spurgeon on this walk.

17. *The Sword and the Trowel*, May 1892, 247.

18. Mrs. C. H. Spurgeon, *Ten Years After*, 167–68.

19. Comparing the dates of various accounts of Spurgeon's death, it is evident that though Susie attended the memorial service in Mentone, prior to Spurgeon's body being transported to London, she did not attend the funeral services in London. See Ray, *The Life of Susannah Spurgeon*, 240.

20. Mrs. C. H. Spurgeon, *Ten Years After*, 171.

21. Ibid.

22. Ibid., vi–vii.

Chapter 13: A Lady of Letters

1. *The Sword and the Trowel: A Record of Combat with Sin & Labour for the Lord* (London: Passmore and Alabaster, 1865–1904), January 1899, 9.

2. Ibid., November 1903, 555.

3. Mrs. C. H. Spurgeon, *Ten Years of My Life in the Service of the Book Fund: A Grateful Record of My Experience of the Lord's Ways, and Work, and Wages* (London: Passmore & Alabaster, 1887), 27.

4. Ibid.

5. Ibid., 305.

6. Ibid.

7. *The Sword and the Trowel*, December 1895, 624.

8. Mrs. C. H. Spurgeon, *Ten Years After!: A Sequel to "Ten Years of My Life in the Service of the Book Fund"* (London: Passmore & Alabaster, 1895), v.

9. *The Sword and the Trowel*, November 1903, 553.

10. C. H. Spurgeon, *C.H. Spurgeon's Autobiography: Compiled from His Diary, Letters, and Records, by His Wife, and His Private Secretary* (London: Passmore and Alabaster, 1897–99; repr., Pasadena, TX: Pilgrim Publications, 1992), 2:293.

11. Ibid.

12. Mrs. C. H. Spurgeon, *A Cluster of Camphire: Words of Cheer & Comfort to Sick & Sorrowful Souls* (London: Passmore and Alabaster, 1898; repr., Springfield, MO: Particular Baptist Press, 2016), 1–2.

13. Mrs. C. H. Spurgeon, *Ten Years*, 206.

14. Mrs. C. H. Spurgeon, *Ten Years After*, 84.

15. "C. H. Spurgeon," Hymnary.org, https://hymnary.org/person/Spurgeon_CH.

16. Mrs. C. H. Spurgeon, *A Cluster of Camphire*, 31.

17. Ibid., 32.

18. Ibid., 3.

19. Ibid., 4.

20. Ibid., 7.

21. Mrs. C. H. Spurgeon, *Ten Years After*, vii.

22. Ibid.

23. Ibid.

24. Ibid.

25. *The Sword and the Trowel*, December 1903, 615.

26. Ibid., December 1895, 624.

27. Ibid., 624.

28. Ibid., 625.

29. C. H. Spurgeon, *Autobiography*, 2:293–94.

30. Mrs. C. H. Spurgeon, *Ten Years*, 161.

31. Ibid., 162.

32. Ibid.

33. Ibid.

34. Mrs. C. H. Spurgeon, *A Cluster of Camphire*, 90–91.

35. Ibid., 91.

36. *The Sword and the Trowel*, April 1899, 164.

37. Mrs. C. H. Spurgeon, *A Cluster of Camphire*, 92–93.

38. Ibid., 93.

39. Mrs. C. H. Spurgeon, *Ten Years*, 26–27.

40. Ibid.

41. Ibid., 27.

42. Charles Spurgeon did not focus on writing his own autobiography, but he did leave behind contributions that Susie and his longtime secretary Joseph Harrald included along with their own. Of Spurgeon's chronicles: "In the occasional intervals of comparative leisure that he was able to snatch from his busy life's labours,—and mainly in the bright sunshine at Mentone, —he recorded many of the principal incidents in his wonderful career. As each one was completed, he used joyfully to exclaim, 'There's another chapter for my Autobiography'; and had he been spared long enough, he would doubtless have given to the church and the world a full account of his life as it appeared from his own standpoint. This he has virtually done from the commencement of his public ministry, though not in the connected form in which it is now interested" (*Autobiography*, 1:1). Spurgeon considered that *The Sword and the Trowel* was "in some sense our autobiography" (*The Sword and the Trowel*, January 1885, 25). Tom Nettles writes that "much of the

material collected by his wife and his assistant J. W. Harrald for Spurgeon's posthumous *Autobiography* first appeared in this monthly pastoral missive" (Tom Nettles, *Living by Revealed Truth: The Life and Pastoral Theology of Charles Haddon Spurgeon* [Fearn, Scotland: Christian Focus, 2013], 9).

43. *The Sword and the Trowel,* February 1898, 51.

44. Ibid., 52.

45. Ibid., January 1899, 9.

46. Ibid.

47. Ibid., September 1899, 486.

48. Ibid., November 1903, 555–56.

Chapter 14: Planting a Final Seed

1. *The Sword and the Trowel: A Record of Combat with Sin & Labour for the Lord* (London: Passmore and Alabaster, 1865–1904), May 1896, 217.

2. Ibid.

3. Ibid.

4. Ibid., May 1896, 218.

5. Ibid.

6. Mrs. C. H. Spurgeon, *Ten Years After!: A Sequel to "Ten Years of My Life in the Service of the Book Fund"* (London: Passmore & Alabaster, 1895), 94.

7. Ibid., 94–95.

8. *The Sword and the Trowel,* May 1896, 218.

9. Ibid.

10. Ibid., 219.

11. Ibid., Preface, 1896, iv.

12. Ibid., September 1896, 508.

13. Ibid., 509.

14. Ibid.

15. Ibid., September 1896, 508.

16. Ibid., 509.

17. Ibid.

18. Ibid.

19. Ibid.

20. Ibid., September 1896, 508.

21. Ibid., 495.

22. Ibid.

23. During my research, I attended a service at Beulah Baptist Church and was warmly welcomed by the pastoral staff and members of the church. The building is much the same as it was in Susannah's day. The songs reflected biblical truth, and I appreciated hearing an evangelical sermon that was faithful to the biblical text—this over 120 years after Mrs. Spurgeon's confident assertion concerning the future of the church. The Rev. Dr. Graham Holliday is the former Senior Minister, and he was trained for the Baptist ministry at Spurgeon's College (originally, the Pastors' College). The associate minister is Rev. David Lockwood.

24. Michael Bradshaw, *Beulah: Yesterday, Today and Tomorrow, 1896–1996: The Story of Beulah Baptist Church* (self-pub.,1996), 16.

25. *The Sword and the Trowel,* January 1897, 9.

26. Ibid., May 1897, 213.

27. Ibid., January 1897, iii.

28. Bradshaw, *Beulah,* 16.

29. *The Sword and the Trowel,* May 1897, 215.

30. Ibid.

31. Ibid., 215.

32. *The Sword and the Trowel,* May 1897, 212.

33. Ibid., 213.

34. Ibid., August 1897, 441.

35. Ibid., 466.

36. Ibid., 467.

37. Ibid., 469.

38. Ibid., 469–70.

39. Bradshaw, *Beulah,* 16–17.

40. *The Sword and the Trowel,* September 1898, 498.

41. Ibid., 499.

42. Ibid.

43. Bradshaw, *Beulah,* 20–21.

44. From a photograph that this author took at Beulah Baptist Church while conducting research for this book.

45. *The Sword and the Trowel,* September 1899, 487.

Chapter 15: Seeing the King and His Glory

1. Robert Shindler, *From the Pulpit to the Palm-Branch* (New York: Gospel Publishing House, n.d.), 122.

2. C. H. Spurgeon, *C.H. Spurgeon's Autobiography: Compiled from His Diary, Letters, and Records, by His Wife, and His Private Secretary* (London: Passmore and Alabaster, 1897–99; repr., Pasadena, TX: Pilgrim Publications, 1992), 2:299.

3. Mrs. C. H. Spurgeon, *Ten Years After!: A Sequel to "Ten Years of My Life in the Service of the Book Fund"* (London: Passmore & Alabaster, 1895), v.

4. Ibid., vi.

5. Ibid.

6. Ibid., vi–vii.

7. Ibid., vii.

8. *The Sword and the Trowel: A Record of Combat with Sin & Labour for the Lord* (London: Passmore and Alabaster, 1865–1904), March 1902, 116.

9. *The Brooklyn Daily Eagle*, June 1902, 24.

10. From a brochure held at the archives of The Southern Baptist Theological Seminary.

11. Ibid.

12. *The Sword and the Trowel*, November 1903, 556.

13. From a letter held at the Metropolitan Tabernacle, London.

14. To read more about the challenges of the Metropolitan Tabernacle after Spurgeon's death, see two books by Iain Murray, *The Forgotten Spurgeon* and *Archibald G. Brown* from The Banner of Truth Publishers.

15. *The Sword and the Trowel*, May 1899, 211.

16. Ibid., 211.

17. Ibid., 212.

18. *The Los Angeles Times*, September 17, 1900, 5.

19. Ibid.

20. *The Sword and the Trowel*, January 1900, 42.

21. Ibid., March 1900, 193.

22. Ibid., May 1900, 242.

23. Ibid., May 1901, 217–18.

24. C. H. Spurgeon, *Autobiography*, 2:180.

25. Mrs. C. H. Spurgeon, *Ten Years,* 251.

26. *The Sword and the Trowel*, November 1903, 556–57.

27. Ibid., 557.

28. Ibid.

29. Charles Ray, *The Life of Susannah Spurgeon*, in *Free Grace and Dying Love* (1903; repr., Edinburgh: The Banner of Truth Trust, 2013), 247. The lines quoted by Susannah are

from a hymn by John Newton. See John Newton, "Be Gone, Unbelief; My Savior Is Near," http://www.oremus.org/hymnal/b/b004.html. The lines are engraved on the grave that she shares with Charles.

30. Ray, *The Life of Susannah Spurgeon*, 247.

31. *The Baptist*, October 30, 1903, page 281. This newspaper clipping is held at the Metropolitan Tabernacle, London. All future references from *The Baptist* are from this edition.

32. *The Sword and the Trowel*, November 1903, 557.

33. Ibid., 551–53.

34. *The Baptist.* See previous reference for details.

35. *The Sword and the Trowel*, December 1903, 599.

36. C. H. Spurgeon, "The Cleansing Fountain" by William Cowper (1779) in *Our Own Hymn-Book: A Collection of Psalms and Hymns for Public, Social, and Private Worship.* (London: Passmore and Alabaster, 1885), 288. The common title today for Cowper's hymn is "There Is a Fountain." Spurgeon included it as "The Cleansing Fountain."

37. *The Sword and the Trowel*, December 1903, 599.

38. Pastor John Clevely, current pastor of Beulah Family Church, made church records available to me that record Susie's membership at Beulah Baptist, Thornton Heath, from late 1889 until her death in 1903. Initially Susie attended services as she was able; later her health prohibited attendance. However, she remained involved in the church via supporting various ministries and through her financial contributions. Susie's name also remained on the church records at the Metropolitan Tabernacle until her death. Correspondence between Beulah and the Metropolitan Tabernacle (MT) reveals that the MT disputed that Susie was ever a member of Beulah. Susie also presented Beulah with an organ, which is surprising since Charles did not employ musical instruments at the MT.

39. Thomas L. Johnson, *Twenty-Eight Years a Slave* (Bournemouth, England: W. Math & Sons, 1909), 86.

40. Ibid., 88.

41. Ibid., 104.

42. Ibid., 143–44.

43. https://www.thegospelcoalition.org/article/why-american-south-would-have-killed-charles-spurgeon/.

44. Thomas L. Johnson, *Twenty-Eight Years a Slave*, 237–38.

Epilogue: The Legacy of Susannah Spurgeon

1. C. H. Spurgeon, *C.H. Spurgeon's Autobiography: Compiled from His Diary, Letters, and Records, by His Wife, and His Private Secretary* (London: Passmore and Alabaster, 1897–99; repr., Pasadena, TX: Pilgrim Publications, 1992), 2:11. Emphasis mine.

2. Susannah Spurgeon, *Free Grace and Dying Love* (repr., Edinburgh: The Banner of Truth Trust, 2013), 101–102.

3. C. H. Spurgeon, *Autobiography*, 1:69.

4. Charles Ray, *The Life of Susannah Spurgeon*. In *Free Grace and Dying Love* (1903; repr., Edinburgh: The Banner of Truth Trust, 2013), 191.

5. Ibid., 192–93.

6. *The Sword and the Trowel: A Record of Combat with Sin & Labour for the Lord* (London: Passmore and Alabaster, 1865–1904), December 1903, 607.

7. C. H. Spurgeon, *The Metropolitan Tabernacle Pulpit: Sermons Preached and Revised by C. H. Spurgeon,* (Pasadena, TX: Pilgrim Publications, 1970–2006), 27:42.

8. C. H. Spurgeon, *Autobiography*, 2:11.

9. Mrs. C. H. Spurgeon, *Ten Years*, 80. Though Havergal and Murray are sometimes associated with the Keswick movement, one should not conclude that Charles and Susie were sympathetic with the movement as a whole. For Spurgeon's views on the Keswick movement, see Peter Morden, *Communion with Christ and His People, The Spirituality of C. H. Spurgeon* (Eugene, OR: Pickwick Publications, 2013), 223–57. Susie was also greatly influenced by Luther, Calvin, and the Puritans. She considered that Puritan literature should be read due to "their Scriptural expositions" and that such books should be "prized far beyond the hazy and questionable utterances of the so called 'cultural preachers' of the day." Susie cannot be accurately characterized by a "let go and let God" theology as some modern Keswick adherents are sometimes described.

10. Mrs. C. H. Spurgeon, *Ten Years of My Life in the Service of the Book Fund: A Grateful Record of My Experience of the Lord's Ways, and Work, and Wages* (London: Passmore & Alabaster, 1887), 83.

11. Ibid., Preface, iii.

12. Mrs. C. H. Spurgeon, *Ten Years After!: A Sequel to "Ten Years of My Life in the Service of the Book Fund"* (London: Passmore & Alabaster, 1895), 21.

13. Mrs. C. H. Spurgeon, *Ten Years,* 337.

14. *The Sword and the Trowel*, August 1904, 414.

15. Charles Ray, *The Life of Susannah Spurgeon*, 250.

16. Ibid.

17. "The Banner Book Fund," Banner of Truth, https://banneroftruth.org/us/about/the-banner-book-fund/.

18. Mrs. C. H. Spurgeon, *Ten Years After*, 37.

19. Ibid., 38.

20. *The Sword and the Trowel*, December 1903, 606.

21. Excerpt from a letter held in the Angus Library at Regent's Park College, Oxford, England. Used by permission.

22. *The Sword and the Trowel*, December 1903, 607.

23. Ibid., November 1903, 551.

24. Lewis Drummond, *Spurgeon: Prince of Preachers* (Grand Rapids: Kregel, 1992), 230.

25. C. H. Spurgeon, *Autobiography*, 2:21.

26. From a letter held at the Metropolitan Tabernacle, London.

27. Susan Valerie Barker, "Susannah and the Lemon Tree": Mrs. C.H. Spurgeon's Book Fund, *Baptist Quarterly* 48, no. 4 (2017): 159–67, DOI: 10.1080/0005576X.2017.1376536.

28. *The Sword and the Trowel*, December 1903, 603.

29. Charles Ray, *The Life of Susannah Spurgeon*, 250.

30. *The Sword and the Trowel*, December 1903, 608.

31. Ibid., December 1903, 602–604.

32. Mrs. C. H. Spurgeon, *Ten Years*, 396.

33. *The Sword and the Trowel*, December 1903, 604–605.

34. Mrs. C. H. Spurgeon, *Ten Years*, 396.

35. Words carved on Susie's monument at the West Norwood Cemetery.

Acknowledgments

1. Lyle W. Dorsett, *A Passion for Souls* (Chicago: Moody, 1997), 291.

To learn more about Susie Spurgeon and author Ray Rhodes Jr., visit:

www.rayrhodesjr.com or www.susiespurgeon.com

You can also follow the author here:

www.facebook.com/susiespurgeonbook
Twitter: @susiespurgeon1
Instagram: susiespurgeonbook

ENTER THE REMARKABLE UNTOLD LOVE STORY OF CHARLES AND SUSIE SPURGEON.

Yours, Till Heaven invites you into the untold love story of Charles and Susie Spurgeon to discover how the bond between this renowned couple helped fuel their lifelong service to the Lord. Discover how Charles and Susie traversed the challenges of physical affliction, popularity, controversy, and other trials together with a heavenly vision.

978-0-8024-1952-1 | also available as an eBook

> "Only God can justify the ungodly, but He can do it to perfection. He casts our sins behind His back; He blots them out. He says that though they be sought for, they shall not be found."

– C. H. SPURGEON

MOODY Publishers®

From the Word to Life®

In an age of limited travel and isolated nations, C. H. Spurgeon preached to over 10,000,000 people in person—sometimes up to ten times per week. It is in this classic work that Spurgeon most clearly presents the message of salvation—man's ultimate need and God's unique provision—both simply and sincerely, for honest seekers and zealous witnesses alike.

978-0-8024-5452-2 | also available as an eBook

DISCOVER THE INCREDIBLE JOURNEY OF ONE OF THE GREAT SOULS OF HISTORY

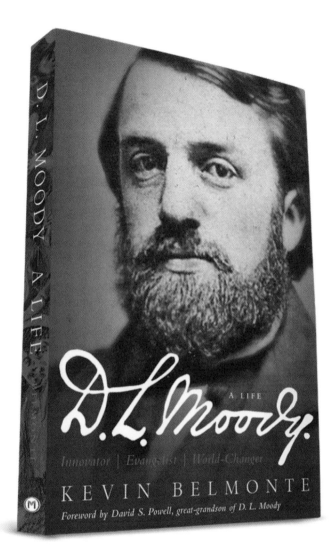

D. L. Moody was the visionary educator and evangelist of the nineteenth century. Long before radio and television, he brought the transformative message of the gospel to millions and the mission he started in an abandoned saloon drew children by the hundreds. Drawing on the best, most recent scholarship, *D. L. Moody—A Life* chronicles the incredible journey of one of the great souls of history.

978-0-8024-1204-1 | also available as an eBook